The Child's Discovery of Himself

THE CHILD'S DISCOVERY OF HIMSELF

Edited by
Clark Moustakas

738732

MISSOURI WESTERN COLLEGE
4525 Downs Drive
ST. JOSEPH, MISSOURI 64507

Jason Aronson, Inc.
New York

Copyright © 1973, 1966 by Clark Moustakas
(Originally published as Existential Child Therapy)

Library of Congress Catalog Card Number: 73-81215
ISBN: 0-87668-108-9

Manufactured in the United States of America

❧ *For Jimmy Hudson*
who lived as he died
with the gentle, compassionate
spirit of love

❂ Preface

THIS BOOK BRINGS TOGETHER original contributions in which each psychotherapist explores his experience with a child who represented a significant challenge, provoked unique encounters, and initiated a process of awareness and enlightenment. For the most part, observation and analysis are in the background; immediacy and I–thou are central.

Each illustration is unique and offers an opportunity to see the living dimensions of therapy, to participate in an encounter with genuine persons, to comprehend the child's life with the therapist and witness directly the evolution of his selfhood. The focus is on the immediate process of human engagement and commitment, where the integrity of the persons and the flow of life between them is the primary ingredient, rather than any theory or concept or preconceived plan. Episodes of critical meaning are presented to reveal the essence of therapy that involves real people in real situations. Significant moments that vividly disclose the central themes and issues in the confrontations between therapist and child are accented. Wherever possible, the actual dialogue and commentary are retained, so that unfolding life can be perceived in the living processes, components, and transactions of the two human beings.

The chapters by Antonia Wenkart and Eugene Gendlin touch on the underlying roots of theory and experiences that clarify the process of therapy and present a way of understanding the growth and transformation of the self, a way of visualizing and conceptualizing the shift from static, meaningless, restrictive living to creative self-expansion and self-realization. These chapters reveal the essential dimensions and conditions of the authentic human relationship and its healthy emergence and growth.

In the course of creating *Existential Child Therapy*, help was needed in many places. I wish to thank Pauline Park Wilson Knapp, President, and The Merrill-Palmer Institute for continuing to support the idiosyncratic philosophy and way of life reflected here in the face of growing pressures for conformity. I express my appreciation to Melvyn Baer for his encouragement in times of delay and for his marathon proof reading; to Roseanne Ellicott for her original typing of my cramped and often-changed manuscript; and to my wife, Betty Moustakas, for being present, often silently and affirmatively, throughout the numerous transformations of this volume. I also thank each author in the book for patiently struggling with me to create a structure that would present the life of encounter and dialogue in therapy, for being willing to reorganize, restructure, and rewrite until a genuine, revealing form emerged.

Detroit, Michigan Clark Moustakas
December 1965

❈ Preface to Second Edition

A FEW YEARS AGO a radical change occurred in the focus of my work with children and families. My energy and effort shifted from primary involvement in child therapy to concentrated attempts to humanize learning in elementary schools. My major commitment was with groups of young children in primary classrooms. Art, music, movement, drama, and literature were the basic media for integrating human values into the learning process. Though it was possible and necessary to relate to individual children in the classroom in facilitating emotional freedom and full development of potential, these relationships never achieved the depth and significance of the person-to-person dialogues and actions that are a part of therapy. In time, classroom changes occurred in children and teachers toward significant self-awareness, effective communication, and a learning process that respected individuality, uniqueness, and difference. Even so, something was missing. I began to experience the loss of the privacy and depth of the gradual, unfolding life with one other person. I missed the conflict, struggle, and crisis, the awakening of new spirit and energy; the new creations that in the past had brought intensity and special meaning into my life with children. I realized that although my work with groups was challenging and rewarding, these experiences could never substitute for or replace the intimate life with one other person. So I returned, in some measure, to involvement in child therapy where the conditions and values can make the setting a sanctuary, where a life grows in distinctive and unique form because child and grown-up will it, shape and fashion it, create it in their own way.

The person-to-person process, in a controlled and private setting, still represents an incomparable way of coming fully to know another human being and of coming into the full range and extent of a relationship. Thus, with renewed conviction and value, I introduce this edition of *The Child's Discovery of Himself*. Here are examples of what life can be when it is lived deeply and fully between two persons, when there is an unyielding commitment to freedom, individual integrity, and personal growth.

Detroit, Michigan
June 20, 1973

Clark Moustakas

✺ The Authors

EUGENE D. ALEXANDER is Administrative Director and Chief Psychologist, Child Guidance Center, Harrisburg, Pennsylvania.

FREDERICK H. ALLEN, who died January 15, 1964, was a child psychoanalyst at the Philadelphia Child Guidance Clinic and a pioneer and innovator of clinical theory and practice in psychotherapy with children.

DOROTHY W. BARUCH, who died September 4, 1962, was a clinical psychologist in private practice, working with children and adults in individual and group therapy, with a special interest in psychosomatic problems.

CHARLOTTE BUHLER is a clinical psychologist in private practice in Beverly Hills, California, and is also Assistant Clinical Professor of Psychiatry at the University of Southern California Medical School (Emeritus).

HANNA COLM, who died March 20, 1965, was a clinical psychologist, at one time Director of the Munich Child Guidance Clinic and later consultant at the Washington School of Psychiatry and child and adult analyst in private practice.

EUGENE T. GENDLIN is in the Department of Psychology at the University of Chicago and Editor of *Psychotherapy: Theory, Research and Practice*.

RICHARD C. KOGL is a child psychoanalyst who supervises psychotherapy with adults and children at Napa State Hospital, Imola, California.

EVE LEWIS is a psychotherapist at the Exeter Child Guidance Centre in England and visiting lecturer at the C. G. Jung Institute in Zurich, Switzerland.

CLARK MOUSTAKAS is a faculty member at The Merrill-Palmer Institute in Detroit and is engaged in teaching of graduate students and in psychotherapy with children and adults.

ANTONIA WENKART is a faculty member at the American Institute of Psychoanalysis, a Training Psychoanalyst, and Attending Psychoanalyst at the Karen Horney Clinic.

Contents

PREFACE *vii*

PREFACE TO SECOND EDITION *ix*

THE AUTHORS *xi*

Introduction: The Existential Moment 1

1 The Dying Self within the Living Self 9
   Clark Moustakas

2 Little Mocking Bird 30
   Dorothy W. Baruch

3 Just a Stupid Little Boy 45
   Richard C. Kogl

4 The Self-Defeating Search for Love 78
   Hanna Colm

5 Therapy in an Existential Crisis 102
   Charlotte Buhler

6 In the World of Silent Dialogue 119
   Eugene D. Alexander

7 Therapy as a Living Experience *134*
  Frederick Allen

8 Initiation of an Obsessional Adolescent Boy *152*
  Eve Lewis

9 Individual Psychotherapy as an Obstacle to Growth *177*
  Clark Moustakas

10 The Child Meets the World *191*
  Antonia Wenkart

11 Existentialism and Experiential Psychotherapy *206*
  Eugene T. Gendlin

INDEX *249*

Existential Child Therapy

❋ Introduction: The Existential Moment
Clark Moustakas

IN EACH LIFE, there are moments that leave an imprint in the mind and heart and spirit, moments that transcend lesser times and enable a person to stretch beyond what he has known, into a new realm of discovery. In such moments, the person feels his feelings; he hears his own inner dialogue; he feels his footsteps and knows them to be his own. The individual trusts his senses to guide him in the right direction. He forms words that build bridges to deeper regions of his own being and strengthen his relatedness to others. What he says and what he does and what he feels really matter.

In place of the habitual dead happenings, in place of the routine patterns and habits, in place of systems of definition and function bounded by proper time and proper place and proper role, a real person emerges who is suddenly present in the world, ready to collaborate with life, ready to use his resources for self-growth and for fundamental ties to nature and the universe. The individual no longer gets in the way of himself; he knows what he wants; he is aware.

It is this moment of awareness and discovery and presence that I call the existential moment; it is the moment when a person recognizes his own existence in the world and the unique and incomparable nature of that existence.

The existential moment does not refer to a time dimension. It may be of brief or of long duration, but the time element is not the crucial factor. Rather, it is the living, growing self of the person, the authenticity of the individual, that takes on a meaning and a value. It may be a moment of realization of who one is, a sudden understanding of life, an awareness of the rightness of a value or conviction or decision. It may be a moment so utterly revealing that it will alter one's destiny or a moment when an apparently enduring value is destroyed.

The existential moment is a time of discovery that life may be a form of death or that death is not the end or terminal point, but a point in the process of life. It is a moment of self-disclosure in which a new and distinct feeling emerges, in which a beginning identity is formed, in which the inner self is experienced in depth; or it is a moment of awareness of the emptiness and futility of a life without value.

The existential moment is a moment of pure feeling, a moment of reflection and solitude, a moment of wonder, joy or grief, an experience centered in a particular self; it is my sorrow, my elation, my despair, my excitement, it is a feeling which infuses my entire being.

The existential moment is sometimes the beginning of a new conviction or commitment emerging from a distinctive and particular identity. Such moments provide substance for searching, struggling, feeling, asserting, yielding, facing, and choosing a direction that challenges and enhances realization of potentialities both in the individual and in his growing relationships.

In therapy, it is a moment when the child and the therapist are in full communion. Martin Buber describes the kind of communion that enables the child to develop his creative powers:

> Because this human being exists: therefore, he must be really there, really facing the child, not merely there in spirit. . . . In order to be and to remain truly present to the child he must have gathered the child's presence into his own store as one of the bearers of his communion with the world, one of the focuses of his responsibilities for the world. Of course he cannot be continually concerned with the child, either in thought or in deed, nor ought he to be. But if he has really gathered the child into his life then that subterranean dialogic, that steady potential presence of the one to the other is established and endures. Then there is reality *between* them, there is mutuality.[1]

The therapist living existentially with children transcends schools of thought and adheres primarily to value and to discovery of the meaning inherent in evolving life. Such a person is sensitive to the growing nature of his own self and his own real feelings. He is willing to plunge deeply into life with a child, to venture into new and unknown regions of experience, to risk his own identity while searching and struggling and inquiring into the depths of a troubled mind and heart. He is willing to live the moment and believe in the creative value of spontaneous, emerging life, long before he fully understands what he lives and long before the hidden pieces of the puzzle are revealed. Crisis, shock, confrontation, resistance, struggle, rejection, defeat as well as joy, silence, the excitement of discovery, the peaceful smile, the gestures of affirmation and growth—all these enter into the process of therapy in which real persons rather than ghosts engage in the challenging struggle of wills and the ennobling pursuit of meaning and value in living.

---

[1] Martin Buber, *Between Man and Man*, translated by Ronald Gregor Smith (London: Routledge & Kegan Paul Ltd., 1947), p. 98.

The therapist is sensitive to the self of the child, to the healthy and sick components of behavior, to the means that suddenly emerge and enable a particular child to stop fighting against his own unique selfhood, to stop battling himself and the world, and to begin to actualize his own special potentialities. At times, there are deep issues between therapist and child as they reach from the depths of hostility and despair to discover a healthy way of life. The therapist must be willing to face the child in these moments. He must be willing to take the path with the child and not be defeated by the severe feelings of hatred and hostility that the child expresses along the way. The therapist who lives in the existential sense maintains his own uniqueness, meets the requirements as they emerge, faces life openly with a willingness to recognize his own limitations and his own uncertain, groping nature in a life that has never existed before, with a child who is entirely new, no matter how much his behavior may appear like that of other children. Such a therapist remains with himself, utilizes his own being as the central resource. He does not adhere to vested schools, although in practice he reflects his background and his affiliation. But this reflection is incorporated as one dimension of the self. He, the therapist, stands out on his own firm ground, not in terms of ideas, content, material, not in terms of facts and figures from a dead record, not in terms of concepts and theory; but he stands out, exists, present to his self as a whole, integrated being, present to his own resources as they emerge and unfold in his experiences with the child. He is committed to spontaneous, flowing, human processes and potentialities that are engendered and sparked in the communion of a significant relationship. I am not speaking of course of the existential analyst or of existentialism as such, which too often has been a system of unreal (though often imaginative) happenings and events, of odd stresses and strains, of weird themes, of behavior more thoroughly examined and analyzed than the impulses and instincts of traditional analysis.

In experiential therapy, there is a time of crisis and a time of tranquility, a time of confrontation, and a time of encounter. In the confrontation, there is an open facing of a painful issue or conflict between two persons. The child must be free, must even be encouraged to maintain his own identity, his own ideas, his own perceptions of reality, no matter how distorted they may appear to the therapist. The resources and talents and potentialities of the therapist, his entire being, must be present, facing the child, encouraging him to unleash deeper and deeper feelings, to express his anger, his rejection, rage, sarcasm, belittlement, to express all of the negative components of a frightened and angry self. In such a moment, the therapist is present as a real human being, feeling and experiencing with the child. As powerful as the altercation may be, as violent as the child's attack may be, the therapist never loses touch with himself as a person, never fails to stay within the relationship, never surrenders his conviction that the child has capacities and resources for healthy self-emergence. He remains with the child and enables him to come to terms with his own rejection, immorality, or hatred, not by utilizing a dialectical maneuver or a professional technique, but by bringing to the child the full resources of a real self, interested and committed to the child's well being. In this moment of crucial meaning, the relationship unfolds into more and more meaningful and deeper regions of communal life. There is a release of feeling and tension, a movement toward growing awareness and insight, and a sense of responsibility. The confrontation is a way to deeper intimacy and relatedness, to authentic life between persons. The therapist must be courageous enough to live through the suffering and unknown factors in the confrontation with the child, trusting enough to let the breach heal through silent presence and communion when words and dialogue fail, strong enough to maintain his love and respect for the child whatever else may be canceled out in the issue or dispute. The therapist never loses sight of the fact that the child is seeking in his own way, however fragmentary or futile or destructive it may appear, to find an authentic existence, to find a life of meaning and value, and to express the truth as he sees it.

In the encounter, child and therapist meet in full harmony and communion. The encounter may be an exchange of brief duration. Yet, in the moment, there is full human expression and depth. Sometimes, it is a simple sharing, a feeling of intimacy and unity between the therapist and the child where all subject–object, self–other, and individual–universal dichotomies disappear. It is an immediate, imminent reality. However alienated or detached a child may be, there remains within him an entirely unique and particular substance that is his own, intact and inviolate, an individuality that can be recognized and called forth in the encounter. Such a moment is a creative experience in which there is a dropping-off of conventions, systems, and rubrics and a letting-go so that the child reveals his real self openly and directly and the therapist enters the reality of this self-disclosure in a living sense, in terms of the conditions and requirements intrinsic to the situation. Openness, receptiveness, commitment, involvement, relatedness are all significant aspects of the encounter. In the encounter between therapist and child, each person enters into a meaningful tie, where mental power and compassion mingle. No matter how complicated, how discouraging or frightening, no matter how uncertain the therapeutic process, even during the most prolonged plateau, the possibility for encounter is present if the therapist's courage and strength and perceptiveness are available, if his resources for spontaneous engagement are present. The life of therapeutic encounter is a two-way process. It is a person-to-person meeting in which child and therapist collaborate in their search to unravel the hidden meanings; to clarify the distortions and confusion; to disclose real feelings and thoughts in a closed and fragmented self; to create a climate of learning, where conflicts, challenge, and emerging insight and awareness integrate with sensitivity and compassion in restoring a child to mature and healthy self-hood. New potentialities are actualized in the solitary inner dialogue and in the exquisite fullness of communal life.

The therapists in this book come out of different experiences and disciplines. When they speak about therapy and therapeutic process, they hold different views and different theories, but their own integrity and daring are more important than schools of thought and professional ties. In the living encounter with the child they are not bounded by any theory or system, but they live in accordance with self-values and are open to spontaneous perceptions and insights, open to the unexpected, to new awareness and awakening. They stand out uniquely, individually, personally, living spontaneously and arbitrarily. They follow no rule or custom or technique but only the guiding spirit of the integrated self and the direction of their own senses. They are willing to accept the inspirations and the creative developments as well as the consequences of a life based on meaning and value and the emerging, unknown dimensions of real experience.

1

❊ The Dying Self within the Living Self

Clark Moustakas

JIMMY CAME TO ME, quiet but with the spirit of the West wind. He entered gently, with swift steps, his movements registering a zest for life, a vibrant joy and enthusiasm. His entering the room was like radiant light being introduced, and suddenly the lifeless toys, the sand, the water, the guns—everything—took on a vividness, a brightness, a human meaning. I could feel his presence infusing energy into the formless shapes and the impersonal forms. Somehow, when Jimmy arrived, a new world opened up and I became aware of a vital existence unfolding before me. In him, I saw a new eagerness expressing itself with total commitment. Jimmy's joy in being with me in the playroom was instantaneous and filled me with wonder and awe. He helped to make my life with him one of value and excitement and frequent surprise. I knew from our first moments together that this was to be no ordinary experience in play therapy.

Jimmy was unlike any child I had ever met before. As each child is unique and differs from all others, Jimmy was unique. But his being in therapy was unusual in another sense. An unqualified diagnosis had been made: Jimmy was suffering from a treacherous and fatal disease; he was dying of a rare form of blood cancer. The onset of the illness was sudden and unexpected, and the leukemia was rapidly taking over. So, Jimmy, who had been a healthy, robust, and active child, at the age of seven was doomed to die of an insidious disease which in a matter of months would vanquish him and destroy his vitality, his way of being in the world.

Jimmy's therapy started in a children's hospital one dark afternoon in a small room while Jimmy and his parents waited for the final report on a bone-marrow test that had been done that morning. As we played a game together, Jimmy was engrossed in moving the wooden pieces to successful completion, while I was very much involved in the meaning of the moment. I watched Jimmy. I watched the other children crowded into a small room, all waiting for examinations that would reveal their fates or indicate at what point they were in a process that would eventuate in death. Slowly, gradually, other children noticed Jimmy and me in the mass of people. They created a circle around us, and, feeling the invitation that came from us, they soon joined us in the game. The excitement of the play compelled the attention of many of the fifteen or twenty children in the room. A sudden quiet ensued, a stillness following the noise, as the children took their turns in the moves or watched as others played. The tensions melted, a calm atmosphere resulted, and the children played in a relaxed and enjoyable way, temporarily forgetting the ordeal that was to come, not even hearing the painful screaming of youngsters in the background, in the consultation rooms. But, I felt an unshakable sadness knowing the grief and tragedy contained in the room.

Thus, my first hour of "therapy" with Jimmy did not occur in the private setting of the playroom. Nor did we have the usual toys, materials, and space. Just the contrary; we used what was available—a small room, crowded with children and their mothers. And we had only one item, a game, which we stretched enough to enable five others to play, a game that included many others who stood by and watched. Yet I am not speaking about a game. I am pointing to an experience in psychotherapy with children, an experience not in the usual or prescribed professional pattern or mode. The therapeutic value of the experience was immediate. These children found a way to live, to be active, to use their energies constructively, a way that temporarily alleviated the painful waiting and the terrible anxiety in facing the unknown. Obviously, the conditions were far from ideal for group therapy; yet the results were immediate. A situation was created in which these children could exist in a meaningful way. An adult was present, interested in them as individuals, concerned that these children were all dying of cancer and listening and attending to each one, caring and wanting to enter and perceive the particular world of each child, even when it was only a momentary glimpse, a momentary communion.

The initial hour of therapy with Jimmy did not end with a game. The hemotologist called Jimmy's parents. He wished to talk with them alone. Gently, he informed Jimmy that it would be necessary to give him a blood transfusion. Turning to me, the physician asked that I assist by remaining with Jimmy while he received the blood. In the meantime, he could have his private talk with Jimmy's parents in another room.

In this way, the second phase of my first "hour" of therapy with Jimmy began. I went with him to the special room. As we walked, I sensed his growing anxiety. When we entered the room and saw the bottles of blood, his body tightened visibly throughout, and a dark look of violent dread crossed his face. A shadow passed between us, a foreboding expression which spread so completely that neither my words nor feelings could break through this catastrophic moment. All I could do was stand by and wait until the first overwhelming swells of fear subsided. After several minutes passed, in which Jimmy stood in a kind of paralysis, he recovered enough strength to get up onto the table, but his fear remained, and his body was tense throughout.

Getting the needle into one of Jimmy's veins was an ordeal. He screamed again and again. Unfortunately, the physician himself was unsteadied by Jimmy's reaction, and his aim was off the mark. He made numerous probings with the needle before he could make a successful entry into the vein. During this time, Jimmy's emotional state fluctuated between extreme fear and extreme anger. Each time the needle stuck him, he yelled and jerked violently. The physician tried to convince him that the needle would hurt him only a little, but this infuriated Jimmy. He screamed repeatedly and threatened to get off the table. He demanded that his mother and father be allowed to come to him, but the doctor told him that his parents would not be permitted to enter the room until the blood transfusion had started. During this time, I held his hand and tried to comfort him. In words, I tried to tell him that I knew it must hurt very much. My attitude throughout was to remain with Jimmy, with his experience. I did not talk about the realities involved. I did not attempt to convince him that the blood had been ordered to help him get well. I did not explain the plan of treatment. It was not information he sought, but escape from this terrifying situation.

I remained with Jimmy, as one person with another, facing a crisis in life. I remained with his perceptions, with his feelings. As far as it is humanly possible for one person to be in the center of the world of another, I was there, offering myself, my skills, and my strength. It was Jimmy's experience that mattered to me. At times, I reflected his feelings of fear and anger, but these reflections did not contribute much in helping him to face the situation with courage. I did not believe that his fear and pain could be assuaged, but rather that he had to live with them, in all the intensity of his experience, before the severe, terrifying threat could be altered.

Finally the needle was successfully introduced into the vein, and the flow of blood from the bottle into Jimmy's body began. I read to him during the transfusion, and, although he was still experiencing great fear, there were moments when the reading compelled his complete attention. He interrupted the story at one point to ask why the doctor had been so clumsy in getting started. I encouraged him to talk about this experience, and he expressed considerable feeling that the physician could not understand his fear or pain. Jimmy imagined changing places with him. He thought that the doctor would know how it felt if he could be pierced with a needle several times.

Soon after the transfusion began, Jimmy's parents returned. Their eyes were filled with tears, and their faces with grief. No words were needed to tell me that the tentative diagnosis of leukemia was confirmed. Immediately, Jimmy's mother took my place, standing by him resolutely, with an expression of determination and strength. For the next ten minutes, I remained with Jimmy's father in the corridor, trying to enable him to regain enough strength to be able to face Jimmy with the new knowledge that was as irrevocable as death itself. There is no way to describe the acute physical suffering and mental anguish that Jimmy's father experienced, a torment so great that his whole body shook in waves of grief, so great that he pounded the walls of the hospital. In such a time, one can only stand by and wait for the process of self-healing and self-unity to return, wait as the person lives with the tragic fate until he is able to live in the world again. The meaning of such a situation is beyond therapy, beyond any intervention or help. Only the process of life itself, the restorative powers of the individual self, can enable the person to live again. This he must choose to do. No outsider can render him whole, can integrate him, can do what only he can do for himself from within the depths of his own suffering.

When Jimmy's father had recovered himself, he entered the room where Jimmy was. As the door closed, I saw them embrace with silent tears flowing between them. This was now a time for the family to be alone, a time to live with grief that was to be the beginning of the end—the end of a pattern of life that held so much beauty and love and serenity. It was in this way that my first "hour" of therapy with Jimmy came to a close.

Each week I brought my kit of games and books to the hospital to live with Jimmy and his friends while they waited for their medication and treatment. The children greeted me as I arrived; and, though the therapy could not alter the slow death facing each of them, it served a temporary value in immediate, concrete moments in the hospital. The anxiety, the tension, the horror disappeared for a while; and in their place joyful voices rang out; eager children participated in challenging games. Active involvement replaced passive, fearful waiting; and the atmosphere of the room changed. Being in the hospital during this hour took on a new meaning, not a succumbing to the inevitable, but a spirit and an enthusiasm for living characterized this group of children. I established a relationship with each of them, a relationship in which each child could express himself, his experience with the illness and at the hospital. Usually the children made only brief personal comments during the course of our games, but occasionally a child spoke at length. After the first meeting, I did not participate in the games unless another player was needed. I sat with the children attempting to relate to each child, with a glance, a gesture, a word. After the first hospital experience, I did not assist with the blood transfusions again. Jimmy's father and mother remained with him during these experiences.

The weekly meetings continued at the hospital for about six weeks until Jimmy achieved a remission. Then Jimmy and I met in the therapy setting described in *Psychotherapy with Children*.[1] Though I understood that Jimmy was dying, though I had been told that within a year the leukemia would completely ravage his body, I could never integrate this knowledge in any living sense. It remained outside, as an ominous idea that threatened and needled and brought occasional images of terror. But only rarely did this knowledge create a shadow between us; only rarely did it bring a darkness that would prevent full human communion. Of course, the disease increasingly affected Jimmy, debilitating him in some ways and creating pain. But it never reduced him to a passive, mechanical, dependent existence. On the contrary, he remained spontaneous, autonomous, active, in touch with life in an imaginative, flowing sense.

My mode of living with Jimmy meant remaining within his world, stretching with him to new horizons of experience, pursuing with him new ideas, developing new facets of self and society, engaging in activities and projects, and encouraging spontaneous, active expression of feelings. Within this pattern of philosophy and value, and mode of existence, a relationship evolved in therapy in which Jimmy came to express his anger and resentment and fear against all the

---

[1] Clark Moustakas, *Psychotherapy with Children* (New York: Harper & Row, 1959).

inhuman devices in the world, against the impositions of hospital superstructure, against dishonesty and unnecessary hurt, against cruelty and torture. But, at the same time, Jimmy came to be forgiving; he accepted and valued his life at home, in the hospital, and in school. With amazing perceptiveness, sensitivity, and insight, he could recognize the limitations and imperfections of people in his life. But he could also express an unusual degree of sympathy, understanding, and respect even for those who misunderstood him or treated him unkindly. After he had related an unpleasant or painful experience, Jimmy would often say, "He's not being very good to himself" or "He's not treating himself in a kind way." Thus he understood that the self who treated the other cruelly and destructively brought suffering upon itself in the form of a diminished and fragmentary life. The self at odds with the world was beset with internal warfare.

I wish to repeat that I never thought of Jimmy as a dying person. I never met him with the feeling that this hour might be our last. Even though the possibility of Jimmy's imminent death always remained, the reality of our moment-by-moment life was all that mattered when we were together. The reality we shared was too much in the stream of life, too lusty in its quality, to be primarily concerned with decay and death. When I met Jimmy, I just met him. I just went on living with him, and the living was the center of our existence, as it always is when there is a sense of wholeness and unity and mutuality between people. And, as in all living, we had our confrontations and our issues, our conflicts and disagreements; but we also had our moments of joy and communion. I did not deny either the healthy or the sick components of Jimmy's world. These dimensions of himself merged and mingled freely, as we lived.

There were those who treated him as though he were dying; and there were those who treated him only as a healthy, flourishing individual. Some recognized only the health, and some recognized only the illness. But, within Jimmy, there were both components—the healthy, growing self and the dying person. These worlds existed side by side, or they merged in experience. The reality that he *was* embodied contrasting moods and contrasting emotions, darkness and light, a sense of pessimism and defeat and a feeling of hope and of glory. Who could meet him in these varying dimensions of himself and not know the exhilaration and joy as well as the discouragement and despair? But to meet him either as a dying person or as a person growing solely in a healthy, normal way automatically meant denying the reality of the other world, of the different centers of his existence.

No method or medicine could free him of his pain or suffering. While accepting the efforts of others to help him, Jimmy somehow maintained contact with himself. He continued to feel the pain. He tells about his experience with a hypnotist in the following conversation:

Dr. Wright will hypnotize me again tonight so I won't feel the needle any more.

And, when he hypnotizes you, do you feel the needle?

Yes, I do. I feel it, and it hurts.

And you're scared when the doctor starts to pierce you?

Yes, I am. Dr. Wright is trying to help me so I can take the transfusions better.

What is hypnosis, Jimmy?

It's a kind of sleep that helps you not to be afraid. But it doesn't work with some people. Some people go on being afraid.

Are you afraid, Jimmy?

Yes, I am. I am afraid.

Jimmy's hours of play therapy were important to him. They represented in philosophy and structure a place where he could create a world of his own, in his own way and in his own time. Here he lived in accordance with his own interests, by his own values and ways. The privacy, the consistency, the emotional climate, the presence of an adult totally interested, committed, and concerned—all combined to enable Jimmy to express openly the inner life he experienced in the hospital, in his home, and at school.

The meetings in the playroom differed radically from those in the hospital. In the playroom, we were alone in an expanded universe of space and resources that offered a wider degree of genuine choice. Here Jimmy could make decisions that more fully challenged him. He could initiate a theme in conversation and know that he had my complete attention, know that he would not be interrupted.

So he entered the playroom with great exuberance and delight. He husbanded his time, treated every moment as precious. He was keenly aware of time, often verbalizing his feelings that he had so much to do, so much living to embrace within a single hour. With Jimmy, there was never preparation, never getting ready. He plunged into experience and remained actively involved as a self from the first moment to the last.

We met fifteen times; during each meeting Jimmy emerged with new facets of identity, with new means of encountering life, with new ways of being and relating in the world. At the center of Jimmy's existence was a great energy that sometimes unfolded in quiet construction projects and sometimes was expressed in hysterical, hyperactive movement from item to item and brief activity to brief activity. There were periods of heightened joy and laughter, and there were episodes of frustration and anger. Within these two modes of relating to the world, Jimmy's behavior was characterized by a high degree of self-consistency, involvement, and commitment. He persisted in following his own directions rather than conventional signs, and he insisted that he could overcome any obstacle he encountered. Quitting, being defeated, or failure to see a self-chosen activity through were simply not characteristics of his life. He often said that it was the attitude which counted. He simply would not and did not give up because he believed that he could solve any problem he met, if not in the standard way, then by his own standards. He was satisfied that, if he stayed with a problem long enough and had enough patience, a solution would emerge.

The sessions with Jimmy began with quiet construction projects. These projects generally involved the building of models. Jimmy worked in a serious, methodical way. When he chose a model, he chose one that would challenge him. He commented as he looked them over: "That one is too easy for me" or "I want one with more pieces" or "This is just right for me." He stayed with the model he chose until he completed it, although occasionally this required two or three weeks. While he was working on a complicated, difficult model one day, the following conversation took place:

That's a rough one, Jimmy.
Ya. (*Pause.*) But if I don't finish it today, I'll work on it next time.
It's a real challenge.
I'll be up to it.
Yes, I can see that you will.
No fun doing the easy ones.
No, not for you.

Jimmy worked in an orderly way. He would open the box, lay all the pieces before him, study the directions, and then begin to work. He worked like a craftsman, being careful to use just the right amount of glue and fitting the parts with precision. As he put the pieces together, he encountered problems; but each time he stayed with the problem, puzzling it out and seeing a way to proceed. As the pieces began falling into place, I could feel a growing sense of excitement in Jimmy. He would often remark enthusiastically, "Well, at last I got that one" or "I see ya! This is it." Obviously, during these times, Jimmy was a self-directed child. He knew what he wanted to do, and he pursued his tasks with diligence. He did not wish or need help. He wanted to find a solution that fitted his own sense of harmony and unity within the experience. There were times when I had to take hold of myself to keep from telling him how to proceed, especially when he had experienced considerable frustration and failure. Fortunately, I did not intervene. And, in every case, Jimmy discovered his own way, even though it did not always conform to the directions.

I learned from Jimmy the value of waiting and having patience, of living with a child through defeat, and of permitting a child to come to terms with a problem or issue in his own time and in his own way. I learned that my commitment to Jimmy involved a human presence, being there with him as he lived, groping with him, sharing his struggle, accepting and supporting his decisions, his way, not manipulating or directing, but simply standing by fully committed to him as one person with another.

My concern occasionally focused on a different dimension of Jimmy, his physical health. There were times when his breathing became labored, when he coughed heavily and repeatedly. But when I asked him if he wanted to rest awhile, he shrugged off my suggestion, even found it difficult to understand. After our first few meetings, though occasionally I was bothered by what appeared to be an uncomfortable physical tension in Jimmy, I did not comment, but rather learned to live with the discomfort, as Jimmy did.

During the fourth meeting in the playroom, Jimmy began

to express feelings of hostility. The shift from model building to aggressive activity occurred gradually. At first, he wanted only to try the guns and rifles and darts. He used the typical targets. Then he began shooting Bobo, the comeback clown. This sequence of starting with the usual targets and then directing his shooting at Bobo continued over the next four meetings. Each time the intensity of his attack on Bobo increased. I offered numerous interpretations during these outbursts! I remarked, "Sometimes when someone hurts you, you feel like you would like to get even"; "You seem to be especially angry today"; "Perhaps you're mad at the whole world today." Jimmy received these comments silently.

Soon the attacks shifted from the standard targets to Bobo exclusively and then tentatively, but definitely, toward me and from me to other figures in the room. He shot all of the "bullets" for all of the guns in the room, first at Bobo and then at me. He repeated this sequence a number of times. Then Jimmy selected a doctor and nurse figure. Repeatedly he shot down these figures. Finally, he returned to Bobo. He punched Bobo severely. He kicked Bobo, jumped up and down on it, punched it in the nose, and threw it across the room. He choked Bobo until it collapsed to the floor. He took a heavy board and clubbed Bobo over the head several times. He carried Bobo to the sandbox, poured sand on its head. He took a shovel and beat Bobo over the head with it. He took Bobo by the neck and strangled it fiercely. He bit Bobo, chewed its nose, and slashed it viciously with a shovel. Finally, he dragged Bobo to the steel vise, opened the vise, and squeezed the head of Bobo tight in it. While Bobo hung precariously in the vise, Jimmy made clay balls and heaved them into its face. He loaded a Ping pong rifle and emptied it into Bobo's face. He left Bobo, got a nursing bottle and squirted it into the face of the doctor and nurse. Then he squirted the faces of the family figures. He picked up the stethoscope and brutally poked it against the doctor several times. At the end of the hour, Jimmy carefully stood up five figures: a mother, father, two girls, and a boy. With the Ping pong rifle, he shot them down one by one, with the exception of the boy. Then he remarked, "Only one child, only one child left." He looked at the clock, and, seeing that his time was up, he left the room.

In the next session, Jimmy began a furious attack against me. First, he shot rubber darts at me. When he hit the mark, he laughed and shouted almost hysterically, "Ha! Ha! Ha!" Next, he selected the bow and arrows. He came toward me and aimed directly at my face. He approached within two feet of me and was about to shoot. The following conversation occurred:

Maybe you want to eliminate me altogether. (*Pause.*) I'd rather you didn't shoot me in the face.

(*Jimmy hesitated. We stood facing each other for several moments.*) Well. (*Then he dropped the bow.*)

(*Jimmy picked up a metal pistol and threw it at me. He followed with a number of other objects. Then he turned to other figures in the room.*) Doctor, Father, and Mommy. (*Jimmy picked up a Ping pong rifle.*)

And do you plan to shoot all three?

Ya, in three shots. (*Jimmy loaded the rifle and shot all the "bullets" but missed the figures. He loaded again and shot. This time, one by one, the figures went down.*) Psh-h right down! (*Jimmy's voice was heavy. He coughed repeatedly. The coughing became particularly bad.*)

You really aren't feeling well today.

I have a cold. It started last Friday and it isn't getting any better.

Jimmy picked up a machinist's hammer, looked in my direction, then moved away, and began pounding a table. He turned his attention to Bobo, pouring sand and water over it.

He slashed Bobo with a plastic sword, kicked it, jumped up and down on its face, and squeezed it into the vise. As he attacked Bobo, he shouted over and over again: "Wowee!" "Wowee!" He threw a rubber knife at Bobo and cut fiercely at its head. Suddenly, he looked startled. His entire emotional mood changed. He was visibly disturbed and unhappy.

Oh, look, now I've put a hole right through there. Can you get a piece of tape for that so I can fix it?

You want to repair it?

Yes, I do.

I got a repair kit and Jimmy patched Bobo and blew it up. This was characteristic of Jimmy. Even in the moments of strong anger, he did not wish to destroy; and, when he did, he tried to repair the destruction. Next he selected a car model and worked until the end of the hour. As he left, he said, "I'll take this one home to my sisters."

From this point on to our last meeting, these attacks continued reaching a peak in the tenth meeting and subsiding considerably by the last. Between the aggressive outbursts, Jimmy returned to construction of models. He also painted and constructed objects using wood, nails, and tools. Occasionally he used clay and tinker toys.

What was the meaning of the episodes of extreme anger that at times bordered on rage? Although it is possible to speculate with hidden dynamics, with psychic traumas of early childhood, with concepts of deprivation, rejection, fixation, and other similar notions, there is another way of viewing the meaning of Jimmy's behavior, a way that for me is direct and consistent with the current reality. The catastrophic condition was not in some faraway repressed conflict in the family nor in the parents' treatment of Jimmy nor in the birth of his twin sisters. The tragic condition was ever present, imminent in Jimmy and inescapable. The irrevocable catastrophe was that Jimmy was dying. Jimmy was becoming increasingly debilitated. He was being pierced and poked with needles. From week to week, he lived in fear of the blood transfusions and the other horrors involved in leukemia. In brief, his world had been shattered, and none of the people in it were quite the same. Everyone had changed in some very important ways, particularly his mother and father. Jimmy himself had changed. There were many activities—running, riding a bike, even walking—that other children take for granted and that Jimmy could no longer do. Many, many days, he was unable to attend school. He was no longer a peer among peers, a friend among friends. He was now different in a critical way from all other children at school and in his neighborhood. This was the irrevocable tragedy of Jimmy's life. Even with great effort on the part of his parents, his teachers, and others to treat Jimmy as a growing person, there were many times when his condition required special handling, when he became the exception, when adults responded to the dying self inside the living self and treated Jimmy accordingly.

The irrevocable, inescapable disease and all the resulting changes it brought into Jimmy's personal and social world created pressures and tensions, daily frustrations, and daily ordeals. There had to be an outburst. There had to be a safety valve. There had to be a release. And Jimmy was too controlled, too sensitive, too kind, too considerate, to let the explosion occur in the hospital or in his home or at school. So, he used the playroom as his safety valve. Here, the strained, intense feelings could be expressed.

I believe that as the disease spread, as the pain and suffering increased, as Jimmy was more and more restricted from a spontaneous life, as he was exposed to continual hospital treatment, and deviant school and home life, Jimmy's tensions mounted, his anger increased, and the explosions in the playroom occurred unabated. My acceptance of these attacks, not only against the items in the playroom, but also against me enabled Jimmy to feel increasingly free to express himself and to relieve himself of the pent-up feelings and frustrations. Once the hostile outbursts got under way, Jimmy reached a peak of intensity of feeling. As the feeling was expressed and accepted, in the meaningful framework of relationship therapy, Jimmy relaxed and returned to constructive projects with models, with paints, with wood. The sequence was the same: aggressive attacks followed by constructive projects. Almost without variation from the fourth meeting to the last, Jimmy began the hour by expressing feelings of anger and ended the hour by working quietly, immersed in his projects. The pattern was reversed when he had been absent for many weeks. Then he began with a construction activity, slowly moved into hostile play and ended the hour with a work project.

Jimmy's illness prevented him from coming each week. The fifteen meetings occurred over a span of seven months. When he missed for long periods, he always commented on it, often as he entered the room, saying, "I haven't seen you for quite a long time. I missed coming here, but I'm glad I'm here today."

Jimmy's crisis was a crisis of life and death. He lived in the midst of an existential dilemma, and that dilemma revolved around the question of death. But this issue was not only an issue of death. He did not just die as many people do. Perhaps there is no ordinary death, but the unique character of Jimmy's situation is that he was actively involved in the process of dying while he was also involved in the process of living.

Jimmy did not know he was dying, in words. He had not been told, and he did not verbalize such knowledge. But he knew in the meaningful sense, from within. He knew in the deepest regions of his being, from the experience of his own senses—not consciously, not in the usual way of knowing, but from the radical shift that was occurring in the primary components of his life. The inner battle between the healthy cells and the cancer cells was being waged, and the disease was gradually but definitely taking over. He was aware of his tragic condition in the existential sense, as intrinsic knowledge, not by diagnostic labels. His fears and his desires came out clearly in one of our final meetings, after he had expressed considerable hostility in his play. He picked up the stethoscope, and, placing it next to my heart, he listened. Then he put it over his own heart. His breathing was heavy and labored. He seemed greatly frightened.

It sounds like a terrible storm.

Yes, I can believe it does.

Here, you listen to my heart (*Jimmy handed the stethoscope to me.*)

Are you worried that your heart will break like a storm? (*Long pause.*)

It sounds like thunder. (*Jimmy picked up the nursing bottle and looked at me.*)

Would you like to drink from it?

Of course not; I'm already seven years old. You trying to give me the baby treatment?

Well, once you were a baby, you know.

But not any more. That was before the girls came.

When you were a baby, you were alone and you were well taken care of.

Well. (*Pause.*)

Sometimes?

Yes. Especially, once every year.

When you got sick?

(*Laughing.*) Uh-huh, not when I got sick.

When, on your birthday?
No.
Christmas?
No. It happens every year just once.
And you love it.
Yes! (*Emphatically.*)

Jimmy never explained what he meant, but it was my impression that he was speaking of a great, rare euphoric moment that transcends all lesser moments rather than of a specific occasion or event.

Jimmy's sensitivity, his unusual awareness, and his depth of insight into so many aspects of human life placed him beyond the ordinary. He saw facets of behavior, nuances and meanings in personal situations, that most people overlook. And he had a deep interest, more than this, a genuine compassion, for other human beings. His gentleness and sensitivity meant that he could not express his growing hostility toward the disease and the treatment in any direct way, at least not with the persons most immediately involved. This was the secondary crisis he faced within himself. For Jimmy, there was an unwritten moral law that one simply does not condemn or attack the people one loves, one does not trespass the ingrained moral signs; the voice of inner conscience must not be violated. This attitude became deeply ingrained, out of seven years of life in a gentle, compassionate family. Angry explosions, violent outbursts, physical aggression, or corporal punishment simply were not a part of his life. From his beginning, he knew the meaning of kindness; he experienced quiet, gentle sounds and movements; he lived in an altruistic world. He was not taught or commanded to be gentle. He simply absorbed this quality as a natural outcome of living in a world of tender ways. For Jimmy, this gentle passion was perhaps the organizing principle of his life. His deep conviction was that he could not hurt those he loved, those who cared for him.

But, in the playroom, Jimmy could express the two basic dimensions of his nature: the sweet, gentle, soft, noble feelings for his fellowman and the violent anger engendered by the disease itself, by the dying aspects of himself, and the concomitant treatment, the piercing and probing, the mechanical pushing, the injections and transfusions, and the frustration and anxiety that revolved around the plan and program of medical therapy, and the manipulation and deception that were sometimes used to persuade him to accept treatment. In the playroom, his outcry against the injustices in his world could be heard.

The four figures most directly and most frequently the center of these attacks were his doctor, father, mother, and therapist. These were the primary adults in Jimmy's life. These were the four people connected with his illness and with his treatment. And although these persons provided the climate in which he was cared for and nourished and loved, although these adults were within the matrix and substance of Jimmy's life, they were also directly connected with the painful, paralyzing feelings, with the discomfort and suffering.

Jimmy could not explode at home or at the hospital, but in the playroom he came to feel that this other world in which he lived, this world of anger, of hostile and destructive wishes and impulses, could be expressed in the receptive atmosphere of relationship therapy.

In Jimmy's world, he could not fight those who took care of him. Somehow, this was a principle he would not violate. But it was this world which therapy recognized and encouraged and enabled. And through the process of expression of the frightened, angry inner self, Jimmy arrived at a sense of harmony and a restoration of inner peace, which, of course, was partly destroyed as the disease flared up, as he reexperienced the hospital routines, as the fear and pain surrounding his illness intensified, as the shots and transfusions were required. These gains were never fully destroyed, but they were not accumulative. However, Jimmy's hostile outbursts reached a peak during the course of therapy and then subsided significantly.

In both of these contrasting worlds, there were dimensions of Jimmy that remained embedded in fibers of his identity. He had a zest for life, a ringing laughter, and impish, gleeful eyes. But beyond all of the observable, describable characteristics, there was a certain unique substance, a certain way of being that was always present when Jimmy entered a room, a personal identity that had never existed before and will never exist again.

We lived together in the two worlds—the world of creation and the world of decay—and we lived moment by moment, each moment containing its own unique meaning and relevance. Each time, there was always the present moment, only the present moment. It was this moment which counted for us, which created the bond between us. This moment existed complete in itself even though we both knew that it might be the last. But, knowing or not knowing, all we could do together was to live, to embrace with full commitment who we were and who we could be within each experience as it unfolded in the present. It could not have counted any more fully or be lived any more fully than it was, even if we had known that any particular moment was to be our last. Each meeting was crucial and lived within the existential crisis which made our therapy a unique encounter. We went on in this way, living concretely, two human selves intertwined in a beautiful but tragic destiny, until the final moment came and Jimmy returned no more.

2
Little Mocking Bird 🌸
Dorothy W. Baruch

SINCE I AM LIVING on time that medical science enables one to borrow these days, I keep asking myself: In what there is left to me, shall I write poetry? Or a novel? Or the things I've wanted to put into other books, but which were too startling? Not to be spoken of. At least not as I hope to speak, of truth about children, which sounds as if truth were stretching on an unsteady tiptoe.

As fiction anything goes these days, but not as truth, when the truth holds a shock about the thoughts of a child. A child must pathetically hide inside him the monstrous things, the preposterous giant imaginings, the incredibly serious wonderings, the crazy sounding but poignant longings. For fear of ridicule, he must hold these in. For fear of being met with astonished condemnation.

I have great feeling for parents who feel they know so little, who fear they can't do what they need and want to do for their children. "It's always hardest with your own." Parents are eager and hungry to know. But, for too long they have been made to feel unable to handle what they deserve to know. Parents are puzzled. They worry over their own strictness (there's been so much said about "freedom"); sex in their children (so much about freedom here too); masturbation; delinquency; hostility, most of all.

They worry whether they are good parents, whether they love enough? They doubt themselves in this when they feel the outcroppings of animosity toward their children that most parents feel at times. They worry whether their children love them enough. And they doubt this love when a child gives frank expression to the hostility within him. They fail to realize that at least some of the child's grievances are unrealistic: the result of not having imagined wants fulfilled.

There should not be the need for children to bury feelings and fantasies that breed troubles when unaired. There should be more earnest and knowledgeable attention, more hearing, more understanding that goes forth at a quiet pace to meet our children's feelings.

All people with children can give themselves to this: parents and teachers who care for most of our children throughout their years of growing, doctors and clergymen, people in many professions. Because they are human and have once been children themselves, they hold within themselves the ability to understand children's feelings.

We can all understand. We can all listen and hear.

But first, the clogging wax of ignorance must be removed from our ears. We must emerge from behind our bunkers of adult defense against a child's indecencies, monstrosities, preposterous leanings—and discover how to make peace. We can become less offended by the raw inner stuff of childhood's emotions, less skeptical of their presence, if we are given the chance.

This is a dream for the future, but not too far distant. Some of us have already opened the gates toward understanding. Some have already made the beginnings of showing children that what they have in their minds can be accepted so that it comes to confuse and worry them less, so that the normal problems of childhood remain normal, so that much of what is unhappy, unpeaceable, unproductive is prevented before its underground root-branchings have spread.

What can I do? What do I feel "called on" to do, as it were, in the time that I still have? The closest I have come to it is a kind of going back over experiences I've had as a therapist . . . a kind of informal talking with parents and teachers, other therapists, and people in other professions who are interested in children, about what children feel and think and don't ordinarily talk about but want desperately to have us understand, about us, too, and our adult reactions and the things that keep us from understanding, and what we perhaps can do to open our hearts.

> We have come to this day
> > of astronauts . . . of missiles . . . of men with
> > > machines
> > who handle with sureness
> > the finger-tip message of death.
> And yet—
> > as man and woman,
> > fathers, mothers, people with children—
> we are at a loss.
> > > From our shut-in places of silence we ask:
> > > What to do about feelings that keep us apart?
> > > > Anxiety. Anger.
> > > > Anger that we have arrived at this pass.
>
> We have come to this day
> > of science . . . of computations. . . .
> > > And yet as man and woman,
> > > > we are still searching
> > > > for ways of saying with trust,

> "I give myself to you
> without fear of losing myself."

We have come to this day
   uncertain of paths
   to loving our children
   with warmth that endures
   those times when warmth lags.

     We have come to now—
       at last knowing we must
       find in the message of human to human
       more sure, tender touch.

There are so many things a child thinks and feels and dares not talk about, that he holds inside. If he so much as lets one of these push timidly out of its hole, he catches our look, our horror, our indignation, or our amusement. Not the listening attentiveness that trouble deserves.
   Children want us to listen and to hear them.
Why don't we?

   Too little time?
   Too busy?

What they feel should not be said, isn't fit to be heard. The little animal in them should keep out of sight.
   But perhaps with more honesty: We are afraid.
   The fear of our own feelings—and of our children's as an echo of what ours may have been—keeps us from doing the very things we most want.
   How do we know what children feel?

   The child therapist has an ear to their heartbeat . . .
     And so let us talk about—
   What the therapist hears
   What this can mean to children—

Here I think of a child, a very disturbed child, possessing many of the fantasies and feelings typical of "normal" children, but so intensely loaded that they might seem quite otherwise.

When I went into the reception room, the mother was showing the child a magazine. My eyes took in the two blond braids, ends tied with pink bows. The spotless white pinafore ruffled over the shoulders. The starched pink dress.

The mother looked up. "I forgot to tell you," she said in her too sweet voice, "Timmy wanted to do this today. He just loves to dress up like a girl."

In the playroom I stared at him and muttered half to myself, "I wonder does Timmy really like it so much?"

He stared at me. Opened his mouth. Blinked his eyes into the unseeing squinch of tightness his mother had described as the tic that lately had come with increasing frequency when he tried to talk and could not get out his words.

I wanted to open my arms, to hold him to me, to say to him, "Look, all of this isn't you!" But I didn't follow my instinct. I was stupidly stiff. Letting protocol steer me, I pointed to the box of playthings on the floor.

He stood looking down at it. "I—I—I c-c-can't get my dress dirty."

And suddenly I was free from protocol. The dress be damned. The important thing was the boy! And aloud, "To hell with the dress then. Take it off if you'd like. And do what you, yourself, want."

He burst into peals of laughter. He shook with laughter. Doubled over in giggling. Then stood straight and tall. "To hell with the dress." And off he went into peals again.

He pulled at the apron strings. Pulled apart the beautiful bow his mother had so carefully tied. Very soberly he undid the dress. Pulled off the braided wig. In the sunsuit he'd worn underneath, he sat on the floor, looked up at me and declared, "I'm your little mocking bird. To hell with the dress!"

When his mother had come in initially, she had told me about his blocked speech, his tic, his bed-wetting, the masturbation she "was afraid he engaged in" in spite of her warnings that if he touched himself he would make himself sore and might—vaguely—"suffer permanently." He would beat himself over the ears, cupping his hands. (I thought: Perhaps so as not to hear.) She mentioned his unaggressiveness with the other children in kindergarten. His timidity with them. His fear of being "picked on." His lack of standing up for himself. But what she did not mention was the dressing-up business. Nor that his father had blown up at her, "If he turns out to be a homo I'll kill him. Or at least disinherit him."

"Not that his father ever really has liked him," she added at the time she told me this.

During her pregnancy, Beth "knew" the child would be a girl. She dreamed of dressing her little girl to perfection. "All pink and white and ruffly!"

When she saw her baby after its birth, still in the delivery room, her head "half-woozy," she'd looked at him and had thought, "That pink thing. How beautiful!" And quickly, "How vulnerable. How awful for me to have to be responsible for that!" But, "I learned how to take care of it. To wash it. To keep it clean." And now with Timmy at five and a half, she still held his penis when he urinated. "He can't steer it himself."

"Don't touch!" she would tell him. To him, she seemed to be saying, "It's not yours to steer." His wetting "in his sleep" was a kind of protest to feel that he still had what it took to make him whole physically. A kind of avowal of himself, which he dared not avow in his waking moments.

He was part of her. She was teaching him to read. Taking

his brainpower to herself with great pride. She wrote notes to me from him that I discovered he knew nothing about. And yet she wrote in first person singular and signed his name. (He is mine! He is me! My son! But dress him up, Beth, so no one can see. Turn him into—My girl!) Men were no good. But I sensed from what she had said and from the expressiveness of her face and body that slumbering in her was the wish for a man warmly beside her, a grown man, not a small boy. Some day perhaps this wish would emerge. But meanwhile, for her with her therapist and for her son with me, there would be long, struggling days.

Just as for his own preservation, he had felt he needed to stay part of his mother, so now Timmy felt he had to stay part of me. "I am your mocking bird." (As if he were saying, "I cannot be me, freely moving in my own direction. I must follow you.")

Inside myself I had to keep saying, "Go gently, gently. It will take the long, gentle plan. He will need gradually to separate himself from you. But he must do this without feeling rejected. It will give him protection for a while to be part of you-who-can-release-him. This will help him gain courage to release himself from a part of someone who cannot yet wish him Godspeed on his own. Sooner or later, he will need to find that he does not have to remain part of me to be safe, that he can be a separate person, and that I will still protect him as one human being protects another in need." I would have to watch for the clues, the cues, the signs, even the smallest, that would show his readiness to take his first independent steps. And I would need to open gates and structure the situation from time to time in order to lead him ahead.

With his funny little gnome face and cropped sandy hair, he would look up at me—this very disturbed five-and-a-half-year-old child. "I am your little mocking bird."

So began his persistent siege. He would remain a part of

me. He would sit as I sat, stand in whatever pose I happened to stand, pretend to write when I wrote. . . .

I remembered he had been afraid to get his dress dirty. I wondered if I might utilize his wish to imitate me to help him past this fear into an introduction to greater freedom. So I hauled out the clay bucket from its corner of the toy closet and felt a hand beside mine on the handle. He was hauling too.

Dump out the moist clay. Dig in. Dig in. My hands digging.

His hands dug too.

Finger paints slurrfing on paper.

No pattern. Just action. With me hoping he would go into patterns of his own.

Finally one day I said to him, "Perhaps today, my little mocking bird, you can choose something you'd like to play with."

"Can choose something you'd like," he echoed seriously.

I nodded.

He nodded.

"You can take it out now yourself."

"Out now yourself."

Glancing at him I thought I detected a wicked, small smile.

"You—you," I laughed gently and I think tenderly—at least that was the way I felt. "I think you want to be a real mean little mocking bird."

"Mean little mocking bird. . . ." He was grinning broadly. Then the giggle burst forth.

Moving swiftly, he took out one thing, another. Everything. Everything. Piling things high on the floor.

Then, looking at me he struck my pose again. "Your mean little mocking bird," he grinned.

He loved words. "I think you want to be my ex-asp-er-ating little mocking bird."

"Exasperating," he said. And he was. The fact that I was accepting his wish to be a nasty little mocking bird, a naughty little mocking bird, a teasing, angry little mocking bird, seemed to give him more courage.

The hauling out of things moved from its formless clutter. He would touch something, take it out, put it back.

"You seem to be looking for something?"

"Looking for something." But this time his words were not just an echo. He spoke them without my questioning intonation. He was talking with his own positive voice.

In the next session he asked for finger paints. And he painted a picture. (He was six now.) It was, he told me, a girl in a pink dress sitting on the toilet. And it was, quite distinguishably. Then carefully mixing a darker pink with his finger, he made a stroke between the girl's legs. "Her pink stick," he said. Then squinched up his eyes.

Back and forth. It always goes that way. A spurt of courage. A sputter of fear.

He looked dejected. He touched one thing. Then another on the toy shelf. Lifted it. Put it down.

"Do you want something, Timmy? Can I help you find it?" I rose and went to the closet.

He looked up at me. Started to cup his ears, as he did when he would beat at them. But this time it was an abortive gesture. He dropped his arms, leaving his ears free to hear. Then he put one hand out slowly toward me and pulled me gently to a chair.

And then, wordlessly, he opened his pants. Took hold of his penis and showed it to me. Barely above a whisper he asked me, "Is it an all right pink stick, Dorothy?"

Perhaps I should have said, "Why do you ask, dear? Tell me about it." But I didn't. I felt this was not a time to explore. But a time to confirm. I nodded. "I think it's a wonderful pink stick."

"Do you?" with puzzling incredulity. "Do you really like pink sticks, Dorothy?"

"Yes," caution to the winds. "Yes, Timmy, I do."

And suddenly the gnome face gave way to the face of a boy.

He never showed me his penis again. He didn't seem to need to. He came to the same point in other ways. There was, for instance, his play with the bird.

He went to the toy closet and got it from the box, where it lay with an assortment of molded animals. A tiny bird. He went after it deliberately, knew exactly where it was so that it was apparent he had seen it before but had not dared take it out. He stroked it gently. Cuddled it fondly in his hand. Touching it, beaming. "We won't let anybody hurt our bird."

He wanted me to help him shape a clay nest in which the baby bird could lie "safe and hidden" and to fasten this onto the wall high in the toy closet, where no one could reach it. And he exacted a promise from me that I would not let any other child bring in the ladder to "even peek."

Next session he asked me to bring the bird down to be fed. "Those chocolate kisses." He knew they were in the candy box in the cupboard. He'd discovered them when the cover had rolled off the box on one of his days of dragging things out indiscriminately. But he had never asked for any candies for himself. Now, however, his bird should be fed. "See, Dorothy. See how he opens his mouth!" With this, he stretched his own neck in a birdlike gesture and opened his own mouth demandingly wide for me to drop the chocolates in. He stood back. "Now lap-sit him carefully. Don't let him fall."

He handed the bird to me. Watched me cuddle it, rocking the tiny thing in the palms of my hands in my lap. He sighed deeply. Smiled.

But then his eyebrows puckered together. And in a far-off

voice he said, "My mother, you know, she's not a very lap-sitting woman. I don't think she was a very lap-sat girl."

For weeks, each time he came, he checked immediately, the anxious lines vanishing when he found the nest still there. "There are bad people after birds, you know. There's one bad boy in school. He's a grabber." (To his mind, his mother in disguise? This could be one reason why he had been so afraid of other children in school.)

For weeks he had me tend the bird, lap-sit it, feed it. "We wouldn't let anyone hurt it, would we?"

He used the "we" continuously now. I listened carefully to find out its meaning. He did not use it as the editorial "we," meaning "I." It was rather a replacement of his being my mocking bird, except that as part of me now, he did not just follow and imitate. He could at times suggest for himself what he wanted to do.

He played a lot with the "wild zoo animals." "The monsters! They eat people up." Suddenly stopping with eyebrows drawn, looking up at me anxiously, "We won't let anyone hurt our bird? Feed him now, Dorothy." Seeking with his own open mouth the comfort of being protectively fed.

He made lumpy monsters of clay. "They get themselves filthy. But, Dorothy, we won't let anyone hurt our bird. Feed him now, please."

Comforted and protected, he grew in inventiveness. Made up his own private set of animals. "The zoo-poohs." Among them: The great, ferocious "sharkers" with enormous "toothful mouths." And the fast-running, fast-swimming "baby grumpets" with many arms. "*So in case the sharkers bite off an arm, then one of the other arms can take over its work.*" And then, with the thought of an arm being bitten off, "*Cuddle him, Dorothy. Feed him. Feed him.*" Again and again: "*We won't let anyone hurt our bird.*"

The "we" still made us one. He and I, amalgamated, were

strong enough to circumvent hurt. But by the same token, the "we" was also a kind of resistance to going further on his own. For one thing, it was safer than soaring on spreading wings to the place where he would come upon his view of his mother's fantasies and to the place where his own accumulated anger would bring its explosive dangers to light.

For awhile, I used the "we" with him. I hoped he would feel that even though I understood its meaning to him, still to me it meant something different. It meant: *You, Timmy, supported by me who am bigger and stronger and have the authority here; we together can keep you safe while you confront these fantasied dangers and discover that what you imagine is not actually fact.*

I fed the emotionally hungry, bird-mouthed Timmy and cuddled the little bird. At the end of each session, at his request, I helped put it safely back in its nest. And in my strongest voice I reiterated, "No, we will not let anyone hurt him." Until one day Timmy took the little bird from me. Lifted it high above his head. Soared around the room. Jubilantly. "*See! See! He can fly now, Dorothy. He won't need his nest any more.*"

When he came in for his next session, he was noticeably anxious. Out of the cupboard with this and that. This and that. Dropping a cluttered heap on the floor. Skittering. Settling down on nothing.

It is usually this way. Back and forth. A spurt of courage. A sputter of fear.

What fantasies, I wondered, were frightening him? We had to get at them. This clutter obscured them. It did not reveal.

He'd been cuddled. Fed. He'd relived, as it were, a more satisfying babyhood than he'd had originally. It was time now to move on. He'd signaled his readiness when of his own accord he'd discarded the nest.

"Such a mess!" I mused aloud, viewing the muddled heap. "It looks like a junk heap that a bird might think it could hide in. But not a very comfortable one." And to Timmy, "I think you'd better choose some one thing you'd like to play with, or two, or three. You decide which. And then I'll help you put the rest away."

He sat dejectedly on the floor, stared in front of him, and didn't even look up at me.

I sat down on the floor beside him, put an arm around his thin little shoulders. "I think you're kind of scared."

He was ramrod stiff. But almost imperceptibly he shifted and leaned against me. So I sat there with him a few long minutes. And then I said matter-of-factly, "There! Let's get going. I'll get back to my chair and my note-taking. And you put your thinking cap on and choose what to play with."

"Which two things? . . ." in a whisper. And half-heartedly, "The clay, I guess. And the bird."

When the clutter was cleared, he looked at his two things, the mound of clay and the bird. But his shoulders were still droopily hunched.

"I think maybe you're still pretty scared."

"The little bird is," he nodded. "He wants to go back to his nest."

"I know," I said, this time addressing the bird. "I know you want to go back to your nest. But I know too that you're strong enough now to be able to fly."

"B-b-but," with hands over ears. "H-h-he wants to go back."

"He's awfully scared not to."

He nodded tearfully. Rose. Came and stood beside me. With the shy touch of uncertainty he pushed my hair from my ear, and he whispered into it. "But you don't know what he'll do if he flies." And then, moving around so he could watch my expression, he brought it out with a rush, looking petrified as he did so. *"The little bird'll doodoo right down on mean people's heads."*

I put my head back and laughed, and he laughed with me. "We thought that was funny," he chuckled.

"Yes," I said, "we did. And I think too that every little bird I know, naturally wants to do that when he's mad."

He was quiet and thoughtful. "Will you lap-sit him now again?" (Would I care for him still after glimpsing his hostility?) "But of course."

Pathetic little Timmy retreating, like the bird wanting to go back to its nest. Or further back, to a state before birth. But even in his backward-going, he had taken a tremendous step forward. He had said, *"You keep him there, safe for me."* We were two separate people! Timmy was at last acknowledging that he himself had his own identity, which he could look to me to protect.

One day the toy delivery truck, he declared, was a "Dorothy truck." He placed one of the dowels in it. Then he had the "mother fire engine" chase after the delivery truck. "She's going to try to steal the stick."

"But the truck isn't going to give it to her. It's delivering it to Timmy. That's the person it's for."

"Oh!" he exclaimed. And his mind made a jump seemingly disconnected but in actuality triumphantly sound. "Oh!" he exclaimed. "I just thought of my monkey. Did you know, Dorothy? He's ready now to be born a boy."

When he had the monkey out of my pocket, he inspected it critically. "It's not right," he said. "He has no sticking-out pink stick." And with a tinge of anger at me, "Can't you get him one?"

In some way I would.

Between then and the following session I puzzled and experimented. How would I do this? Finally, by putting a pin into the body of the monkey in the proper place and covering it with pink, waxy, hard clay that held firmly, I'd done what he asked.

Timmy came in. "Did you? Did you do it?" Doubts mingling with eagerness.

When he saw it he threw his arms around me. "He has it! He has it!"

He reached for the monkey, his face radiant. Held it in one hand and with the other hand proudly touched its most treasured part.

Timmy placed the monkey on the stool next to my chair. And there it sat during many sessions. A kind of symbol of his own right to be. Monkeyish. Monster and gentle creature varying. As he expressed it himself later, *"Both the bad and the good. Like me. I'm both the bad and the good. I'm the director, you see, doing both parts. So both have to naturally be parts of me."*

With both bird and monkey, by keeping the token of his body's wholeness, he came to feel that he could grow more whole in being himself.

3

❦ Just a Stupid Little Boy
Richard C. Kogl

TO MOST ADOLESCENTS, the world is a jungle and home is a garden. A garden ill prepares one for life in the jungle. There is a hothouse artificiality about home, but there is no such artificiality in the jungle of one's peers. In the jungle, one must test and prove oneself to know one's worth, to feel secure, to grow and live. And so the teenager runs from the safety of the family circle to the demands of his circle of friends. Perhaps, his friends give little warmth or recognition, but they provide the promise of life as it really is, the future as it really will be. Repeatedly, the adolescent comes back to the haven of the garden of his home, only to leave again and return to the jungle of his reality.

However, some teenagers perceive the world as a particularly harsh jungle of competition or, worse, as a sterile wasteland, empty of rewards or nurture. Even more than most adolescents, such a troubled youngster needs an adult to show him how it is possible to survive, grow, and live with dignity in an essentially hostile world. An adult shows this by words and deeds, but especially by being an honest and open person, someone with whom the adolescent can identify.

If the troubled youngster sees the world as a hostile place and if the only adults in his life, smothered in their own self-deception, provide him with empty jargon and false gestures, but not meaning, the young person develops a feeling of helplessness, insignificance, meaninglessness. Out of these feelings may grow a need to deny powerlessness by an act of strength and to express anger at the ungiving world by an act of defiance. These needs are fulfilled by delinquency. Delinquent behavior is defiant and provides a narcotic illusion of power and significance. Delinquent behavior becomes the means of concealing one's vulnerability and meaninglessness.

Traditional treatment often fails with such a person. He distrusts what is thrust upon him by the adult establishment he has come to despise. He is, because of his youth, too bound to the present to deal with such abstractions as past and future. He is not in the mood to talk about troubles if at the present moment he is content. He cannot schedule himself to talk about himself and his feelings at an appointed hour one or two or three times a week. Furthermore, he perceives the silence of noncommittal, nondirective techniques as indicating adult indifference. He cannot grasp the peculiar rules of the traditional psychotherapeutic game.

The Children's Center at the Napa State Hospital in California has attempted to avoid some of the disadvantages of traditional treatment. For the most part, the youngster chooses which adults he wishes to have as friends, and the youngster moves into these relationships at his own pace, carefully evaluating the staff member from a safe distance before coming close.

Most of the time, the behavior between the adolescents and adults is a casual, friendly bantering. Superficially "no treatment" is taking place. However, such an interpretation of "no treatment" is as much a misreading of significance as saying that nothing is taking place at those times when the analyst is silent during the fifty-minute hour. The apparent chaos of a ward of the Children's Center contrasts with the apparent decorum of the analyst's office, but the essential process is not so very different. In both settings, there is an opportunity only a small part of the time for words or actions that have optimal therapeutic impact. The form, content, and timing of those words or actions will depend to a large degree on the alertness, skill, investment, and commitment of the therapist. A therapist may goof off with impunity in either setting, but, in either setting, he has the opportunity for significant beneficial impact.

At the Children's Center, the peer group has as important an influence on the individual adolescent as elsewhere in the world, but instead of having an effect at cross purposes with adults, the group of patients identifies with the staff. The group of young people has accepted certain of the values of the staff—that it is worthwhile to understand oneself so that one may live a richer, less self-destructive life. A new patient identifies with the group, including the group's feeling that it is valuable to talk to adults in order to obtain better understanding and meaning, and the new patient also identifies with the trusting and affectionate group feelings toward the staff.

The adults at the Children's Center are aware of the total living situation—the twenty-four-hour life of the young people. If discontinuity, the requirement to play a variety of roles, is an aspect of the sickness of our times, then at least for some young people, office therapy may reinforce the compartmentalization. At the Children's Center, adults are perceived as quasi-family members or friends. Each ward becomes an extended family. There is less need for a variety of roles and masks. At the Children's Center, the peer-group jungle and trustworthy adults exist in the same setting. There is no need for the adolescent to split his world. Strong adults are standing beside him in the jungle, helping to show him how to survive and flourish.

There is no typical patient to exemplify the principles of treatment at the Napa Children's Center. Each young person is unique, and the impact his sojourn at the Center has upon him can fit no pat formula or prediction. A great number of the troubled youngsters who come to Napa are termed juvenile delinquents. That term is a legal label and is essentially meaningless psychiatrically. It seems even more devoid of meaning when one confronts the flesh-and-blood persons who bear the label. Real people don't conform to a framework of terms and concepts, scaffolding that the mind uses in an attempt to approach a grasp of reality. So it is paradoxical, but not really strange, that the boy to be discussed in this chapter well illustrates the therapeutic impact of Napa upon the delinquent despite the fact that technically he was not a delinquent.

Ron Jennings spent most of 1963 at the Children's Center at Napa. He was fourteen, but his intelligence and a serious demeanor born of depression made him seem years older. His father was an habitual criminal who had never held a steady job. He was a cruel and brutal man. When Ron's mother entered the hospital for the boy's birth, she had a black eye and a broken nose, results of a family altercation.

During his infancy, his parents separated, and when he was five his mother remarried. That marriage ended when Ron was eleven. Divorce resulted after the stepfather broke the mother's arm and struck her with his fist.

In October 1962, Ron was accidentally struck in the head by a baseball. He sustained a concussion; and, one week later, for the first time in his life, he had a convulsion. A brain-wave test performed a few days after the seizure demonstrated an abnormality on the left side. The brain had been damaged. Ron was placed on anticonvulsants.

Five weeks after the head injury, Ron threatened to kill himself with a butcher knife, and later that day he climbed an eighty-foot tree and said he was going to jump. He was placed in the county hospital for a week.

In January of 1963, when Ron returned to school, his teachers noticed that he had changed. He was belligerent with them and with the other students, and at times he was depressed.

On January 15, Ron was found standing in the middle of a highway defiantly daring traffic to hit him. After this incident, he was brought to the Napa State Hospital, where in the admissions suite he said, "I don't care what happens to me."

During the first week on M-6, the adolescent boys' ward, Ron's depression began to lift somewhat, but he was aloof and condescending toward both adults and youngsters. Gradually, he relaxed and became friendly. His intelligence won him the attention of several adults. His enthusiastic description of past antisocial exploits won him the regard of his peers. Although he attended group-psychotherapy sessions regularly and participated actively in them, he showed no desire to talk about any fears or worries. He maintained a pose of defiant bravado. Ron seemed particularly cool toward me in those early months, and, only later, did I recognize that he feared my powers as a headshrinker—I might challenge the illusion of health that he was attempting to create.

At Ron's case conference in March, it was decided that he should remain in the hospital for a longer period of time. He had improved superficially, but he was too guarded for any of us to feel assured that his depression was gone. In the weeks following that staff decision, his forced cheerfulness dissolved. He became quiet and pensive.

Then one spring morning as I arrived for work at the Children's Center, I found Ron waiting for me at the entrance of the Children's Center Administration Building.

"Can I talk to you, Doc?"

It was not a convenient time for me to talk with him, but it was so unusual for him to make the request that I acquiesced.

We entered my office. Ron's expression was serious, intent, and tense. He was silent for a few moments, apparently deciding how to begin. The May sun had begun to whiten his blond hair. His blue eyes had the coldness they seemed to retain in all ranges of his moods from cheerfulness to sadness. He licked his lips. His voice was strained.

I don't want to go home anymore. (*He stared at me, waiting for my response.*)

Do you mean to be discharged to your home or to go on visits or what?

Both. (*His voice was without emotion.*) You see, Doc, whenever I'm at home, I get such strong thoughts about killing myself. If anything, even the slightest little thing, goes wrong, I think that I'll kill myself, and I'm afraid one of these days I'll do it.

What kinds of things go wrong?

Anything. You name it. An argument with my brother or my mother, not doing my homework right, anything like that. Any mistake I make makes me feel I'm not worth a shit, and I think the world, especially my mother, would be better off without me.

Are these feelings worse lately?

Yeah. (*Ron paused, apparently wanting me to ask the questions.*)

Any idea why the feelings are worse lately?

(*Ron nodded and then started to speak more freely.*) I guess you know my mother is divorced. Well, she's been going with this guy, and he's a pretty nice guy. Well, a couple weeks ago he got married. (*The boy stared at me.*)

You mean, he married someone else?

(*Ron nodded again.*) She had no warning he was going to do a thing like that. It was a surprise, and it's got me shook, Doc. You see, a couple years ago she tried to kill herself, and she would have if my brother and me hadn't been there to stop her. Well, Doc, what if she tries to kill herself now? I'm not around to stop her. (*There was genuine anguish in his voice.*) And another thing, now that my mother's boyfriend has married someone else, I'm afraid my mother will marry some other man who'll be as bad as my real father. I'd kill that bastard. Honest, Doc, I'd kill him—not for anything he did to me but for what he did to my mother.

What was that?

He threatened to kill her.

Ron then explained that another reason he was sad was that his grandparents had recently divorced, and even more important Ron's girl friend Candy had broken up with him at the previous Saturday night dance.

And yesterday she got transferred to the Adult Service because she's sixteen.

Why did she break up with you?

Well, she's a lot like me. She feels that she's no good for people just like I feel I'm no good for people. She told me she wanted to break up with me because she was afraid she might hurt me. Candy thinks she might kill herself someday. If she did, well, she knows that, if I were still in the picture, it would hurt me a lot. (*Ron's voice had softened. He swallowed.*) Doc, I know if I go home, I'll get all the money I can and run away to someplace like New York, and after the money's gone, if things don't work out, I know I'll get rid of myself.

You mean kill yourself?

Yes.

Then it's important that you not go home—at least not until you're feeling better.

(*Ron nodded agreement.*) You know, Doc, this is the first time

I've been honest about myself and really opened up to anybody. I think we should talk often—perhaps every day for awhile. Okay. (*Ron left the room.*)

About a half hour later Ron wanted to see me again.

After I left your office, I went over to school. I started thinking about Candy, and then I started cutting my wrist with a pair of scissors. (*He held out his left hand to show me the fresh red nicks on his wrist. Ron's voice was serious but calm, almost matter of fact.*) Could you put me in a side room, Doc? That way I won't have a chance to do any more of this sort of thing.

Yes, and I think you should be on some medicine to help you feel better.

Arrangements were made for Ron to be transferred to a side room on M-6, a room that could be used for seclusion if necessary. About twenty minutes later, I visited Ron in his room.

I think it would help if I could talk to Candy.

(*I thought about this before answering.*) I'll see whether it can be arranged with the Adult Service. It may take a day or two.

Later Jean Ammon, the M-6 psychologist, and I discussed this and decided that it would be desirable for Ron to visit Candy. Jean agreed to speak with Candy first and then take Ron to the ward to visit the girl.

On the day following our conversation, which Ron characterized as the first time he had really opened up to anybody, the boy looked more relaxed and less depressed, but he asked to remain on heavy sedation. He made no overture for a long talk with me, and I decided it would be best to wait. In the afternoon, Jean Ammon took him to see Candy. Jean told me that after the visit he looked less sad, but he complained of feeling worse.

A weekend passed, and on Monday Ron cut his wrists with a piece of broken glass. The cuts were not deep, and he was cooperative in having the wounds dressed.

I saw Ron in his side room. He was half reclining in the bed, staring ahead with a sullen, stubborn expression. He immediately showed me his newly acquired superficial lacerations.

I'm going to do it again, Doc. (*This was said between a threat and a boast.*)

What are you trying to prove? (*Ron looked at me blankly.*) Are you trying to hurt Candy?

(*His answer was soft, without insolence.*) Not consciously.

What are you trying to say to people by cutting your wrists? To me it says you feel very sad, very unhappy, but there must be more you're saying.

Candy thinks I'm a little boy. She said I was just a stupid little boy. (*His eyes filled with tears.*)

And by cutting your wrists or killing yourself, you can prove you're a man?

(*He began to cry.*) I'm not just a stupid little boy, but that's what Candy says I am.

After our talk, Ron relaxed, but at five o'clock in the afternoon, as I was preparing to leave for the day, he smashed his hand through a window. I returned to the ward and found him seated in the treatment room. A technician was holding a gauze dressing on the injured hand. I removed the dressing. Blood flowed freely. The boy had incised his index finger to the bone and into the knuckle. The white of the joint cartilage glistened in contrast to the surrounding red.

So I'm just a little boy. She thinks I'm just a little boy.

Ron's injured hand was repaired in surgery, and he was kept overnight on the surgical ward. When he returned to M-

6 on the following day, he was heavily sedated. There was danger that if he further damaged his hand or if the wound became infected, he would lose the use of his index finger or it would have to be amputated.

He slept for most of the next forty-eight hours. When he awakened, he spoke with me in the ward doctor's office.

I still feel like killing myself. I'm afraid I'm going to do it, Doc, and nobody can stop me. (*He looked at me with an expression in part challenging, in part appealing to me to prevent his suicide.*)

If these feelings continue, Ron, we'll have to put you in restraints and perhaps start shock treatment. I'm not going to let you die.

I don't want shock treatment. I want to see Candy. I've got to see her. (*There was a pleading note in his voice, yet there was a certain falseness about his emotion.*)

Why do you have to see her?

So she won't kill herself.

The other day, you were angry at her for saying you were just a little boy.

I still am angry. (*Ron slurred somewhat drunkenly.*) But I want to see her.

When you're in better shape and in better control of yourself, I'll try to arrange for you to visit her again.

Ron moved slowly, somewhat unsteadily. As we left the M-6 doctor's office, he again asked if he could see Candy immediately. I said no. Ron turned away from me and started pounding his injured hand against a cracked window. The technicians stopped him. I ordered Ron put in restraints. In part, I felt he had called my bluff.

He struggled as the restraints were applied, but as soon as he was in bed, he relaxed and said he was going to take a nap. He asked me to please awaken him when his favorite technician, Mrs. Campbell, from Ward M-5, came to visit him. He closed his eyes and fell asleep, looking very much the small child, blond, almost angelic.

In the afternoon I visited Ron again. He was awake, and he smiled wanly. As I took his arms out of restraints, he cried softly. These were not the earlier tears of anger and frustration. He was a little boy, and yet he cried adult tears of weariness with life.

There's something I don't understand, Ron. Candy says you're just a little boy, but she confides suicide thoughts to you. People don't confide suicidal thoughts to people they think of as children.

I don't know. (*Quietly*.)

Ron required restraints during much of the following weekend. At times he jumped on his bed to reach the ceiling light fixture, hoping to electrocute himself. Unknown to him, that was not possible, but there was danger that he would fall and hit his head. When in restraints, he pulled his hands tight in the cuffs until both his injured and uninjured hand turned purple.

Ron refused to eat until his best friend on Ward M-6, Keith Thomas, offered to spoon feed him. Keith kidded Ron about his being drunk, and both boys were comfortable with this justification for Ron's dependence. Keith commented with pride to the staff and the boys, "I'm the only one Ron will eat for."

Ron was no longer the tough, sophisticated teenager. He was too proud and fearful to depend on adults, to accept the nurture he deeply craved, except when he was drugged or depressed.

But Ron's behavior consisted of much more than a plea for nurture. He seemed to be saying a great many conflicting and contradictory things all at once. He wanted to be helpless. He wanted to be all powerful. He wanted to die. He wanted to control through intimidation. I was confused. There were many manipulative elements in his behavior, and I was reluctant to be taken in or be conned. I didn't know to which aspect of his complex behavioral message I should respond. So I did the safe thing. I maintained distance. I was reluctant to make a mistake, so I avoided becoming actively engaged. My pride as a therapist, my reluctance to risk, interfered with my being a therapist.

On the following Monday, while he was being returned from surgery clinic, Ron tried to smash his head through the window of the ambulance. On the ward, he refused to eat for the psychiatric technician who was assigned to stay with him. He threw his food at her. However, he did continue to allow Keith Thomas to feed him. He made repeated suicidal gestures and was again placed in restraints, and again he pulled his hands in the restraints, cutting off the circulation. His hands were swollen and purple.

The chief technician of M-6 complained to me that the ward was not equipped to handle a patient like Ron. Because of the physical makeup of the ward, there was too much danger of successful suicide. I agreed with him and was relieved to have reason and justification for transferring Ron off M-6 to an adult ward designed to reduce suicidal risk.

Mike O'Connor, the director of the Children's Center, concurred in the decision, and Ron was transferred away from M-6, but after he was gone and our anxieties had subsided, I began to doubt the wisdom of my action. I visited Ron on the adult ward. He was in belt restraints, but his arms were free. He was happy that I visited him, and he wept out of loneliness for M-6.

All my friends are there. It's the first place in my life where I've had any friends.

I assured him I would try to return him to M-6 soon.

Later in the day I spoke with Mike O'Connor. "I feel very strongly that I was reacting to the general anxiety of the Children's Center about Ron Jennings when I decided he should be transferred. Suddenly, it seemed as if a great number of different people were worried about the fact he wasn't getting better, if anything, was getting worse. It seemed as if rather quickly the feeling on M-6 changed from seeing Ron as a challenge, in the good sense of challenge, to an attitude of defeat."

Mike nodded. "Those aren't forces one can fight. It's better to go along with them. Once the attitude had changed, M-6 probably couldn't do any more for Jennings. Wisdom consists of knowing when to drift with the dominant forces in your environment and when not to."

I wanted to believe Mike's reassuring words, but I couldn't. The chief technician of M-6 had stated that the physical makeup of the ward has been the critical issue making Ron's transfer necessary, but it had not been. The issue had been the psychological makeup of the ward. I had been unable to commit myself to the total involvement Ron's behavior demanded, and my reluctance and indecision led to a loss of direction, a loss of confidence in their own abilities on the part of the M-6 technicians.

I was troubled and confused. I had played it safe and lost. But why? A therapist's pride, reluctance to make a mistake? Yes, this, and also the fact that my thinking had been hobbled by having labeled Ron "brain damaged." A baseball hit his skull in October. One week later he had a convulsion. The electroencephalogram proved his brain had been damaged. I had labeled Ron brain damaged with some kind of superimposed depression. I tried to fit his behavior into the theoretical framework such labeling provides, and this framework limited my freedom of response. I quibbled with myself about whether his behavior was organic or psychological, and while I had split academic hairs at a safe distance from the boy, the situation had deteriorated. I had missed the complex metaphorical question that he was asking me. I had responded with silence. I had played it safe and lost an opportunity.

On the first Sunday in June, five days after he left M-6, I visited Ron on the adult ward for a second time. He was rather cheerful, out of restraints, strolling around the ward. He grinned.

> I feel back to usual, Doc. Can I go back to M-6 tomorrow?
> Soon, but I can't promise it will be tomorrow.

It was almost two weeks later that he returned to M-6. His smile was broad.

> Boy, I sure missed M-6. Don't get me wrong, Doc. The people on the other ward treated me real good, but here is where my friends are.

While Ron was on the Adult Service, I arranged for one of the psychology graduate students to see him. Mr. LaFollette's first interviews with the boy were successful, and this pleased me. Knowing something was being done for Ron helped assuage the vague feelings of guilt I had. However, within a few days of Ron's return to M-6, Mr. LaFollette complained that the boy wasn't volunteering much anymore. He showed progressively less desire to speak with Mr. La Follette. I talked with Ron about this.

> I don't have any problems now, Doc. I've got nothing to talk about. Anyway, it makes me feel sort of like a freak, being called off the ward to go over to see Mr. LaFollette. Most of the other guys don't get called off the ward. And another thing, he talks so slow and quiet, and he's so polite to me and so careful what he says to me. He treats me like I'm some sort of nut.

Mr. LaFollette said he was disappointed at Ron's lack of motivation. "Dr. Kogl, Ron told me he has nothing to talk about. I told him I wouldn't set up any more appointments. I said he should contact you if he wants to see me any more." The student shook his head in discouragement. "It would be easier if he were ten or twenty. Past and future problems don't have much significance for him. They would for an adult. It's very difficult to do therapy with adolescents."

"It's true that a teenager usually reaches out for help only at times of immediate distress, but there are other times as well. The trouble is that the opportunities are rare and fleeting and can't be forced into a schedule. Being on the ward, being available to them as much of the time as possible makes it more likely that a significant encounter will occur, but even then one misses many, many opportunities. You see, with these kids, sustained contact doesn't occur. They come and go, set their own pace, choose when they want an adult's help." Rather sadly, recalling my own behavior a few weeks earlier, I added, "And then finally when they do ask for something meaningful from you, you may not hear them."

"But how can I cut down his negative feelings about being a patient in need of treatment? How can I make it a high-prestige rather than a low-prestige situation?"

"The more you can avoid the conventional therapist's role, the better. Most teenagers see that as a pretty phony role, and perhaps it is. Many of the boys consider it a special treat to go for rides. You might drive him to the lake on the grounds or go for a walk with him."

"Yes, maybe I'll try that." The student sat silently for a few moments. "I've never met a kid quite like him. He's so adult acting in many ways."

"That's part of the problem. He's afraid to let his guard

down and become dependent on you. To him that would mean becoming babyish, in other words vulnerable. That's something that scares him."

As I spoke the words, I recognized that not only Ron was afraid of being vulnerable, but also Mr. LaFollette was afraid of being vulnerable, just as I had been. I wanted to say something to the student to help him, to drive the fear away, but there were no comforting words. I still possessed the fear myself, as does every therapist. The events in May had sharpened my awareness of that fact. But each therapist has to choose for himself whether he will run from frightening vulnerability or whether he will find courage to stand and expose his soul to another human being for that is what an honest encounter involves. I could not make such a choice for Mr. LaFollette. I could not even recommend.

Mr. LaFollette did not continue seeing Ron, and Ron did not ask to see him. I was disappointed. Ron was in need of help. Although he was passing through a period of calm, the explosive self-destructive potential remained. I was sad that despite Mr. LaFollette's sincere interest in helping Ron, I could not enable the student to depart from conventional notions of therapy enough to demonstrate a commitment to Ron rather than to a role.

For the next two months Ron was relaxed and cheerful, enjoying his many friendships at the Children's Center. He spoke a little about himself, tentatively, to his favorite technician Nadine Campbell, but his conversations with me and the rest of the staff were guarded despite the surface appearance of casualness.

On the second weekend in August, a few days before his next scheduled case conference, Ron had a fist fight with a new, tall, fifteen-year-old patient. After the fight Ron smashed his fist into a window, acquiring a collection of superficial cuts. He spoke of suicide and complained to the technicians that he was losing all of his friends. I spoke to him on the Monday morning following the incident, and he asked about his case conference, which was scheduled for Thursday.

What's going to happen to me, Doc?
It depends a lot on you, Ron. Do you feel ready to be discharged?
No. (*He held up his bandaged hand.*) And maybe this will convince 'em I should stay in the hospital.
I think you could have convinced us with words. You didn't have to do that.

Ron shrugged.
Keith Thomas, Ron's best friend, was scheduled to be picked up by his family that evening. He was being discharged from the hospital. I imagined that Ron had Keith in mind when he complained that he was losing all of his friends.
That evening, a few hours before he was to be discharged, Keith left the weekly Children's Center dance and sat on a bench on the grounds and cried. He didn't want to go away from the Children's Center. Earlier in the week, he had threatened to get in trouble purposely so he could be sent back to M-6, and now he announced to his friends that he was going to run away.
Ron was worried. He was certain Keith would steal a car and perhaps get in serious trouble. After nervously waiting for ten or fifteen minutes, Ron left the hospital grounds in the hope of finding Keith and inducing him to return. He searched without success. Unknown to him, Keith had changed his mind and instead of running away had walked to Ward M-5 to say goodbye to the technicians.
By the time Ron Jennings returned to M-6 in the middle of the night, Keith had been gone for hours. His family had picked him up as scheduled.
Ron's concern and devotion were not surprising. It had

been Keith who had spoon fed Ron two months earlier, when Ron refused to eat for anyone else.

Ron sadly reported the events of the evening to me on the following day. He also told me more about why he had been upset during the weekend. His new girl friend, Debbie, called him a stupid little boy.

With some surprise I said, "That's exactly what Candy said last spring!"

Yes. (*Ron sighed.*) A while back, I told Debbie how shook I got last spring when Candy said that. So this weekend when Debbie got mad at me, she said the same damned thing—the same damned thing! (*He pounded his fist on the desk for emphasis.*) And it was just after that that McNellis and I got into a fight, and that's why I got mad and smashed the window.

On the following morning as I drove up to M-6, Ron Jennings met me at the car and started to ask for something. Then he stopped and said, "Forget it."

What were you going to ask?
I was going to ask you to drive me to the canteen.

Ron rarely asked favors of me, so to his surprise I replied, "I'll take you." In the car I asked him how long it would be.

About five minutes.
Well, I'll drop you off at the canteen, and you can walk back.
(*He was silent for a few moments.*) If you'd do me another favor it would only take one minute instead of five.
What favor is that?
Buy a pack of cigarettes for me.
(*I pondered this a bit. It was irrational, but my impulse was that I should.*) Okay, I'll do it.

On the ride back to the ward after purchasing the cigarettes Ron said, "You could get in twice as much trouble for doing that."

How do you mean—twice as much trouble?
Well, not only are you an adult buying cigarettes for a minor, but you're an employee.
I guess you're right.

Then Ron asked if the two M-4 girls who had run away on the same evening Keith had been discharged had been found.

I don't know. I don't believe so.
What'll happen to them when they're found and brought back?
I don't know.
You see, Doc, the reason I'm kind of specially curious is that I helped them get away.
You did?
Yeah, you know when I was leaving to look for Keith? Well, I ran into them, and I helped them.

He volunteered no more information, and I said nothing.
Group therapy began as soon as Ron and I arrived on M-6. He again brought up the topic of the M-4 girls and wondered what would be done to him for his part in helping them run away.

I don't know.

Harvey Bernstein, a small, querulous patient, was irritated by this.

Tell the truth, Dr. Kogl. What will happen to Ron?
I'm really not sure—I don't recall anything quite like this coming up before. There isn't any standard punishment.

(*Ron stared at me seriously and spoke quietly.*) You let us do anything, don't you?

I don't think so. Why do you say that?

He answered by holding up the cigarettes I'd purchased for him.

In the afternoon Ron wanted to speak to me alone. The two M-4 girls had been returned to the ward. As punishment for their runaway they were to be restricted to their ward for one week and were to go to bed at 7 P.M.

Now just hypothetically what if an M-6 boy went over to M-4 between 7 and 8 P.M. and got caught talking to one of the girls through the window? What would happen to him?

He'd probably be put on restriction himself—maybe for a week—which reminds me, you seemed somewhat disappointed this morning that I didn't have any punishment for you for your having helped the girls run away. Maybe you should be restricted to the ward at 7 P.M. every evening this week.

I wasn't disappointed there was no punishment.

But you said I let you boys get away with anything.

I really didn't help them much. I just told them to duck when I saw the security patrol car coming, but after the girls left I started worrying. (*Ron's mood had changed from cockiness to seriousness.*) I figured what if something happened to them or what might happen to them when they come back—I had heard about some of the girls I knew here who are now on the Adult Service—I heard they ran away and when they came back they were pregnant.

It sounds to me as if your worrying has already punished you for what you did Monday evening.

Yeah. (*His face was sad.*) That's right.

Well, you know Bernstein asked this morning what your punishment would be. I think discipline and punishment are mainly for kids. Being disciplined is an easy way of paying for having made a mistake. But as an adult, when you make a mistake, you worry and feel sorry, and that's a lot harder. It probably would have been easier for you if there'd been some punishment for helping the runaway rather than having to worry about it.

That's true. (*He nodded.*) Well, what if I do go over and talk to the girls on M-4 tonight?

(*I stared at him and smiled slightly.*) Ron, it seems to me you're setting up a kind of trap for me.

Why? (*His eyes were wide. He had an innocent expression on his face. At such moments, Ron could manage to look cherubic.*)

You've been saying I'm too easy on you, and now you tell me something wrong you intend to do. It seems in a way that you're asking me to prevent you from doing it. If I do prevent you from doing it, by restricting you to the ward this evening, you'll holler at my being unreasonable—unfair for taking advantage of something you told me in confidence. But if I don't restrict you, you'll think, "That bastard doesn't care what I do or care anything about me."

No, I. . . . (*Ron paused, swallowed, stared at me intently, was silent for a few moments, and then spoke.*) You've got me dead to rights. (*He stared at me longer.*) That's how I did have it set up.

And which way did you want me to react?

I think . . . (*He looked down at the floor and slowly returned his gaze to mine.*) the way you did—that you saw through it and understood. (*He smiled slightly.*) You know I thought that if you didn't stop me from going to M-4 and if I got caught and if it fouled up my conference by my getting in trouble, I'd have thought "that son-of-a-bitch wrecked everything." (*He stared ahead, pensive and serious.*) Was that pretty juvenile of me to set a trap like that?

No. It's not juvenile. It's actually more what adults do. A child is interested in being loved and accepted. If he has that, he's happy; but an adult wants respect from someone whom he respects. If someone is nice to you but you feel he's weak or a pushover, it doesn't mean much—the kindness doesn't have much value. You were testing me to see whether I was worth respecting and whether I cared about you. Teenagers do a lot of this because they hope to find honest, strong adults who can help guide them, help make sense of the world and sense of life. A child isn't aware of the kind of confusion and contradiction in the world that makes an adolescent test an adult the way you did. What you did was decidedly not childish.

(*Ron nodded rather gravely. Then his manner brightened.*)

You know, Doc, we've been good friends now for about seven months, but I really don't talk much about myself to you. I've been wondering if maybe I'm making a mistake in putting all my feelings in my new girl friend. I'm afraid it'll be just like it was with Candy. Maybe I'll lose everything again.

I don't think it's exactly the same as it was last spring because this time, in addition to having a girl you love, you've got friends you trust and rely on. You didn't have that much before. So now the risk of losing everything isn't as great.

There wasn't really anybody else in my life but Candy then, but that is different now. (*Ron smiled.*) What about my going over to M-4?

Do you still need me to take some action about it?

No, not really—I don't plan to go over there. Say, Doc, you don't have to answer this because it has to do with another patient, but what's Tom Richards' diagnosis? Is he brain damaged or what?

I'm sure Tom wouldn't object. Yes. He's brain damaged—that's the basic problem, but his brain damage interferes with learning. Yours is much milder and doesn't have any effect on your learning.

Why does Richards act so goofy?

When people are brain damaged at seven or at seventy, they feel they've lost something or lack something, and that makes them sad.

Yeah, but Richards is joking and kidding all the time.

That's a good way of covering up feeling sad or feeling you're lacking something. For example, if you ask a seventy-year-old person whose memory is getting poor, "How long have you lived in this town?" he may just joke and kid around and give you no straight answer. Then if you say, "Well, that's all very funny, but I really want to know how long you've lived here," he may become cross and irritable. Then if you insist he tell you, he may burst into tears and say, "I can't remember." People like Richards need to cover up feelings of being inadequate—hiding them from themselves and others. Silly behavior is a good way to cover up.

(*Ron stared at me seriously.*) That's what I did when I was in the hospital before I came to Napa. I talked funny and acted nutty and silly around people, but when I was alone, I'd cry.

It had been a valuable conversation with Ron. It had been a significant encounter. He tested me, thought he found me to be weak, then found me to be strong—a strong person who was concerned about him and committed to his well being.

In individual outpatient therapy, it would have been considerably less likely that I would have been forced into this sort of crisis. I would have had less to say about discipline, less to say about the mundane considerations of everyday life.

It takes a long period of seemingly doing nothing in order to build to the point where a highly significant encounter of the kind I had with Ron Jennings in mid-August becomes possible. Such an encounter may occur at any time, and one must always be ready for it. It is more than merely the timing of an interpretation. Instead, it is being aware that a significant confrontation is occurring and then responding to that confrontation not with technique and gimmicks, but with honesty—the honesty that grows out of one's struggle for self-knowledge and out of one's struggle to find meaning in life.

In the following weeks, Ron showed a warmth toward me that I had not previously seen. His friendliness for the most part took the form of good-natured teasing of me. He avoided long talks about himself.

During the first week of September, apparently for no reason other than to prove his toughness, Ron Jennings beat up Bob Cavanaugh, another M-6 patient. They were the same age, but Ron was taller and heavier and more muscular. Usually they were on good terms. After the fight Cavanaugh sobbed. Jennings listened to the admonitions of the technicians with disdain.

On the following day, Ron talked to Jean Ammon. He complained about the classes to which he had been assigned in the hospital school.

I don't want to go to this school. I'd rather do my regular school work on the ward, and if you guys don't let me drop school, I'll fix it so you have no choice.

What do you mean?

I'll get out of the kids' unit and back on the Adult Service.

How will you do that?

By attempting suicide.

It sounds as though you feel you can manipulate everyone in order to have your own way.

That's right.

Later, at five in the afternoon, Ron asked me to drive him to the canteen to buy cigarettes. I refused because I had a very different feeling about the significance of his request than I had about the similar request in August. In August, he had wanted evidence that I was concerned about him, concerned enough to break a rule for him. Now it seemed he was not asking for evidence of my concern. Instead, I felt he was testing me to see whether I were spineless and weak, someone whom he could intimidate and control.

On the next day, I received a phone call from the school. Ron refused to attend his classes. I discussed the problem with the chief technician of M-6, the psychologist, and the social worker. The social worker commented that Ron's forthcoming visit with his mother might be the reason for his increasing irritability.

As the four of us were discussing Ron and how best to cope with his negativism, the ward called me. Ron had just smashed a window and had run his forearm along the jagged glass acquiring a three-inch gaping laceration. Before I returned to the ward to suture the wound, the four of us agreed that Ron was out to test us to the limit. I suggested that he be placed on tranquilizers and restrictions. If this were not adequate, we would use restraints and seclusion. I felt no conflict, no confusion about the emphatic stand I was taking.

I closed his wound with six sutures. He was contrite and friendly, expressing concern about his mother's reaction when she would come to pick him up and would discover his injury. I was pleasant to him but noncommittal. The appropriate time to talk about significances was not while the boy's blood dripped. I didn't reprimand him, but I sutured without procaine. He didn't complain, but at one point, he said he was afraid he would faint. Later he told me he had been shaking throughout the procedure. Perhaps it was cruel to avoid the use of local anesthesia, but I did not wish to blur the reality of his act. Some would have anesthetized and scolded. I chose to allow Ron to feel the pain. The consequences of his behavior in terms of reality were more pertinent than any sermonizing from me.

I left Ron in order to attend the weekly meeting of the M-6 technicians, explaining that I would see him as soon as it was over. At the meeting, the technician Joan Elgin described how Ron had told her, while they were waiting for me, that he wished to telephone his mother so that she wouldn't be surprised by his injury when she came to visit. Mrs. Elgin blandly replied, "Oh, I don't think she'd be too surprised that you would do a thing like this. Anyway, hearing it by phone, she would probably think it was more serious than it is." Ron continued to want to phone. Mrs. Elgin rather impulsively asked, "Ron, do you want to hurt your mother?" He answered quickly, "Yes, maybe I do."

"Did he say why he might be angry with her?" I asked Mrs. Elgin.

"No, he didn't, but Mrs. Jennings has taken him on very few visits, and when she does, she doesn't take him home. They go on camping trips. Ron, his brother, and Mrs. Jennings. Ron says he believes this is because his dog is blind or perhaps dead and that his mother doesn't want him to find out."

I glanced at the social worker. "Is there anything to this?"

She shrugged. "I think that the more basic issue is that Mrs. Jennings fears that if Ron comes home on visits, it will be hard to explain to the neighbors. You see, she has told everyone he's visiting relatives out of state, but she hasn't wanted to tell Ron this because he might feel stigmatized."

"My God. Isn't all this lying worse?"

I told the technicians that we should be firm and decisive in our handling of Ron because if we seemed indecisive, he would be confused and feel a need to test us more. "However, I don't mean to say that all of his behavior is manipulative. It starts out that way, but once the process is under way, it becomes a frenzy. He can no longer simply choose to stop."

Jean Ammon agreed. "Basically Ron feels helpless. Much of his behavior of trying to control and manipulate is to cover such feelings. Yesterday he told me that when he has to go along with rules and decisions that he has had no part in making, he feels like a puppet on a string."

I discovered that not only were my reactions and the staff's reactions to Ron's self-mutilation different from the confused impotent response we had made in May, but that the boys on M-6 had a different attitude also. One of them asked in regard to Ron's cutting himself, "Why would a guy do a nutty thing like that?"

After the intershift meeting, I found Ron sitting solemnly

in the day hall of the South Wing watching a television panel show. He bounced up brightly in response to my invitation to talk, and he came along readily, almost eagerly. In the office he stretched himself on the examining table.

Now you can psychoanalyze me.

(*I didn't join in the light-hearted mood. My attitude was firm.*) What's getting you so upset?

I think it might be my mother's visit this coming weekend. I'm getting more and more excited about it. (*His answer was in a serious tone.*)

I've noticed you've been more excited—beating up Cavanaugh, things like that.

Yeah.

What about this school issue—not wanting to go to classes here? Is that bugging you a little or a lot or what?

Well, it's about equal in importance to my mother's visit.

As far as school is concerned, at conference the staff felt you should attend our school plus doing extra work. Evidently there was some misunderstanding, and you thought you wouldn't have to attend classes.

That's right.

I personally don't care one way or another. You can discuss this with the teachers. Actually I'd be willing to suggest you not go to class if I were sure your reaction was merely anger about this misunderstanding, but I'm not at all sure it's just that.

What do you mean?

Sometimes a kid makes an issue out of things as an excuse to rebel.

(*Ron looked at me with curiosity.*) Sometimes a kid wants to test who is stronger—he or the adults around him. If that's what you're doing, getting you out of classes may just mean you'd have to find something else to make an issue about, continuing to test us, trying to find whether we're a bunch of weak pushovers or if we're stronger than you.

I think what's important to me is that other people are playing fair with me.

Yes, I know that's very important to you, but whether adults are strong or weak is important to you, too. That's what puts people like Mrs. Campbell or Dr. Ammon or me on the spot. If we try to play fair, you may think we're weak. If we act strong, you feel we're not playing fair.

Most of the time, I feel people are playing fair, and I play fair with them, but then what happens?

What do you mean?

Why do I start getting concerned about whether adults are strong or weak?

I'm not sure. Sometimes when a kid has too much responsibility too early in life, he develops this kind of a problem. Part of him is afraid he isn't strong enough, isn't enough of an adult, so he needs to convince himself he's stronger than others, stronger than adults.

That's probably why I get such a kick out of conning adults. It makes me feel stronger than them.

Then you don't have to feel scared. The only trouble is that there's another part of you that would like to feel there are adults around whom you could trust and who are stronger than you. When you con people, you feel good at first because it makes you feel strong, but down deep I think you feel disappointed in them. You cross them off your list because you can't turn to them for help when you need it. Conning is like taking heroin: it gives a pleasant kick at first, but the long-range effect is bad—a letdown.

So in a way, I'm addicted to conning. (*Ron smiled.*)

In a way. You keep trying time and time again to find out whether adults are weak and worthless or strong.

There are only two people in my life who ever caught me at conning them—and that was Mrs. Campbell and you. Do you think that means you are the only two I could turn to when I need help?

I don't know.

I think maybe so. Ever since I was eight, when my parents got divorced and my mother went to work, I've had to take care of myself and my younger brother and sister, but I don't remember feeling I wasn't adult enough. I always felt I could do anything. Could this other feeling be unconscious?

Yes, very often it is. What makes me suspect it's there, even though you don't feel it, is that your behavior says two things at once. When you smash windows, threaten suicide, and get everyone to cater to you, on the one hand, you're saying, "Look how strong I am, I can run the show"; but you're also saying, "Look at me. I'm running wild. I'm out of control. I need someone to stop me. I need someone to control me."

Do you think there's some kind of pattern—something that sets it off when I act this way? Could we go over my chart and see what seems to cause it?

We could. Perhaps we should, but I think we already have some clues about what sets this off. When you're playing fair with people and trusting and depending more and more and then someone does something to hurt—like with Candy . . .

When she called me a baby, a little boy?

Yes, that hurt, and perhaps it hurt you more than it would the next guy because it came close to what your own fears are about yourself. It was too close . . .

To the mark?

Yes.

And then I broke windows and cut my hand to prove I was important.

(*I nodded.*) And with this recent school issue . . .

You know what I thought when I found out I was assigned to those classes? I thought those bastards all ganged up and did this to bug me.

No, it wasn't like that. We didn't all gang up on you, but maybe it was something almost as bad. There was a mixup—a breakdown in communication—and that shouldn't happen. Being lost in the shuffle is about as bad as being ganged up on.

But I shouldn't have jumped to conclusions. (*He sat and stared ahead, deep in thought.*) You know my mother is supposed to visit me every two weeks, but it comes out to every six weeks. (*He was silent again.*) I don't like it.

I understand that, when she does visit, she doesn't take you home.

Well, you see, Doc, I think my dog is blind or maybe dead and she doesn't want me to find out and get upset. You know whenever she had bad news for me she'd always say, "Ron, I've got something bad to tell you and something good to tell you," then she'd maybe say that my pet mice had died but that she'd bought me something special I'd been hoping for. She was always good to me. I love her, but in a way, it was wrong for her to buy me things when something bad happened.

Why? What was wrong about it?

Because it wasn't her fault the mice died or whatever the bad thing was that happened.

I think you're right. She meant to be kind, but in trying to cancel out the unhappy things in life that way, she was setting up a sort of false promise.

I don't get you, Doc.

I mean there was bound to come a time when something bad would happen that she couldn't make up for.

You know, a few years ago my stepfather's family tried to turn me against her. They told me I was adopted, that my stepfather wasn't my real father, and they got me to spy on her, to check on where she went and who she saw, and I phoned them and told them. Then as a reward for all of that spying, after saying all those bad things about her to me, they gave me a shotgun and shells. You know, maybe they were trying to set it up so I'd shoot her. I didn't feel it at the time, but now I think they used me all that time. They just used me.

It sounds as if they did use you.

Like playing with me, like a cat with a mouse. Later my mother told me that my stepfather hadn't been my real father, but I already knew.

How did you feel about her not having told you?

Not good. It was sort of as if she were just playing with me, too.

I can understand after the way your stepfather's family used you that you would have a fear that adults can't be trusted, that you have to be stronger than they are.

I wanted to be independent. I still do, but I want to have some people I can trust and rely on.

I think you should be independent and also have some people you can trust.

If there's nobody you can trust, you're all alone in the world.

Afterward Ron spoke excitedly with the technicians about our talk, and he repeated much of the content of the conversation. The next day, Ron was in good spirits. He said that we had identified his basic problems and, therefore, he had no need for the tranquilizers I had started.

I think you know yourself better than anyone else does. If you say you feel O.K. and don't need medicine, I'll cancel the orders.

I'd like to phone my mother today so she'll know about my arm before she comes tomorrow. I'll explain it's just a minor cut so she won't worry.

I don't think it's such a good idea to call her. No matter what you say, she's likely to exaggerate it hearing about it by phone.

Yeah, I guess you're right. Say, Doc, could you explain something? When I took psychological tests when I first talked to a psychiatrist, they asked me to draw a picture, anything, so I drew a picture of two guys cutting down a tree. What does that mean? What can you tell from that?

What do you think it might mean?

Well, I'm not sure who the two guys are supposed to be. Maybe they could be my father and my stepfather. (*Ron paused and thought about this.*) And maybe I'm the tree. Does that make any sense?

I think so. Does it make sense to you?

Sort of. I guess I've always been afraid of being cut down. That's why I try to be smarter than adults. (*Ron lit a cigarette and exhaled slowly.*) But, Doc, can you see any reason why I should be afraid? I can't even remember my father, and my stepfather was never rough with me. He didn't especially have much of anything to do with me. Why should I be scared of them?

Who ended up living with your mother?

Neither of them. She divorced them both. My mother lives with my brother and me and my sister.

When you first described the drawing of the tree and the two guys cutting it down, I wondered whether it might represent you and your brother cutting down your father or cutting down your stepfather.

Maybe. You mean because both of them are gone, and we remained?

Yes. Possibly the drawing represents a question: Are you going to chop down Father or is Father going to chop down you?

(*He stared at me with special interest.*) What do you think I should be when I grow up?

(*I recalled questions about chemistry he had asked me in recent weeks.*) A doctor.

You mean it?

Yes. You could easily handle the course work.

I know I could in a way, but sometimes I think I'd fail at anything I'd try. Then at other times I think I'll be—well—someone outstanding, like a genius.

Only those two extremes?

Usually. Sometimes it's not so extreme. I would like to be a doctor.

Well, that's in the middle. You don't have to be a genius to be a doctor.

Why do I usually go to extremes like thinking I'll be a failure or a genius?

What do you think?

I don't know.

Yesterday we talked about how you resented feeling used. Maybe it's tied in with that.

How?

Your mother never had a very successful marriage. Sometimes, a mother whose marriage isn't successful has a lot of daydreams and wishes about her son. Maybe it isn't you who feel the need to be a great man. Maybe it's your mother's need.

And if it's her wish not mine, then I might feel used by her if I work to try to be a great man? Say, Doc, do you think maybe that's why I'm always wrecking up my hands?

Why?

Well, if my hands are all goofed up, there are a lot of things I can't do.

Ron and I spoke frequently after that interview. Soon after it, he announced that he was ready to leave the hospital, and I agreed. He went on a two-week home visit, and he returned feeling cheerful and content. Arrangements were made for his discharge. Approximately one month after the conversations in which Ron had talked of feeling used by adults and had talked of the possible significance of damaging his hands, he left M-6 for home.

It had taken a long period of observing me before Ron dared to test me, and although I hadn't responded well to his efforts to involve me in May, I hadn't failed entirely. He tried again. In August and September, I understood his metaphorical language, and I responded to him in ways which told him that a strong adult who knew the realities of life was his honest ally committed to his well being. He had discovered someone upon whom he could rely, someone whose support was not contingent upon his remaining a perpetual child or upon his becoming an adult too soon. I agreed with him that the world was a jungle not a garden, but I showed him that I was not overwhelmed with fear of the jungle. One can grow and live a life of dignity in the jungle. This I believe, and this faith I was able to impart to Ron.

4
The Self-Defeating Search for Love ❀
Hanna Colm

LIVING, BEING HUMAN, implies limitations. Each person must come to terms with his limitedness, with the fact that he does not know where he comes from, who he is in terms of his capacities and abilities, and where he will go—his fate and the meaning of his life. This is the over-all existential limitation, the nonbeing in living. In the course of his life, man will make what he can out of the unknown challenge that is given him.

In addition to the existential limitation, there are limitations inherent in the specific situation into which each man is born and which, in the course of his living, he learns to accept. Or, he denies the limitations and strives to achieve the impossible; then, the only avenue of escape is neurotic defense.

In clinical experience, one often witnesses the struggle against limits. This is particularly true of families with adopted children whose personal history and hereditary background remain unknown to parents. Interwoven with the refusal to accept this limitation of not knowing the child's background is the fear of allowing the children to experience any kind of rejection or frustration.

In this essay, I am presenting such a family, a family in which the parents were obsessed and tormented with the anxiety of not knowing where their children came from, of seeing each of the children as a single, loose leaf with the tree to which he belonged missing. They reacted much more severely than natural parents who also have doubts about their children's inheritance.

The adopted child, in turn, does not know his parents and his immediate roots. He struggles painfully with the knowledge that his real parents rejected him and gave him away. His life often becomes a constant struggle to win total acceptance and unqualified trust. The limitations of adoption do not mean that the family is doomed to develop neurotic ways of living. Yet *if* the parents believe that life should be perfect, that life should not have limits, they will be caught up in an endless effort to learn what they cannot know and to make up for what cannot be restored. As a consequence, the child will refuse to accept his own specific limitations and the limitedness with which life challenges every human being. He will strive again and again to prove himself. He will repeatedly test the acceptance of his adoptive parents and will be unable to understand and integrate the primary rejection that came from his real parents. Rejection thus becomes actually and constantly a destructive factor in the living of the adoptive family.

It was precisely this kind of situation that was the focus of my deep and meaningful moments in therapy with Bobby and Gavin X. Both of these adopted children had developed school difficulties; but because twelve-year-old Bobby had begun to wake up with nightmares, at first, only he came for therapy. Bobby came to me after a bewildering series of family events. His adoptive mother had been married to Mr. Y at the time of the adoption of both boys, but her husband had very suddenly died. In grief and depression, Bobby's mother had withdrawn from the children, leaving them emotionally bewildered and alone for long periods of time. Sometime later, she married Mr. X who, though he tried to be a good father, was at times rejecting of the boys and their problems.

Mrs. X had grown up in a puritanical New England family where there was little display of affection. She found it difficult to express her feelings. She had a gruff, dark voice and often sounded rough when dealing with the children. But the roughness was only surface, for she had a deep concern and identification with the children. She sought to understand their primary rejection and make sure there would be no more of it. She was determined to make a perfect world for her children, to be a perfect mother, to raise perfect children in a perfect, never-rejecting mother–child relationship. Instead, the result was a controlled relationship—unspontaneous and planned—to which the children reacted with problem behavior. Mrs. X did not recognize that the problem behavior was a response to lack of trust in spontaneous living, but rather she blamed it on the children's poor history and poor endowment. The children began to placate for acceptance and repressed their own integrity. Eventually, however, their own individuality burst forth in rebellion against self-denial of the right to experiment with growing up and living. Their response, which was exaggerated, caused the parents great anguish and doubt as to their adequacy.

Mrs. X's preoccupation with the lack of history of these children expressed itself in a continuous round of having them tested and consulting psychiatrists when problems arose. She explained these problems in many ways, wavering from blaming all the trouble on the death of the adoptive father to the fact that she had withdrawn from the children and was deeply depressed. For this she blamed herself; yet like a dark cloud, the suspicion arose that the real trouble came from a very much deeper layer: poor inheritance? poor intelligence? poor beginning? Immersed in her own gloomy thoughts, she missed what the children's way of living was conveying. When, in response to her anxieties and uncertainties about them, the children began to reach out and compete with each other for her, she was completely blind to their hostile interaction.

Mr. X was the youngest of eight children and had never been faced with the need to compete for a "place in the sun." Perhaps, for this reason, he could accept Gavin's pattern of "I can compete only via poor little me," whereas Bobby's big-mouthed, aggressive way of competing was repulsive to him. He had no understanding of the battle these boys were fighting for sole possession of their mother, nor the way she led them into these battles because of her feeling that neither must ever suffer rejection.

Mr. X thus found himself in a situation where he was expected to live up to an image of a perfect substitute father. He was very unsure of his feelings about the children; he pitied them but did not really want them around. He gave them many opportunities to find him unsatisfactory and to reject him.

Though I began therapy with Bobby alone, Gavin often sat in the waiting room with his mother during the treatment hours. From the start, it was clear to me that both boys were actively responding to the parents' anxiety about their endowment, by playing on this anxiety.

When I came into the waiting room to get Bobby for his first hour, he looked at me quite reservedly. He was wearing a high cowboy hat, which he kept firmly on his head. "Status symbol," I thought. I casually put my hand on his shoulder on the way to the playroom. He shrugged me off.

Is this your playroom? (*Immediately, he tried to put me on the defensive.*)
Yes, this is my playroom. As you know, you can play with whatever you want.
Shoot at your lamp? Shoot at your windows? (*He caught me with a pretense full of acceptance.*)
No, I would not let you harm my things.
You are not supposed to get mad at me here.
It *would* make me mad if you shot my place to pieces. Therefore, I wouldn't let you.

He aimed immediately at the lamp, picking a fight with me, showing me the "bad boy." I took the gun away from him and pointed out that there were other things to play with if he wished or he could tell me whatever he had in mind. I explained that there were other ways he could express himself than by destroying my things. As a response to these comments, he began to poke around in the play materials with a contemptuous air. He did not start any real play.

Of course you would not let me break all the toys, or even one.
No. I wouldn't. But what in the world makes you try to make nothing but a policeman out of me? I don't really like to act like a policeman.
Oh.

With these numerous provocative challenges, our first hour came to an end. Bobby arrived for his next hour with his hat still on, and, with a tough expression on his face, he bade a contemptuous good-by to Gavin. I put my hand on his shoulder again. He shrugged it off lightly. Once in the room, he immediately began to shoot, a rough cowboy sort of shooting. He still wore the hat and the tough face. But in the midst of the shooting, suddenly there came from him a few tunes of a song—out of his tough mouth, silver clear pitch. I was touched and acknowledged the gift to me: "Nice song, nice voice you've got." "Yea," he responded. His gift for *what;* I wondered inside: I had not let him run over me in phony acceptance, but, also, I had not believed his shrugging me off.

The next hour he reported, as if his mother had prompted him not to forget to tell, that he had nightmares about a monster.

Oh. How does it look?

Just green.

Green? Just like envy is supposed to look?

Yeah? Well I don't really know. (*Pause.*) Well, what do *you* know about monsters. (*He was challenging me a bit contemptuously.*)

Oh, I know from myself that if I dream about a monster or am afraid of one, it's really something in myself—a monster—that I fear in myself.

Oh, yeaah? (*He began wildly shooting at things in the room, not at the lamp and the windows, but sometimes pointing at my eyes for a second as if to test me in a new way. Then he said that he just did not see why they have to have Gavin around.*)

I tell you the truth. I don't know either, why they got John, my *sec-*ond *fath-er!*

You call him John?

Yeah, because I don't want a *sec*-ond fath-er—really a third! (*Pause.*) And neither do I know what Gavin is good for, that little *adopted* shrimp.

Huh. (*What a contempt about adopted boys, I thought.*) Is that such a terrible thing for you?

Yeah. Would you like to have three fathers around?

Well, you have only one around now, and you have some fun not to let him be your father. You reject him right and left. *You* reject. Is that better than if you feel he rejects you?

Yeah. He brings home a lot of presents, and I know he tries to buy me but I won't let him.

Good for you! (*Pause.*) But let's not forget that thing about Gavin—that little adopted shrimp.

Yeah!

You don't really want anybody around. You really want to have the field alone.

Yeah, that's exactly what I want. Gavin is a pest. (*Bobby told me then of his cat, who "a-t-e" Cynicism, one of her kittens.*) That's what should happen to Gavin!

(*I laughed but immediately grew serious.*)

That *is* a little frightening. What made her do that?

Mom said she could not take care of two.

Oh. (*Pause.*) Do you sometimes wonder what made your first mother abandon you?

I sure do! Do *you* know what made her do it?

No, I don't know either. We often don't know about things and never will. And that is pretty rough, to leave it that way. (*Pause.*) (*Looking at him, I spoke with a smile of appreciation.*) You must have been a very cute baby.

Oh, yeah!

You seem to doubt that. (*Pause.*) Do you sometimes think she rejected you because you weren't nice, you weren't worth her while?

Of course I do. (*Pause.*) You said it yourself; I am a monster!

Oh! (*Pause.*) You seem to want to prove you are one! Is that easier, if you think you know why she might not have wanted you?

Yeah, then I know it. Why?

What do you do, Bobby, when you try to be a monster?

Oh, I just cut a hole into Mother's new shoes or a hole into the bedspread. And, boy, does she get mad at me!

Well, yes, I can see how much you make yourself a monster and how you *make* her mad then. But does that really make sense? You told me also that you love her, and really want her all to yourself.

Yeah. But what made her get John and Gavin? She does not really love me. I *am* a monster. (*Pause.*) I sometimes kick the hell out of Gavin, and does she run over fast and take dear little baby brother in her arms.

You *make* her, just because you can't believe she can love you. And just because you can't believe she can love two or even three people.

The hour was over. Mrs. X and Gavin, who had waited in the waiting room, left with Bobby. Before I was back to my room, I heard a big commotion in front of the elevator. Bobby kicked Gavin away; *he* would push the button. Mrs. X was just about to take "dear little baby brother" in her arms. I jumped over to Bobby and whispered into his ear, "The monster who makes Mom protect Gavin?" "Oh, yeah," he responded.

The next hour was a rough one for me. Bobby let himself be touched on the shoulder, I noticed. "Don't forget it," I said to myself. Bobby, with hat still on, started the hour asking me a question.

You're German, or what *are* you?
I was German, yes, but now (*Pause.*) I'm adopted here.
You put people into gas stoves, didn't you?
No. (*Pause.*) I would have been put into one, maybe, if this country hadn't adopted me.
Oh. (*Pause.*) Were you glad to be adopted here?
Yes, a little, yes, that I could go some place. But it also made me real mean. This was not the country I liked, and I first thought nobody really could like me too much. Everyone asked: "Where are you from?"
And when did you start being less mean?
Oh, when I really believed the people really liked me and wanted me. (*Pause.*) And they want me an awful lot now.
I know. They even pay you a lot of money just to see you.
Does that make you doubt what I really feel?
Yes, a little bit. (*Pause.*) You are not really my friend. (*Suspicion about pretenses, I thought.*)

Yes. Your parents will pay me, because I still need to help you a lot, and I have learned to understand kids and that's what they pay for. (*Pause.*) But they can't pay for what I feel about you.

Oh, you really mean you could really like me even without pay?

I think I do.

What about the monster?

Well, I try to help you with it.

Who tried to help *you* with it?

Oh, the people who understood me and liked me nevertheless. (*Pause.*) I love this country now.

More than Germany?

Just as much.

What about the Nazis?

They are monsters. We helped Germany get them sort of tamed.

Yeah.

At this point, using his language, this child and I had been having a full discussion about the question of love "in spite." We had been speaking of the demonic in him, in me, and in man, of man's destructive side, man's struggle with it, and my respect for this struggle.

The monster-dreams disappeared. He stopped asking for presents when John came home. He began to call John, "Dad."

The next hour Bobby came in singing in his clear young boy's voice.

That must be a joy to your mother, your singing like an angel.

She loves me for it. I know she loves me to be an angel anyway.

Ha! (*This expression just came out of me spontaneously. My use of the word "angel" had set up dangerous alternatives.*) You think she loves you only if you are an angel or sing like an angel?

Of course she does.

That's a bit like what we talked about last time—I like you for the pay.

Oh. (*Pause. Bobby began to tell me that he still is dreaming of robbers, scary dreams.*)

And that says I'm myself a robber? Sort of maybe?

Yeah. If I'm real mad at Gavin or Dad, I just steal money from Mom's pocketbook. She cheated me!

And you cheat back.

Yeah. I still want her alone, I really do.

I know you do. (*Bobby began playing with the toy cash register; he saw some real pennies in the drawer.*)

Give me one.

O.K.

Can I have another one?

No.

Oh, you really reject me!

What! Give me, give me, give me, or else it's rejection! Where did you get that idea from?

From John—his presents! And Mom, when she says, "Yes, Yes, Yes." She never can say "No."

Oh, *that* really makes you feel rejected every time somebody says "No" to you, or does not go your way, or criticizes you. Huh, what a trap you are in! You told me you hated Dad's toys; you felt he tried to buy you with them.

Yeaah.

Well, you can't make me buy you. (*Smiling and pulling his hat down a bit, he put the one penny back. I looked at him and his hat.*) You still can't really trust me yet. (*Pause.*) All dressed up big. I haven't even seen your hair—the way you really look.

Nope!

O.K.

Next time, he came with his hat on again, but during the hour he casually put it aside. I did not say anything; I just looked up to him, glancing over his hair in a delighted way.

He certainly looked handsome. Again, he went to the cash register.

Will you give me a penny? (*Pause.*) Never mind.

What a martyr! How put upon you are. (*Under a rough mask a tiny smile came up as his acknowledgment.*)

Will you read to me?

Yes, I'd like to.

Two chapters?

I don't know yet.

Never mind!

Bang! Rejection! Just when you can't get *all* you want.

Yeah. And if I ask Dad, "Will you do something for me?" and he says, "Later," I just say, "O.K., John."

Yes. That's the same. You got him! It makes you feel like superman, rejecting everybody right and left, if you don't get exactly what you want. I guess it makes you feel *he* is rejected, not you. But I guess it makes you still feel a bit like a superman —even a monster. It's fun; you make John feel guilty. You just made me feel guilty too about the reading. You put that same feeling in between you and me. I don't want to feel guilty about you. I like you. (*Bobby put on his hat, hiding under it, as I continued.*) As if I would not keep on liking you even if you still show me trouble. You think *I* have no trouble left?

Have you? What trouble do *you* have left?

Oh, sometimes getting angry, just like your mother.

You do?

Doesn't everybody get angry at times?

I didn't think *you* would.

Oh, I'm not different from everybody else, in that way.

Oh.

Bobby did not ever bring the hat again. His grandfather became critically ill at this time, and his mother went to New England to stay with him. John was alone with the two kids, and Bobby was obviously appreciative these days to have a dad.

With the death of his grandfather, Bobby opened up the question of dying. He spoke of the death of Mr. Y, with whom he was very close and who had preferred him to Gavin. Then he questioned the value of living.

What's the use, if everybody dies?
What do you mean? It's no use to love people, if then they might die?
Yeah. What's the use?
You mean, you'd rather crawl into the hat and stay very far away?
Yeah.
And what a good time we would have missed, if you had never come here. And you will leave me too, sometime, and still never forget me.
Yeah. But what's the use? (*I had missed something.*)
You mean it hurts, when they die—or when one day you won't come here any more?
Yes.
Well, but that seems to be life: it hurts very much at times, when somebody dies, but we can still love him. Death is not the end of loving. (*Pause.*) I love this country now.
Yeah. I sort of love Dad now.
If you don't need to be superman and tease him and call him John.
Yeah.
I still love Germany, too, *and* this country.
Yeah. This country a bit more?
No. I don't really think so.
Oh. (*Pause.*) How come you didn't ever want to see Gavin? He looks always so sad when I leave for your playroom.
I thought you loved that sad look. You often make him look sad.
I do. But I feel sorry for him.
O.K., let's call him in. (*Hesitation.*) Is it quite a difficult decision, trusting me all the way? (*Bobby went out and got Gavin.*)

Gavin was overwhelmed with joy and gratitude and pussyfooted around in order not to step on Bobby's toes or on mine. Though his mother did not find Gavin difficult to handle, it was clear to me that Gavin also needed help. His mother and I talked the matter over and decided each child would have a half-hour each week alone and one hour together. "Yeah," Bobby said, "that gets me all cheated, having my hour with Gavin." "Yes! And getting you an extra half-hour alone," I said with a twinkle.

During their first hour together, Gavin continued his pussyfooting, quietly and completely obedient to Bobby, waiting for Bobby's suggestions. Just once I said, "Gosh, Gavin, can't you start any investigating of this room on your own? Is Bobby your boss?" All three of us laughed! "Yeah, I am," Bobby answered.

In Gavin's half-hour alone he timidly tried to shoot at a target game, where a Mr. Magoo would jump up and fall down when he was hit. Gavin shot and hit him invariably, and invariably Gavin found himself exactly on the spot where Mr. Magoo would fall down on him. I remarked, "You are pretty good at shooting him off, but pretty stupid at letting him hit you. Funny!" Gavin did not answer. He smiled, shot again, and jumped away from Mr. Magoo from then on. "What makes you do that?" I asked. Gavin made no response.

Gavin spent the rest of the time investigating a cardboard hen with a hole in it. It was a toy for shooting; when a particular spot was hit, an egg would drop out of the hole. I thought to myself, "*He* soon will bring up eggs and questions about his real mother."

The parents' and children's reactions to anxieties were beautifully illustrated in a report Mrs. X had given me about going to get Bobby at the end of his first camp experience. Gavin, who was a member of the visiting party, arrived at the camp and, hanging on to his mother's skirts, went to meet Bobby. He was singing, completely off tune, the songs Bobby usually sang in his lovely voice, the voice which was always so pleasing to Mom. Of course, what Gavin was saying to Bobby with his loud singing was, "I've got her now since you have been gone. Ha! Ha!" The angel-voiced Bobby turned into a little devil. He completely overlooked Gavin—no answer to any of his questions, no hello, no look, no speech. Instantly, poor little Gavin had won the battle. Mr. and Mrs. X were so disgusted with Bobby that they condemned him to bread and water for the return trip. What a guilty victory for Gavin! And what a chance for Bobby to wallow in injustice all the way home!

The same pattern of neurotic interaction emerged in one of my early hours with both boys. It was fascinating to watch it unfold before my eyes. Bobby was a past master at initiating games. He built a big landscape, where enemies could live, hide, and fight. Gavin stood and watched. I stood and watched. And I saw Gavin slowly, slowly moving his foot closer against the big, complicated building that Bobby had just erected for an army barracks. Bang! It collapsed by "accident." Bobby instantly became the monster and threw a stone. Gavin cried out *desperately* and ran to me for protection. Had I not watched the whole thing develop, I would have felt like Mom must have felt a hundred times: "Here Bobby is tormenting poor little Gavin again."

Bobby became defensive immediately, "He is like an idiot. I don't want idiots around!" I said, "Oh shucks, Gavin, that was like with Mr. Magoo the other day, wasn't it? Poor little Gavin (*pause*) or (*pause*) really like superman? He could wreck even big Bobby's building *and* could make Mom come and scold Bobby and comfort *him*." "Yeah," came from Bobby. An embarrassed and relieved smile came from Gavin. At this point, I gave him a short hug—not before, when he had tried to force me into protecting him.

It was very striking that Bobby was always well dressed,

often in a full, expensive cowboy suit and fringed suede jacket, while Gavin came nearly in rags, washed-out and raveled jeans and washed-out shirts with cheap little designs. Mrs. X allowed the boys to choose their own clothes; they chose them according to their "way of being in the world." I had talked with Gavin once about his poor-little-boy, Cinderella clothes. He knew that *he* got the sympathy and protection of his mother and of the guests of the family and that this often made Bobby cruel and mean. And did he know it!

In his time alone with me, Gavin would stand alone and look forlornly at all the toys, not knowing where to begin to play. Now that he *had* what his longing, sad little eyes had told me he wanted when I went off to the playroom with Bobby, he just could not do anything with it. I stood beside him wondering and saying, "It's a bit like with your pajamas. You have some really good new ones, but you'd rather sleep in your shirt and underwear as if you don't really have anything." Gavin would try to play, but I could feel his great effort. Pretty soon he would be clumsy with the toys, as he was with Mr. Magoo, and he would hurt himself. The only thing he did with skill was shooting, shooting into the bull's-eye or at Mr. Magoo—eight, nine, ten times in a row. I would remark, "My, aren't you a good shot," or "That seems to come natural with you, bang, one shot after the other straight into the bull's-eye." For a while he did nothing but shoot, earning lots of praise, his eyes beaming back at me. Finally, I said, "Isn't it really much more fun to be good at something than all this business about 'poor little me'?" "Hm," was all he answered. He muttered something in addition, some sort of baby talk. I could not understand it, and asked that he repeat it. His response was to throw a sudden tantrum. It was another form of "poor me," "poor not understood me," "poor baby me"; he had managed once again not to be understood. All the different forms of it had to come out before he could agree with me that it wasn't really so much fun. The fit that had burst out of him today was something new. I told him I was glad that he could get real mad and show that he wasn't really such a good and meek little boy all the way through. He went back to his shooting, and, lo and behold, no shot went right. He was busy defeating himself. "Are you punishing yourself for the fit?" I asked. He told me that, after he throws a temper fit, he feels that he is a bad boy. His mother does not like him at these times. Yes, that *was* confusing. Mothers like it better without temper, and here I felt good when he showed me strong feelings. But, I wasn't really so fond of temper tantrums either, but more of real and strong feelings. I explained to Gavin that if he wouldn't swallow his strong feelings, all for "poor little me," they might not have to come out with such wildness.

For the rest of this hour, Gavin stood, holding on to his penis, looking self-conscious and bedraggled. He asked feebly if I had a rope. It was fascinating that Gavin was unable to make use of the many toys in the room but had to ask for something not present. His mother had told me that Gavin was often preoccupied with tying ropes around objects as tight as possible so that they would never come off. Seeing him holding on to his penis when he asked for a rope, I realized there must be a connection. With all his interest in being "poor little not-having me," he could suddenly get scared that he would go too far and deprive himself of something that he *did* have and did not want to lose. The conflict was in full bloom.

We talked about his holding his penis. He complained that it really wasn't any good—Bobby's was bigger, Dad's was bigger, and his other Dad's penis was enormous. We talked about his attitude, "I must either have the best or have it all. If I don't, it's not any good; I would rather have nothing." The little superman in him did not countenance any waiting. He had persuaded his mother that any waiting for growing stronger or bigger, any waiting, any place, was rejection, that "no" at any time was rejection. This mother, knowing the children had experienced too much rejection in their early years, did not want them to experience any more rejection. She did not understand that waiting, and disappointments, and "no's" were all part of growing up. Knowing this, I was very much on the light side with Gavin. "Of course you love to have it all the way you want it (*pause*) little superman (*pause*) but all people have to wait at times, all people don't get things just when they want them. Are they all poor and rejected?"

I noticed that a glimpse of a smile went over his face when I used the word "superman." It touched off the real longing behind the "poor me," the longing to be the strongest and even the super-strongest, especially around Mother. Gavin was creating pity and protection in Mom and making Bobby appear guilty and mean; then he felt like a bad boy who needed to be punished. I interrupted this vicious circle in many, many hours of work with him alone and in other hours where both kids acted out the very circle in detail. Here and there, in my presence, Gavin got Bobby in such a rage that I could not but reach out to protect Gavin, or rather to limit Bobby. I never condemned Bobby's anger but curbed the degree of its expression. Most of the time, I did not need to interfere and simply could say, "Gavin, here you nearly got me like you get Mom, taking into her arms poor little Gavin, whom mean Bobby nearly killed. But I don't really feel that you are so poor and pitiful and meek. And I *did* see how superman managed to dig at Bobby till he indeed exploded."

Slowly, slowly this pattern between the two children changed. Gavin arrived with attractive clothes. One day, he told a friend who wanted to tumble with him in wet dirty leaves for fun: "I have a new jacket and don't care to have it ruined." He applied himself better in school and even filled out physically. He stopped thriving on irritating and controlling his mother by putting shoes on the wrong way and then limping around or "accidently" putting shoes on over his pants and becoming the laughing stock of the kids on the street and then coming home with a sad: "Nobody likes me; they all laugh at me." And, indeed, his mother stopped feeling sorry for him and did not need to busy herself trying to prevent the dreaded rejection of Gavin by the neighborhood kids.

Only after his way of handling life failed to be satisfying and successful, did Gavin return to a question he had touched upon in our first hour. This was the problem of the initial rejection in his life: "My real mother did not want me; I'm only an adopted child. From there all my trouble comes." No, indeed, it does not! I wanted to get at his little powerman pattern in living with his present family before I could talk about the mother who had borne him and had "not wanted him."

Now he began to be very much interested again in shooting at the hen, shooting out egg after egg. When he got them out, he again investigated the hole from the right side up and upside down and every other angle. I knew this was anxiety around the birth process, which for him was entangled with the problem: "Why did she not keep me?"

One day after a long time of investigation, he asked: "How does it go with people?" He had not been able to ask this question of his mother, because he sensed the painfulness of that for her, that he had not come out of her. He knew the facts, vaguely, but he was anxious about them. We sat down and each made a man and woman in clay. I showed him what people do when they love each other like moms and dads do. It did not seem funny to him and he did not giggle, as other kids sometimes do. All he said was, "Let's show this to Bobby; he does not know about it this way." We called Bobby, who had been sitting with his mother in the waiting room, and, he remarked loudly, "Oh, yeah!" He let us know quickly that he knew all about it. "Did you?" I asked. "Oh, no, not really," he answered, "but I did talk to boys about it." "Sure you did," I said, "but maybe they didn't really know it all, the way it is. They make it, usually, look silly or dirty."

Bobby stated: "It *is*. What's so nice about it? Mom does not like to talk about it. I know *that*." "Well," I said, "there might be quite a different reason; maybe Mom is sad that she could not be the Mommy who could give birth to you, to Bobby first and then to Gavin. She wanted so awfully much to have two boys and, as she could not have some of her own, she sure was glad that some place there were two women who could not keep their babies and take care of them. She is plain envious of these mothers. Do you blame her?"

At this point, Bobby had lost his pretentious toughness and "know-it-all" attitude. Gavin sat there with a grin, enjoying how much his poor mother, who could not have kids, must have wanted them! And Mother, envious, just like he had been feeling when he first came to the office!

Still the question that was untouched: "Why did our real mothers not want us?" And Gavin, pointing to the clay figure, was now the one who could ask: "Why did they not want us?" She was certainly not a real person to him, and I could not answer this question in a way that would satisfy him. So, I said, "I don't really know what made her feel she could not keep her baby. There are people who keep their babies and are happy with them, and there are people who can't keep their babies and are unhappy about them. There are moms who are longing for a baby and can't have one. I don't really know why that is so, but it was good for your mom to find two babies whose mothers could not keep them." And turning to Bobby, I said: "It was very good for me to have had to leave Germany; it was *the* good luck of my life to become an American then."

In my comments to Bobby and Gavin, no sentimental attempt was made to explain anything away or to explain it all in a reasonable way. My task was to help them accept that life has dark and unexplainable sides and always will have, that we must make the best of the dark moments, not get bitter or defensive about them, not slip into an attitude like "poor me," or "I'm not wanted; I'm the bad one," or "I got to prove I'm perfect against the condemning facts."

Bobby, who had been causing his mother anguish by compulsively cutting plants off at their roots, cut off one more and then stated: "This is the end of *that.*" Gavin, who had been compulsively knotting ropes to anything in sight, stopped this preoccupation; he felt secure enough with his mother and could now trust that she had wanted him desperately.

Bobby reported that he had recurrent dreams from which he always woke up with a sense of despair—of an enormous house, where families live in the country up north, where there is room even for grandparents and great-grandparents, and in this house he was all alone, no relatives, no furniture, poor cut-off Bobby. Mom had tried so hard not to have the children experience this rootless cut-off feeling. She had stressed family relationships in such a way that Bobby had become especially sensitive to her concern.

Now he dreamed of a large house full of antiques. And I spoke to him: "Yes, that's about all one usually knows about one's grandfather and great-grandfather; they are like the antiques people still have in their homes—some have them, some don't." I looked around my furniture: "You see, Bobby, I don't have any antiques around. I like the new furniture better." "Yes, I too," he said. No artificial toughness, no "yeah," just "I too." Life does not *necessarily* require that we have antiques around; it can be lived without *known* roots. It is true that there are no plants without roots—but what does it really matter whether we saw them or still see them or not, if the plant grows strong and self-confident and enjoys growing and is enjoyed in its growing.

The recurrent dream of being lost in an empty old house (where there was room even for grandparents and great-grandparents) changed to a dream of a house in which Bobby stood looking, curious about how many open rooms there were—all to be furnished. What a change in this child! And how much future was expressed in this dream in lieu of the lost, forsaken and empty past reflected in the initial dream.

Finally, in a personal situation, I was able to live out with both boys the way they created tension and disappointment in their parents by means of their envy and destructive competitiveness. Christmas was approaching and Bobby kept making remarks about the big present he had received from his first therapist. I countered these hints lightly, explaining that in Germany we had lighted candles the last hour before Christmas for Advent, and that I would do this with them so that they could see how nice a Christmas candle could be. A few days before Christmas, I bought two small toys, a truck for Bobby and a gun for Gavin.

When the time came and the candles were lit, I brought out my presents. How deep was my disappointment to find that not only did they not care for the candles, but they each stated enviously that he had wanted just exactly what I had given the other. Not wanting to put on a phony front just to save our little Advent celebration, I let them see my disappointment. I wanted them to feel, at this point, what they did to others with their envy. I let them exchange presents, as they wished to do, but I said sadly that I had thought the truck would be just right for Bobby and the cannon for Gavin. Now they made me feel that I just didn't know how to choose the right things for them. This was guilt-provoking —but there *was* guilt to be felt for clinging to the feeling that whatever the other one had was better. To my astonishment they quietly re-exchanged gifts, so that each recovered the one I had originally given him. I ruffled the hair on each head and wished them a Merry Christmas.

Both the parents and the children in this family exaggerated life's unpredictability. There was a lack of acceptance of the negative in living and a failure to recognize that living actually consists of the interaction and struggle between negative and positive forces. Living becomes creative only in the integration and transcendence of the negative. The stalemate develops when parents feel compelled to make good for the obvious limitation in the first love, for the neglect the child experienced in the beginning of his life. As a consequence, the adopted child often responds to this early rejection with insatiable demands and wants, accompanied by feelings of guilt and need for self-punishment, or with an unceasing and futile compulsion to prove himself. Any child, if he is to grow up, must learn to cope with temporary rejection and learn to experience it as a steppingstone toward learning and growth.

For this reason, it is of utmost importance for the therapist not to fall into the routine of traditionally prescribed patterns of acceptance. All too soon, the child will create a situation that warrants rejection; he is alert and sensitive to controlled, phony acceptance; he constantly tests genuineness. He needs to learn to accept genuine undefensive feelings, both positive and negative; and to distinguish partial and temporary rejection from total rejection. He must learn to know genuine love and to realize when he himself makes love impossible.

In therapy with an adopted child, it is more than ever important to show one's basically positive feeling for him, even though he will shrug it off with disbelief. At the same time, one must be able to accept and set limits, to criticize or "reject," since it is the simultaneousness of the acceptance and the criticism that leads the child to recognize and trust the genuineness of the therapist's feeling. This means that the therapist must be aware enough, if he is temporarily drawn into the child's pattern of provoking unreal acceptance, pity, or protection, to catch this in himself and make it a useful experience for the child and for himself. The weight of therapy focuses on showing the neurotic child, in the interaction with his therapist, how his distrusting search for love has actually created for him the opposite of what he really wants. He must learn to accept the inevitability of rejection and the limitations in living.

In the adoptive family, history can become a destructive idol, but it also can become a challenge to greater openness and spontaneous wonder and reverence for the child's humanity, as he grows and as he reveals his being. It is far less important to know the roots of the child's family than it is to be open to the formative "now" of interaction between parents and child. It becomes a challenge for parents to follow the *child's* endowment as it emerges in terms of his own self and not in terms of their own wants and needs. Out of a handicap can come not only a strong urge to identify with historic groups, their own family background, church and general national culture, but also a greater awareness of the creative and destructive elements of the present family interaction and an urge to understand *the voice that the child's living behavior speaks.*

To be able to see one's culture and society and family in terms of its history *is* an important angle of our culture; it gives man the feeling of continuity transcending his small self—it gives him meaning. It gives him the feeling of participation, belonging, challenge, responsibility, and commitment to something greater than he is. It also has its demonic possibilities in that it often turns into a symbol of status and superiority and allows prejudice against another society or nation or family.

In our culture, having a family history is often misused to symbolize not only continuity but eternity. The underlying need is a neurotic pattern of omnipotence as proof against man's feeling of mortality, finiteness, and insignificance. Adoptive parents *must* come to terms with this human need for omnipotence and accept the finiteness of life. They must open themselves to the presence of the child's real being. They must concentrate on understanding the immediate voice of being, interaction, and communication toward a deeper, undefensive, and more fulfilling struggle for the future. In this process, the adopted child, in a deep and genuine sense, becomes a child of their own.

I gratefully acknowledge the editorial assistance of Claire Bloomberg in the preparation of this paper.

5

Therapy in an Existential Crisis ✼
Charlotte Buhler

PHILIP, AT THE AGE OF fifteen, was referred to me by his mother who was extremely bothered by his stuttering. She sought psychotherapy for Philip because two attempts to eliminate the stuttering through speech therapy had failed. The therapy with me continued for a period of two and one-half years involving seventy-three individual hours and forty-five group sessions.

When Philip arrived for his first meeting with me, he had no enthusiasm for therapy of any kind. He was uncertain, tentative, and even loath to get himself involved again in what appeared to be a futile goal. He was a medium-sized boy, with an athletic build, handsome, and unusually serious. He maintained a solemn, sad face during our first hour together, and his stuttering was severe.

Philip's disturbance, his dilemma in life may be viewed in two ways.[1] First, we shall consider briefly his emotional disturbance, problems of anxiety and depression, conflicts with

---

[1] The approach is discussed in detail in Charlotte Buhler, *Values in Psychotherapy* (New York: Free Press of Glencoe, 1962).

hostile feelings and destructive impulses, patterns and habits that had taken root and had created a restricted and immature personality. These emotional factors were responsible for his stuttering and the other restraints and blocks to fulfillment of his potentialities. The emotional disturbance had emerged and developed into full-fledged neurotic traits through a series of early traumatic experiences with his mother, his father, and his grandfather. Second, we shall view Philip's problems in the existential sense, in terms of his shock of discovering that his parents' values were far from healthy, far from good, far from decent and right, the shock of realizing the hypocrisy, distortion, fakery, and lying that surrounded him in his home. The first set of problems affected Philip's emotional attitudes toward himself, his parents, and others; the second were centered in his search for a philosophy of life based on healthy morality, on truth and honesty in human relations.

My main concern in this chapter is with the existential disturbance, its evolution and impact on Philip, his yearning to find a sense of decency and honesty in life. Briefly, however, I shall mention two extremely traumatic experiences that provided the immediate emotional shock and several critical incidents between Philip and his mother and father that significantly altered the entire course of Philip's development.

The Emotional Crisis

The first moment to leave its powerful mark on Philip occurred during World War II, while Philip's father was away from home serving in the army. Philip was about two years of age at the time, and his grandfather lived with him and his mother. A violent, stormy battle ensued between Philip's mother and his grandfather. The screaming became so intense and the gestures so threatening that Philip became terrified. He thought his mother was going to be killed when he saw his grandfather pummeling her. In spite of his great fear, he rushed to his mother's defense. It was a desperate, weak effort that left him completely shaken. While defending his mother in this futile, terrified way, he began to stutter. When Philip's mother described this incident, she said it was one of the most terrible experiences of her entire life. She cried bitterly as she recounted the vicious battle with her father. She felt that she had to shelter her father because he was an indigent man without a place in the world. She said he was erratic and easily provoked, disposed to frequent yelling and temper outbursts that severely disturbed Philip. She felt totally helpless and disabled in dealing with her father during his explosive and violent rages.

The second traumatic event in Philip's early childhood was of an entirely different nature. It occurred shortly after his father's return from service. His father too was given to temper outbursts, shouting in a loud, angry manner, and maintaining a completely dominant position in the family. In spite of these tendencies, it was not his father's aggressiveness which disturbed Philip, but rather it was the drastic and exclusive way in which he possessed Philip's mother, taking her away from him sharply and totally.

Sometime after Philip had come to know me and trust me, with deep emotional involvement, he spoke of the moment that had so markedly affected him. The incident occurred shortly after his father's return from the war.

My mom was standing in front of me; she had no clothes on; my father was lying on the bed and kept saying, "See how pretty your mom is."

I had walked into their room unexpectedly. I was very flushed. I could see her long hair and her smile; I looked away; I was afraid. I felt, even then, that my father made me feel foolish, that he wanted to. . . . I felt it was wrong, that I was not supposed to see her like this and he asked me to see her. I felt he forced me to see her.

What happened then?

I felt he watched me and he watched her. I was up for ridicule at the time. (*Pause.*)

Why do you think he did it?

He thought I was too young to know about sex. I felt it was not right. He might have been trying to make it seem very natural, but actually he showed her off as his. He gave me the impression that he owned her. I had walked in and surprised them.

At that moment I accepted her as his too. They were going to sleep. I was asked if I wanted to sleep with them. I said, No, that I would sleep in my own room.

After that, I started splitting up from them and their things. This thought just came to me now, that this is what I did.

You felt that your father took your mother away from you and you were alone?

Yes, and I accepted it. I decided to be on my own and have no part of them.

This traumatic experience was the first memory that Philip had of his father. But there were many other moments when Philip felt that his father was trying to make a fool of him, when his father maintained a dominant position and made him feel little and inferior.

When he was four years old, he was told that Santa Claus would phone him and ask him what he wanted for Christmas. When he heard the voice on the phone that was supposed to be Santa Claus, he immediately recognized it as his uncle's voice. He answered spontaneously, "Hi! This is Uncle Bill." Unknowingly, Philip had spoiled the adult preparations and plans. His father became quite angry with him and spanked him. Another time, when his younger brother was told he would get a present from a fairy, Philip made fun of the idea and was again spanked.

I was often very mad at him. I thought I would leave home as soon as I could. Once I tried to get even with him. We were all in front of the house, when my father came up and kissed me and hugged me hard. "You broke my ribs," I screamed at him. Inside I was laughing. He was so worried that he had hurt me, he carried me into the house and put me to bed. I howled as if I was in agony, just to hurt him.

The feeling of being made a fool, of being small and inferior, of being cut-off and alone, the feeling that began with the naked scene, prevailed through all the childhood years and into his adolescence. Philip told how his father approached a discussion of sex when he was about twelve or thirteen.

We were sitting in the room watching television. He called me into the kitchen and stood there and just suddenly said, "Tell me all you know about women and sex." It floored me. I thought he was implying I had done something wrong. It knocked me for a loop. I didn't know what to do. Finally, I answered him, "I don't know what to say."

A week later, I had gone to work with him. We were in his office with his friends when one of them remarked that I was a nice person and polite. My father commented, "Last week I tried to teach him the facts of life, but he is too young." He made me feel odd, like a damn fool, as if he wanted to humiliate me. I hated him for a while.

Philip felt that his father had no respect for him. I asked whether his father treated his brother differently. Philip answered in the negative but said that his brother's response was different. His brother yelled back, battled it out with him. Philip believed that this was a better way of relating to his father. He remarked, "It seems my father likes that. He tells me I should stand up for my rights like Billy does. But I don't like to yell. Usually I leave the room and don't say anything."

Philip's relationship with his mother was also fraught with problems and conflicts. His mother constantly nagged him and made him feel obligated.

Every time I want to go some place, she comes up with, "After all I do for you, all you think about is your own pleasure."
What does she want you to do?
She likes me to stay home and sit with her and keep her company. She likes me to watch TV with her. I like to go out with my friends and have a good time.
Do you resent her when she makes you feel obligated?
In a way I do.
You have a conflict about it.
Yes, I feel guilty. She always makes me feel guilty.

Philip has never felt that his parents would stand by him if he ever got into a real jam. He came to believe that his father would insist that he handle any situation or problem by himself.

If I ever got into a bit of trouble, my father would never stick up for me.
You have to stand on your own.
Yes, he has always refused to help me when I am in a jam. Like when bigger kids used to pick on me, and I could not handle it myself.
You felt he deserted you.
That's how I often felt.

His mother also let him down on several occasions, destroying his belief in her and his trust in her. He recalled his mother promising to let him get braces for his teeth and then telling him later that money was so tight that she could not afford to get his teeth straightened. Yet shortly after this excuse, she bought a combination radio and record player. Through many experiences of this kind, both with his mother and his father, Philip increasingly refused their help, detached himself from them and their interests, and became more and more withdrawn, unhappy, and lonely. From the age of eight, he found ways of earning an allowance so that he would not have to ask for money, so that he would not have to be dependent on his parents. In therapy, he admitted that he had been a martyr, that he had gone much too far in rejecting his parents and in attempting to make his own way in life.

Being so severely detached and so sharply independent, Philip could observe his parents' attitudes, he could see their values, their philosophy of life, with all the inconsistencies, contradictions, distortions, and hypocrisies. It is in this realm of an existential dilemma, of an existential crisis, that Philip found himself increasingly opposed to his parents' ways, his parents' ethics, morals, and values. It is in this realm that Philip stood his ground and began to evolve an identity of his own, emerging with a determined sense of honesty, independence, and solitude. It is in this realm that Philip stood out as a unique person in his family.

The Existential Crisis

Philip's parents held to a philosophy of life that was essentially materialistic, characterized by opportunism, exploitation, and selfishness. Philip's father, the owner of a small business, lived in accordance with middle-class circumstances. To improve his business, he used dishonest methods and maneuvers. Occasionally, he discussed his business practices with Philip, presumably as a way of showing his own cleverness and creating a closer relationship with his son. The consequence was somewhat disastrous. Philip was appalled by his father's machinations. Confiding the shrewd business practices merely reinforced the growing existential separation between Philip and his father.

Last winter my father told me that, because business was not good, he called on all the bosses in the area to fix prices. I knew this was dishonest. Why did he tell me about it? Maybe he was showing me how hard he was trying to succeed, but it only made me feel that he was a thief.

Perhaps, in confiding in you, he wanted to make you feel proud.

That kind of pride I can do without.

Why do you think it made you angry?

I always have set my ideals very high, never to lie and cheat. I don't want to. . . . At times, before, they have tried to influence me to do something dishonest, but fortunately I had a mind of my own. They often got mad at me. For example, I would not cheat regarding my age in order to pay reduced fares or lower entrance fees.

Did you ever discuss this conflict in values with them?

I repressed it. I did not discuss my feelings with them or with my friends. Suddenly now it comes to me why I had no respect for them.

How does your mother contribute to the unethical practices in your family?

My mom is a great one for criticizing. She can tear a person apart behind his back in two moments. She is a gossip. I try not to let it rub off on me. When I confront her with it, she says, "What, me a gossip? Not me." My parents put on a false front all the time. Mother always smiles at me, talks sweetly in front of friends. No matter what kind of pest I have been, she calls me a dream child. Not to benefit me, but to let everyone know what a good parent she is. She has to keep a superiority complex no matter what the real truth is.

I get so mad at her at times. I get so frustrated. I hate the way she constantly talks about people. I never say something behind someone's back that I wouldn't say to his face.

My mother tells me that my aunt wears falsies. Why should she tell me that? Is she trying to build herself up more? When my aunt got a new car, right away they told me that she got the cash by sleeping with her boss. I like my aunt very much, yet they try to destroy my feeling for her.

They can hurt you even though you think you are independent of them.

Yes, I am hurt, because they are so dishonest and so false. They are my parents, after all. . . .

It seemed obvious to me that Philip's commitment to honesty was, in part, an expression of rebellion, and a way of feeling superior, a way of gaining a sense of self-esteem. It was his solution to the conflicts with his parents, to being rejected by them. Philip began to condemn their lies after he had been repeatedly hurt by them. Then he began to detach himself, prematurely, before any solid relationships had been built. The first incident that he recalled of being deeply hurt by dishonesty was the hypocrisy around Santa Claus. He remembers that his parents had told him always to tell the truth. Yet he was punished when he openly recognized his uncle's voice. In this experience, he learned that his parents had not been honest with him; he learned that they expected him to pretend; he learned that they did not mean what they said. They wanted him to distort reality at their request and convenience.

I suggested that perhaps he would not be so condemning if he had felt they loved him more or if he had loved them more. He rejected this interpretation saying that for him truth was more important than love.

As we talked one day, Philip referred to a time in his life when he gave up his own values and decided to imitate some of his friends who practiced a dishonesty similar to his parents.

One time in the eighth grade I rebelled against my own standards. I went through a phase of stealing and lying. I saw my friends doing this. I suddenly thought, "It is no use having these standards; they do not help me in school or at home." I thought being different from my friends was of no use.

What happened to you?

It lasted a year, the stealing and lying. Then I began to feel very ashamed each time I stole, each time I lied. I felt it was wrong. I gave it up. From a very early age, I felt I would have to think over my life, I felt I would get no help from my parents. I had to think things through and raise myself and have my own standards.

When I first heard about Santa Claus, I thought it was a terrible lie. I thought about God also as a lie. With Santa Claus, I had never seen a man flying through the sky and I did not see God in the sky so how could he be. At the age of four or five, I refused to attend Sunday School, and I was spanked. I flatly refused. I had no faith in anything. I always felt that there is no hope.

What do you mean, "There is no hope"?

I always felt, that nobody helps you, you aren't given things from somewhere, you have to do it all by yourself.

In Philip's value system, honesty and independence ranked at the top. Undoubtedly these values had their origin in the negative identification with his parents, when he learned to take an opposite stand. The question is, why did Philip choose honesty as the basis of his negative identification? In numerous experiences, I have found that the selection for identification is usually in the direction of an interest or talent which the child feels emerging and growing from within. In other words, the identification takes place in the direction of self-realization. For Philip, the choice of honesty and independence was not only a reaction to the feeling of being unloved and rejected by parents who were not ethical and free, but also in these values he could experience solitude and loneliness and grow from his own inner resources.

Philip's decision to detach himself from his home atmosphere, from his parents, who hurt and rejected him, was the first step in the direction of independence. Independence and honesty provided the ground he chose to stand on. There is every indication in his background that the choice was his own. At thirteen, when he temporarily resorted to lying and stealing for recognition and status, he became aware that this was not his way, that this was not his kind of life. Behaving dishonestly and unethically made him feel "sick inside." He reaffirmed the choice he had made a decade before, that independence and honesty were consistent with his real self, were the only satisfying paths to self-actualization.

Even, in the later phase of therapy, when Philip had worked through the conflicts and problems of his early childhood, when he had learned to accept and appreciate his parents, when he realized that they did have his interests at heart, Philip was still significantly separated from them in the existential sphere. He now could live with them differently in the emotional sense but the existential breach remained the same. He experienced a feeling of love for his parents, but he could not approve of their values, standards, and concepts of life, nor did he wish to identify with them. In contrast, his relationship with me was not based on love, but rather it was based on trust and a belief in my dependability and in my honesty. He considered me a friend. Philip's appreciation of honesty gave our relationship its foundation. In my third meeting with him, he told me he had no confidence in his parents. I asked him if there was anyone he trusted. He answered, "I don't confide in anyone; I have a great distrust of people, always have had a distrust." I pointed out that he had already expressed a number of his deep feelings to me. He explained and justified this by saying that he answered my questions and told me about himself because it was the only way I could help him. But, in my fourteenth hour with Philip, he reversed the earlier expressed attitude. He told me he liked me and that he could talk freely and openly with me. In my twenty-first hour with him, he said he had never before expressed his real feelings to anyone and that he was just beginning to express his feelings with friends. He said he trusted me and could speak to me of his deepest concerns.

While honesty as a value was the cornerstone of our relationship and created a bond between us, I felt that decisive for Philip's existential awareness was a clarification of his commitment to independence as a value. The critical experience in which his father pointedly took his mother away from him initiated in Philip a yearning for independence and detachment. On that day, Philip began to separate himself from his parents. As a solution to the oedipal conflict, certain aspects of the independence ideal reflected their neurotic origins. For example, Philip often described himself as emotionally invulnerable (as a concomitant of the independence value), saying, "I told myself over and over again, 'I don't care and I don't feel.'" His mother told Philip he should confide in her and reveal his feelings to her. But Philip did not wish to step out of his private world.

My mother feels I am ungrateful. She thinks I should tell her my thoughts and feelings. But I have my own ideals and goals, which are different from hers. She feels I am too independent.

I never want to lean on people. I never want to rely on them. If I want something, I go out and work for it. I do not sit around wishing I had it. I do not ask them for it. I guess it comes back to the fact that I don't trust my parents.

They have made you feel that strings are attached.

That's putting it well. . . .

Does your brother react in the same way? Does he feel indebted?

He does not seem to resent it.

He is more trusting and confiding?

Yes, he is.

But your feeling is: "You can't touch me."

In a way, yes. I have always liked to be on my own, completely on my own.

That's pretty hard at times.
It is.

Another facet of his stand for independence expressed itself in Philip's reaction to authority. He frequently stated his dislike for authority. He spoke in a bitter way about teachers who constantly gave orders, saying he did not like being told what to do, saying that he was afraid of the power of the teacher, that for his part he saw his teachers as people who flaunted their authority and, as far as he was concerned, they could all drop dead.

The independence ideal also had its constructive side. Philip could envision his future, could take the initiative in evolving new directions, could determine what he wanted to do.

"I know just what I want to be. I want to be a photographer, and I think I'll be a good one. I don't know how to break into the field of photography, but I'd like to be a free lancer. That's a great challenge, to try all sorts of jobs, shooting pictures from an airplane, going off on dangerous assignments, taking pictures of pretty girls. In this field, I can be my own boss, and I like being my own boss."

After we had started our second year of therapy together, Philip gave me an opportunity to explore more deeply into his attitude toward independence. I began more frequently to use the technique that I call "constructive exploration." I use this technique to complement the initial "analytic exploration" by bringing up certain questions for consideration. The questions are not "suggestive" in terms of any "ought." I do not "influence" a patient's choice of values, as some critics felt. My questions are meant to open new vistas on aspects of life that the patient had not considered or mentioned. This is done sparingly and with careful timing.

The questions of the constructive exploration concern the

outlook on the future. They are reminders of the problem of values, goals, and purposes.

With Philip, the occasion for this arose when he declared one day he wanted to discuss his ideas about independence.

I like to talk about my independence, how I got this attitude, where it came from. I can remember when my mom gave me various gifts, Christmas or birthday or other gifts. Each time, there was an argument, and I was always made to feel obligated. Their attitude seemed to be, "Look at all we have done for you." So when she gave me something, it made me mad. Ever since I was sixteen, I did not take one cent from them. I made it myself. If she gave me a present, I disliked it. I would never use it. An example of how they treated me was my car. When I was sixteen, they chipped in $900 and I had $400. I got the car, but then they said I couldn't drive it till I was seventeen. They stalled and said it was my grades, then they said it was my insurance. I worried so, I got sick over it. When I first went for my license, Mother said the motor vehicle bureau would not let a boy my age pass. But I passed with 98 or 99. All through the years, I developed the idea that, if I wanted something, I had to get it myself.

The car has stood there since we bought it. I cleaned it and waxed it four times a month. I was not allowed to drive it myself. They always talked around things. They never gave me a straight answer. They often lied to me. I feel I don't want their help at all. I refuse their help. I am through. I quit. My parents try to get close to me and get me to confide in them. I completely reject them. When they come to me and tell me what to do and try to run my life a certain way, there is a showdown, revenge, and then I sleep with a smile on my face. Right now I am extremely happy, not lonely as I would be with them. Coming here gives me confidence. It has changed my way of thinking and my attitudes.

You say therapy changed your way of thinking, how?

Well, I understand myself much better. I see all these things clearly and less emotionally.

But in what way is your attitude changed?

I criticize myself now. I begin to understand them better.

But you still want to remain lonely and independent?

Yes, absolutely.

Then what do you want to use this independence for?

Well, I will have my career, my own family and stand on my own.

But what do you want to live for? Do you have any goals?

I have not thought about that. I thought I would just live to be a good photographer.

Philip gradually began to include the significance of relatedness in his list of important values. During this period, he met a girl, whom he came to respect and love. He spoke of their life together, their "wonderful parties at the beach" and joyous activities. For the first time, Philip was enjoying physical closeness, feeling the joy of love. "It seems I am melting," he told me, "I am undergoing a change." He spoke of the future, of the ideal qualities in a girl, of marriage. He began to review once more his relations in his family. He began to see that in many instances his mother and father expressed their love for him, but he had pushed them away. He began to recognize that they really cared for him in their own way, but he still held them responsible for his need to struggle to be valued as a person with talents and potentialities.

They don't take me seriously. They treat me as if I was gliding along in life. They don't acknowledge that I am fighting to make something out of myself. They refuse to acknowledge me as a person. I am still treated as a kid. Perhaps one day, if I am successful, they will acknowledge me. I want recognition, but I want to do good work anyway.

Philip gradually expanded his philosophy of life. The group meetings were especially helpful in this respect. They provided an opportunity to discuss and explore with others existential values, such as freedom, honesty, choice, responsibility, love, and to clarify problems with reference to the individual and society.

Philip spoke of his changed views and values.

A few friends and I talk recently a lot about life, what it is all about. I try to speak my share.

I think you mean, you want to contribute to the efforts of your group; perhaps also to those of the community as we have recently discussed in the group.

I think this is what I mean. My old view about life was that it concerned only me, that it was just what I made of it myself. Now I think of life as working within society and doing my share. My views were very one-sided and selfish. Now they are more open. There has been a change in my sense of values. Coming here has changed my attitude toward life, and strengthened me, and will make me a much finer man and father. Being a good man and contributing to society is my highest value. My second value is progress in school. My third value is finding the right girl. My fourth value is independence. It no longer seems so important. Quite a switch!

Previous to therapy, I thought of life as two things. If I was happy, I had a good life; and if I was sad, I had a bad life. Now I think of life, not as being happy or sad, but in terms of knowledge. This I believe is the key of life. I believe in choosing a goal and working very hard to reach this goal, therefore, bettering yourself. By doing this, you also better mankind, making life better for everyone. I don't think it is important what goal you choose as long as it is a constructive one. To have something to work for and something to believe in, and to achieve that feeling of accomplishment are some of the greatest goals in life.

Philip's ideas about contributing to society, having constructive goals, and working for something he believed in, had been developed in group discussions on what made life worthwhile. Philip was the youngest member of this group and got several of these ideas from others. But the goals of working hard, of bettering himself and making life better for everyone were strictly his own.

We have seen how Philip lived and grew up, torn between fear and rebellion, fighting against hostility and guilt. While emotionally dependent and continuously on the defensive, Philip struggled from his early childhood for existential independence. Honesty and personal independence were his two highest values. He chose honesty in negative identification with his parents. And he chose independence as an ideal of his own.

The psychotherapy of this boy was conducted with two goals in mind. The first was to explore analytically the dynamics of the emotional disturbance. The second was to enhance the values that Philip had set up for himself and to explore constructively their developmental potentials. As a result, Philip is being enabled to grow far beyond the narrow world of his family. His speech is improving, and he is moving toward a wider and freer outlook on life with constructive ideas and values consistent with his own sense of self and self-realization.

6

❧ In the World of Silent Dialogue

Eugene D. Alexander

IT IS DIFFICULT to grasp in words the uniqueness of my relationship with Jerry. In fact, to use words almost does injustice to the relationship, for it was the wordlessness and the reaching beyond words that made our experience so special. The words that I uttered merely reinforced the communion already present. Jerry's own words, when they finally did come, seemed more a condescension to custom than a necessary aspect of our relationship.

With Jerry, there were no sharp encounters, no struggles between therapist and client. There was no testing of the limits of the situation or attempts to define the extent of the therapist's endurance. Jerry did not have to explore dependency feelings or to experiment with the possibilities of transference. Once our relationship was established (the basis for it emerged from the first meeting), each seemed to sense the other's inner self; our relationship enabled Jerry to open up to the depths of potential inherent in our dialogue as two human beings. We became two friends walking down a path, together searching wider horizons. Sometimes I saw and sensed more clearly than Jerry. At other times, he clarified my doubts and my insensitivities. Jerry determined the level at which we shared our beings. At times, he would take a sudden plunge into new and deeper feelings. At other times, he would pause and, for many meetings, savor and explore at one level until I wondered if our relationship had reached its limit. There were times when he touched on feelings that were too threatening or too painful, and he would make a hasty retreat. But eventually he approached depths that neither of us realized existed, and we found ourselves searching out new dimensions. There were few word symbols to clutter up perception and expression; thus, the more significant nonverbal occurrences could be fully experienced.

As I read over this introduction to our relationship, it does not seem possible that I could be talking about a boy who was diagnosed as mentally retarded. Jerry was not only diagnosed as mentally retarded, but spent a year in a class for "trainable-retarded" children, children whose I.Q.'s were evaluated as below fifty. It terrifies me that I, too, came precariously close to diagnosing ten-year-old Jerry as severely retarded.

Our first contact was in a testing situation. It was my responsibility to evaluate Jerry for admission to an educable-retarded class. Jerry struggled through almost the entire administration of the Wechsler-Bellevue with little or no response. Everything I said, everything I showed him, seemed beyond his comprehension, if not downright confusing to him. He was hard of hearing, but he did hear; even so, my gestures and examples appeared meaningless to him. Yet I could not stop. Something inside me insisted that I continue.

He reacted with bewilderment and question to the demonstration of the Block Design, a test of abstract perception, just as he had with all the other tests. But this time there was a difference; he was able to copy the third demonstration.

Then, with sudden insight, as if the capacity came by magic, he was able to complete the next five designs well within the time limits. With this success, Jerry appeared to be a different boy. He seemed to relax. I watched with fascination as he methodically worked out the intricate designs. His complete involvement and enjoyment were quite obvious. He was unable to complete the final two designs within the time limits, but constructed close approximations. As Jerry relaxed, we began to exchange smiles and share the joy of his accomplishment. I think we both felt a bond of closeness. The grin he gave me as he left was free and open. He knew that I realized his true abilities. He knew that I knew he had much more than most people had realized. From this point on, there was a silent understanding between us that nothing could shake.

As I look back to this testing experience, I ponder over Jerry's complete confusion with most of the test items. Perhaps, because of his unique experiences in life, he was unfamiliar with the abstract mode of perception. Because of his difficulty in verbal communication, he had developed his own unique way of experiencing reality. Perhaps, this enabled Jerry to be more rooted in the concrete than other children. He had a greater tendency to perceive in wholes, and perhaps he was confused by the fragmentary, analytic demands of the test. Certainly, for someone who had been accustomed to encounter life directly, a categorical-abstract approach is far removed from reality. Why segment and disassociate a perception when it is obviously "there" in its totality? Why translate feelings into words when they are clearly sensed and understood in their genuine, unspoken form? Ours is a strange world for someone who is deeply in contact with the immediacy of the universe, who is in such close contact with life that he does not abstract and separate himself from the totality.

But why the sudden successes and better-than-average

performance? What motivated me to ignore the rules and continue testing after all the preliminary failures? Did I unknowingly enter Jerry's world and respond to his beckoning instead of the directions of the test? I do not objectively understand my behavior. I can only recapture a vague feeling of being suddenly present in the unfolding life of the other. A sensitivity and awareness was demanded of me that was anchored in existence, not in the rubrics of cognition and language. In me was a sense of something forming, something being born; perhaps it was the uncertain courage to follow a path without knowing why or how or where I was going. As doubts arose, there was a counter feeling of wanting to reach out to an emerging creation. Did Jerry sense my earnest hope, my intense inner urge to help him, somehow, *to become?* Did he sense my own inner experience of faith and conviction and concern, and did this help him to rally his own resources? Did he have to experience repeated failure in my presence to know the meaning of being valued, recognized, and accepted regardless of performance? To know the meaning of companionship, of relationship? Whatever the process, something happened to Jerry, to both of us, that enabled him to achieve, to accomplish what had not been possible before. Exactly what happened remains a mystery, but I believe it was more than the sum of Jerry and me. What happened was between us and beyond us—an essence, an existence that transcended each of us. A human meaning emerged in which two people struggled to reach each other at the deepest levels, a communion that occurs only when two persons are totally and completely alert to each other's being. Perhaps, at the moment of our struggle in the test, a spark of faith leaped from me to Jerry that allowed him to integrate and bring to expression capacities that had long been dormant.

In the hours of our therapy, the key to Jerry's emergence

focused on his feelings of aggression and hostility. Yet these feelings were not the typical intense, aggressive feelings expressed in therapy. It was as though they were not really a part of him, as though he were standing aside wearing someone else's feelings. When he expressed aggression, he looked bewildered and smiled at me in puzzlement. His hostility was not restrained and deeply inhibited, not ready to burst forth violently in a moment of acceptance or encouragement; it was worn on the surface of the skin rather than underneath it. It was a hostility completely alien to his nature. He had to discard these feelings, not in angry outburst, but as he might discard an outer covering to reveal his true self. His feeling of right and wrong was not embedded in a restrictive superego. His conscience was at a much deeper level. He had a way of expressing himself as if to say, "People should not be angry and hurt and destroy. It's not the human way." Jerry was so close to his humanness that his basic nature pressed beyond the conventional standards and expectations and reached deeper into a sense of justice.

In our first meetings, Jerry was reluctant to express aggressive feelings, though his approach to the toy figures implied a need to do so. One day, he set the soldiers in position to shoot the animals. He left them this way until I shouted encouragingly, "Bang!" Almost at the moment of my remark, the shooting began; the battle was under way. I continued shouting "bang" and "grrr" throughout his play, as he shot down the animals and knocked them over. These were our only spoken sounds for a long, long time. Jerry continued shooting until the battle ended with all animals downed. His further play evolved the same theme: he knocked over the soldiers with cars; then he knocked over cars with other cars. Again, he seemed to be expressing detachment or noninvolvement, a feeling that the items themselves were creating battle and war, were moving under their own volition. In a real sense, Jerry was noncommittal in all these actions. He was enacting a scene that had been played many times before, but now he was the director and not simply one of the actors being pushed around. I was delighted in the sudden spontaneity he was expressing, in the release I felt in him. So I continued making sound effects to encourage and even enhance his actions. I made no long comments or reflections or interpretations aimed at promoting insight, just simple sound effects that complemented Jerry's play and added to his sense of courage and abandon. After many more visits, the play took a different turn: Jerry picked up toy people, gazed at them intently, and tossed them gaily into the air.

Another dimension of the world we shared centered in problem-solving situations. Through these experiences Jerry could strengthen his valuing of himself and his confidence in himself. As in the test situation, he initially experienced defeat, followed by struggle, and finally a sense of glory in accomplishment. For example, he worked desperately to put objects together in a particular shape, form, or construction. At times, he appealed to me with gestures, attempting to enlist my aid. But I did not assist him or solve problems for him. I sat by, feeling his struggle and expressing my belief that he could manage on his own. I sensed that his difficulty in handling objects was due to a predetermined attitude, an expectancy that I, the adult, would lose patience and do the task for him. His attitude seemed to be: "Why not fail in a hurry and let *him* do it for me. Eventually, big people get irritated with me and do the job anyway." When he saw that I did not and would not fit the prototype, he was temporarily stopped; but he soon proceeded to tackle the problem on his own. His ability to manipulate objects and coordinate his efforts improved so rapidly that I realized my faith was not the main catalyst in his recovery. It was his growing freedom to be.

As problems slipped away under Jerry's deft fingers, I could feel a relaxation in his body and an expansiveness in his expressive movements. Once the challenge of problem-solving was mastered, a new dimension of Jerry emerged, a warm and intimate sense of humor. His first joke focused on the ridiculous presence of ten toy children and one toy bathtub. He solved this dilemma by putting all of the human figures into the one tub, and then he shared with me a lingering, full-faced grin. Another time, he became concerned about a group of toy soldiers that he had placed in a metal cage. His face lit up, and he smiled at me as he placed a toy toilet in the cage with them. In his silent manner, he had told me that, for the moment, their most pressing problem was solved.

In fact, Jerry spent several hours entertaining me with his "jokes." These episodes were a breathing spell following aggressive play and the struggles of the problem-solving situations. Jerry appreciated my acceptance, understanding, and encouragement, but he also wanted to enjoy the spontaneity and the warmth of human companionship. He wanted to share his light side, his own silent brand of humor. The sharing of the pleasant and comic side of his nature was his way of cementing our relationship and not burdening our friendship with too much of the heavy and serious side at one time.

For some time, I wondered whether we would ever penetrate deeper into his feelings and experiences. But I had to learn to be patient, to wait, to respect his own timetable. When he was ready, he once again began to explore his aggressive covering and painful experiences. During one entire hour, he maneuvered a truck so that it would barely miss the figures of a girl and woman; he carefully and deliberately avoided hitting them. In his own way, he was telling me with whom he was angry. But he was not ready to own the feeling and commit himself to an unrestrained expression of hostility. Would I accept such a strong feeling? Could he dare express the feeling without endangering our relationship? Would he be rebuffed?

My calm recognition and acceptance of his feelings gave him the courage to take the next step. Following his hour of experimental probing with the female figures, he began to crash some of the soldier figures together. At first, I joined in with my usual sound effects. As his feelings became more intense, I said, "Sometimes I bet you wish you could crash real people together like that." This remark precipitated an onslaught. He gritted his teeth and smashed figure against figure for some time. Soon all the human figures were involved in the assault. As the intensity of his feelings waned, I commented, "Sometimes people just start fighting, and it's really hard to understand why they fight." This hit a responsive chord, and, in a concrete way, Jerry began to express what was bothering him. He spent the rest of the hour making a little boy figure and a lady figure fight each other. He had them engage in constant battle. I commented that the mother and the boy were really angry with each other.

Until this point, Jerry had not spoken a single word. I had used words only rarely. I think Jerry would have been very disturbed by too much talking early in our meetings. But now he was ready to follow his feelings more directly. He seemed to have developed more courage and self-confidence. I sensed this growing conviction and value and felt more at ease speaking to him. He reflected my words in his play, showing that they made sense to him. He could hear me expressing his feelings toward his mother and, at the same time, know that I understood and continued to respect and care for him. In referring to his mother in his play, he seemed to be saying, "This is the way life is; these experiences hurt; rejection is a part of my life; I have to learn to live with it."

From this point on, Jerry began to expand his world and to extend his field of exploration. He began to examine and use all of the toys and materials in the playroom. He eyed them closely, felt them, and experimented with them in his play. Once his field of vision and exploration had broadened, Jerry became fully himself and was engrossed increasingly in his own becoming nature. When this began to happen, I experienced many exciting moments with him. But one day in particular stands out as thrilling and encompassing for me, the day that Jerry walked into the room and abruptly began a conversation. His speech was not entirely clear, but I could understand that he was describing a joyful experience with another boy. This was the first time Jerry had spoken to me. Up to this point, he had lived in a world that contained, literally, only silent dialogue. I guess that I was stunned and open-mouthed; but, at the same time, I felt that it was a perfectly natural thing for him to do, for him to speak words to me in just this way. To Jerry I must have looked dazed. His eyes met mine, and he laughed wholeheartedly, with his entire being. It was such a shining victory that tears came to my eyes. I went over to him and hugged him. I just felt I had to do it. "Oh Jerry!" For a moment, an eternity, we were in complete emotional contact.

After this, Jerry talked when it was necessary to communicate in words. His important feelings still transcended words, and many, many silent moments continued to exist. He expressed his feelings through his play, in his gestures and expressive movements, and in his inner bodily self, and I sensed his meanings without question or comment. He had the unusual talent of revealing his feelings in his very being. He had a way of forging beyond the barriers of abstraction so that anyone willing could perceive unity and meaning in his experience.

Our remaining visits were centered in different facets of our relationship and in Jerry's exploration and sharing of his potentialities and attributes. Jerry devoted many hours to drawing. At first, his drawings had a repetitive theme, but once he had gained a sense of freedom, they became quite varied and individualistic. On one occasion, he drew a clock, correct in all details, but he placed it in the sky among moving bodies. He studied his clock and seemed concerned. He looked puzzled for a while, and then, with a satisfied grin on his face, he proceeded to draw jets on the clock. Now it was all right. Now the clock belonged. Now it could stay in the sky in an active way, like the sun and planets. Some of his drawings were whimsical. He would personify objects. He put smiling faces on houses and sad faces on trees. Sometimes he drew without a concrete theme in mind, enjoying the pure experience of color and letting the shape and form flow from the sheer feeling of fun.

At times, he wanted me more actively involved, so he began to make up games that required two persons. We took turns hiding small objects in clay and then trying to find them. We filled up large sheets of paper with x's and o's. Alternately, we gave each other play money, neither of us wanting to keep the lion's share. He cooked and served me many dinners that I ate with delight. We hid objects in the room and spent joyful moments searching for them. Several times, I hid objects on my person. Jerry came in close physical proximity to me, adding to our feeling of closeness. During these hours, we were completely relaxed, enjoying each other's company in a warm, human atmosphere. He learned to tell time, at least our time; without mistake, even to the minute, he always knew when it was time to visit me.

Since the beginning of the school year, Jerry had lived

with his aunt and uncle. His mother had returned to her home and job in another state. When we had reached the peak of our experience in therapy, Jerry departed for a brief visit to his mother and sister. When he returned, he regressed to the hostile attitudes of our first meetings. But this time he was very direct in expressing his angry feelings. Among a group of children, he placed a female figure that he identified as a mother. He used her to push the children and knock them down. I said, "Bad mother." After the mother figure had pushed the children around for some time, he got a knife and stabbed her; then he shot her. I emphasized, "The boy is angry at her and wants to hurt her." Jerry put the mother in jail. I remarked, "She belongs in jail, where she can't hurt children. She can't get along with anybody." At this point, Jerry's attention shifted to the sister figure. He knocked it down and stepped on it. I accented his feeling, saying, "Sometimes the boy has angry feelings toward his sister too. Perhaps he doesn't want her around." Jerry continued to attack the mother and sister figures during the next two sessions, but the intensity of his feelings abated. Gradually these feelings disappeared entirely from his play; they did not return. He knew he would have to live with the reality of a mother and sister whom he felt did not care for him; it was a relief to him to find someone with whom he could share this reality. Expressing his feelings openly and violently eased the pain.

Once again, Jerry returned to his free, expressive play, construction activities, and games with me. His conversations increased as he discussed his drawings and his play and as he involved me in games. Among other facts, he was curious about the denominations of money. He asked me about the different values. He played with the paper money from the toy cash register, calling out each amount and asking me if it were correct. He drew traffic lights, labeling the red light with an "R" and the green light with a "G." He asked me the correct letter for yellow but before I could answer, he said, with an engaging smile, "O.K., I'll use 'P' for pause." During these times, we had sustained conversations, particularly around Jerry's dramatic use of the puppets. We took the child puppets to the zoo and discussed life in the zoo. We went for a train trip and passed through "holes in the mountains." We took a trip to the North and South Poles. He talked easily and openly, using words to inform and question me.

When Jerry came for our last visit, I could hardly believe that he was the same fearful, silent boy who had first come to the playroom almost a year ago. In this final session, he conversed with me naturally and comfortably. Using the puppets, he dramatized in a humorous way various human scenes. We played our hide-the-object game. We had a phone conversation over the toy telephone. As had often been his way, he surprised me by looking up and correctly locating the phone number of a friend. At the end of the hour, he wrote down my telephone number. I remarked that now he knew how to reach me if ever he needed me. It was a panoramic hour of events and a glimpse of our life in review. In our final moment together, we paused in silence. We parted with warm smiles, knowing that this would be our last direct meeting, yet feeling that what we had shared would continue to live.

Jerry's growth in therapy paralleled his growth in the classroom. Some of his first words were spoken in the classroom before he used words in therapy, but many of the changes that occurred in therapy did not show up in the classroom until sometime later. Jerry did not engage in real conversations in the classroom until sometime after our talks in therapy. One day, however, his teacher suddenly realized that one of the voices jabbering in a group of children was

Jerry's. From this moment on, his life of dialogue included words. Jerry raised questions; he expressed his interests; he communicated his wishes in words. He did not talk often, but he did talk. His teacher wondered, as I did, how often Jerry's silence was due to his shyness and his need for privacy and how often it was due to his feeling that words were appropriate only at certain times, only when needed for meaningful communication.

In the classroom, he developed social interests and social responsiveness. He began to play more and more with other children. He especially enjoyed quiet games rather than boisterous activities. He watched other children with interest and participated with them when the social situation contained a genuine value for him.

Toward the end of his therapy experience, Jerry began to read in the classroom. He learned to read by studying each word methodically. His progress was slow, but once he mastered a word it stayed with him. Jerry also developed an understanding of number concepts, using the same painstaking methodical approach in learning number facts.

How much of Jerry's growth was due to his therapeutic experience and how much was due to his stable life with his aunt and uncle and his rich relationship with his teacher? As I look back now, it seems impossible to separate these three major influences in his emergence as a confident, spontaneous person. For the first time, he lived in a home with an understanding male person. His uncle loved Jerry and expressed genuine interest and concern in their relationship. Both his uncle and aunt valued him, understood him, and gave him time and space and a stable family atmosphere in which to grow. Certainly his relationships with his teacher and with his classmates were important ingredients in his steady emergence as a real self, in his steady development of freedom and spontaneity.

What was my effect on Jerry's teacher? I did not offer her suggestions or advice. I did not guide or direct her. I did not provide her with an evaluation or diagnosis. We had many long talks, some about Jerry, some about the other children in her classroom, and some about life and human values in general. We shared our hopes and aspirations, our fears and worries, our disturbance over the mistreatment of children. We discussed the fate of the world and the crises facing modern man. About Jerry specifically? We did not discuss treatment or teaching or education of Jerry. We were concerned when other children manipulated him. We were at times bothered by his passive noninterfering philosophy of life, but we had infinite faith in his potential. We both believed in his individuality, in his being, in the importance of choice, in freedom, in Jerry's becoming. We beamed at his unique and creative expressions. We shared the thrilling moments we experienced with him in his successes. We strengthened each other's values and convictions; we each grew in awareness and sensitivity by exploring our intimate experiences with this unusually silent and perceptive boy.

About eight months after the completion of his therapy, Jerry's teacher wrote to me: "With the advent of the marble season, Jerry has become the life of the room. The kids line up to play with him, and he is having a great time being the center of activity. He laughs frequently and talks a blue streak. Incessantly, he is curious and seeking information. He asks me about maps. 'Can cars drive down here? Is this Africa? South Pole here?' He has five plant experiments going in the classroom. He is filled with wonder and questions as he watches growing life. He asked me how much eggs cost, 'Not the ones you eat but from which baby chicks will hatch.' He is exploring in all directions: 'What's this? This? This? Read this.'"

So Jerry continues to grow and to emerge as a self in his

thirst for new experiences, in his discovery of the wonders of life. His sensitive teacher waits and takes each step of the journey with him. When Jerry is ready, he shows her the way to open up new vistas for him. She follows the path and, at the same time, introduces him to new resources and opportunities.

I like to think that Jerry's therapy experience with me was a catalyst in his emergence, and I believe that it was. I know that from this experience I have become more sensitive, wise, and humble as a person. I am more reluctant to judge another individual on any basis, even in the face of so-called facts and objective evidence. I now understand the vast potential of nonverbal communication and the value of concrete nonverbal awareness. My experience with Jerry has shown me ways of opening up in myself feelings of which I had been only dimly aware. It has reemphasized the importance of patience in therapy, especially during the apparent plateaus and uneventful periods. It has again pointed up the need for patience concerning progress outside of therapy. Even when dramatic changes occur in therapy, comparable shifts may not occur in the school or home for some time. Most important of all, our therapy experience enabled me to know intimately the being of Jerry, to savor his uniqueness, to have a deep relationship with someone special. And, like every human being, Jerry is someone special.

7
Therapy as a Living Experience ❀
Frederick Allen

MY WORK WITH CHILDREN is based on a basic premise: Therapy exists in its highest form and maintains its value to the extent that it is a meaningful and unique life experience. Therapy involves the creation of a special structure in which a troubled child meets with a therapist in such a way that the child's inner life is revealed, in such a way that the child participates directly and actively in the resolution of his own conflicts and problems.

I have chosen to present my experience with Betty Lou as a particularly relevant example of child therapy, consistent with my conviction that the therapist symbolizes life to the disturbed child, symbolizes health in a fundamental way, inviting the child to participate in new experiences centered in self-awareness and self-direction.

Ten-year-old Betty Lou came to me as quite a totalist. In every sense, she was caught up in an extremist position, in an "all or nothing" proposition. She saw life as filled with "shoulds," pushing her in absolute directions. For her, the only possibilities were extremes: Either she must live or die, be safe or daring, win or lose, be cautious or courageous. She could not conceive that life required different solutions at different times. She did not consider the reality of integration, of variation, of between. In her own mind, Betty Lou felt that she was doomed to accept the negative side as the only choice. She felt that there was no alternative but to accept the death forces within her as her fate. Defeat, failure, passivity, hopelessness, fear, and loss were the key themes in Betty Lou's world, the key experiences that predisposed her to view life as a tragedy.

The Family Setting

Betty Lou's family consisted of an older brother and her mother and father. The parents had been married a long time before having their first child. In their relationship, the mother and father had built a life that excluded others. The arrival of the children did not alter this pattern; the parents increasingly encased themselves in their own private world and isolated their children from this world. According to the parents, the children accepted the reality of this world and, up to the time of the onset of Betty Lou's illness, had made satisfactory progress in the home, the neighborhood, and the school.

Increasingly, it became clear that Betty Lou was not evolving in a healthy, productive way in this family atmosphere. In a sense, there was no family at all. There was no unity or wholeness in the family setting. There were two parents exclusively attached to each other, meeting the external needs of their children but rarely joining them in activities, as a unified family. Increasingly, Betty Lou experienced a feeling of separation and rejection and a feeling of threat that reached a peak in the onset of a school phobia, accompanied by nausea and physical illness. She became extremely resistant to the idea of attending school. The fear became so severe that she felt that, if she were forced to return to school, she would become very sick, and, perhaps, die. The school phobia soon required attention from the parents. They had to face the reality of Betty Lou in an entirely different way. Their world of oblivion to others was shattered; the all-encompassing compact between them was broken.

Betty Lou's mother was immediately caught up in the school phobia, and, reversing her attitude toward Betty Lou, she became fully aware of the child as her daughter. Being unable to contribute positive resources and convictions that would enable Betty Lou to come to grips with the problem, she became extremely anxious and over-protective. The father, resenting the threat to his own relationship with his wife, at first was stern and critical of both mother and child. When condemnation did not have the desired results, he withdrew from active involvement in the problem. Another dimension of the crisis emerged when Betty Lou began to project her fears onto her mother. She began to feel that her mother was in jeopardy, that "something" would happen to her mother unless she was constantly at her side. The mother, herself, became caught up in the tremendous concern and promised her daughter that she would never leave the house while Betty Lou was away.

Trapped in this way, the mother's anxiety grew until, in desperation, she sought out therapy for her daughter. Angry over Betty Lou's control of her mother, the father permitted his wife to take this step toward therapy, even though it violated his belief that he could manage any problem by himself.

The clinic required the parents to participate in two exploratory interviews before a plan was created to work with Betty Lou. In the first meeting, however, Betty Lou accompanied her parents, and made it extremely difficult for the adults to talk together. For the second meeting, the parents were told firmly that they could not bring their daughter. This initiated another crisis. The mother was certain that Betty Lou would totally collapse if they left her at home. But, the limit was held, and the parents for the first time began to see that indulging Betty Lou and allowing her to control her mother would further aggravate the problem and entangle the lives of everyone in the family. The parents understood that realistic limits were necessary and that Betty Lou would not perish. With this firm stand, the parents appeared without Betty Lou, and a plan of treatment was established that would involve the parents.

The First Hours with Betty Lou

From the beginning, Betty Lou was eager to come for therapy. In the first hour, she sat somewhat apprehensively in the waiting room; but when it was time to begin, she entered the office with little outward evidence of anxiety. Immediately, she began to describe her illness in school and her fear that something terrible would happen to her if she attended. Then, in explaining why she thought coming to the clinic would help her, she said: "I want to come here to get over being afraid." She agreed with my comment that she felt some of the fear right at the moment with me and that coming was a first step in finding out what she could do about it. This pointed conversation between us paved the way for the main theme of our first two meetings.

Betty Lou's fear centered in the imminent danger that surrounded her mother. She expressed this fear in her questions: "What will happen to my mother if I am not with her?" And, "What will happen to me if something happens to her?" In defense of her own insistence that her mother stay home, Betty Lou explained that her chief motive in remaining out of school was to protect her mother. She felt that she had to build up an elaborate scheme of control which would keep her mother safe. But, she qualified her position by adding, "I could return to school if my mother would promise not to leave the house while I am away." I suggested that perhaps she was also afraid of what might happen to her, that at the center of her own world was a fear of life. As she was not ready to own this fear, she immediately rejected the idea.

She recounted many incidents in the home; each reflected a tremendous concern for her mother and her mother's reactions. At one point, she remarked, "This morning I ate a cookie, and I wondered if I had hurt my mother." In many ways she conveyed the image of herself as undifferentiated from her mother. She expressed the idea that her mother was not actually her mother, that perhaps she was a twin sister. She doubted too that her mother had given her birth and stated quite emphatically, "At times I have the feeling I am an adopted child." As we explored these feelings further, it was clear that she did not really believe in them, but she was playing an imaginative game, letting her fantasy mingle freely and go astray. Rejecting the notion that her mother was in reality her twin, she re-created a twin fantasy, saying that she herself was both twins. I said that I could understand these feelings. One twin in her wanted to grow up, go to school, and enjoy life as other girls her age did; the other wanted to remain a little girl and be cared for and protected by her mother. Betty Lou seemed intrigued with my interpretation but made no comment. To me, it seemed clear that undifferentiated from her mother Betty Lou felt herself to be a person of value, recognized and confirmed. The feeling of separation aroused a feeling of being nobody, at best a twin, but with no adequate confidence of being a unique and distinct person. At the same time, because of its restrictions in her own self growth, she rebelled against the attachment to her mother and retaliated by attempting to control her mother and by trying to keep her mother from being a person in her own right.

At the end of my second meeting with Betty Lou, I told her of the plan to have another conference with her mother and father and pointedly added, "And you will not be there." To my surprise she did not express fear or resentment at being left at home. Instead, she made only one significant comment, "What does my father have to do with this?" I suggested that she had two parents, that they were both worried about her, that they both had a real part in helping her to overcome her fears, in helping her to become a happy person.

At the end of each of the two first hours with Betty Lou, she became openly anxious. She feared that her mother would not be waiting for her. She wanted to stand outside the door of the room where her mother was being interviewed. But, I insisted that she wait in the reception room, conveying, at the same time, my confidence that she could wait alone. Here she made use of my conviction that she could manage on her own, that she could behave in a responsible way.

Conference with the Parents

After two hours of therapy with Betty Lou, a third conference was scheduled with the parents. Although fraught with ambivalence, conflict, and doubt, right up to the last moment, the meeting with the parents came off as planned; Betty Lou remained at home. Thus for the second time, her mother saw that she could stand up to Betty Lou's powers, and in holding firm, she conveyed to her husband that there was a new strength and feeling of hope within her. Again, the mother expressed the fear that Betty Lou would collapse completely if she became firm with her and broke out of the box she was in. But she saw that this did not happen. On the contrary, in spite of the crying and screaming, she sensed that Betty Lou really wanted her to hold to the limits, that Betty Lou really felt her mother's presence in a reassuring way. With these two separations as a beginning, her mother left Betty Lou for increasingly longer periods.

The mother and father began the process of unraveling their own involvement in their daughter's development. It was clear that the independence they had sought was an escape from responsibility, that it had little genuineness or substance. Betty Lou's fear and need to control them had shattered the parents' relationship with each other and had jarred the mother into an awareness of her failure to give her daughter what she needed most—a real mother quality. So, out of guilt, she handed herself over to Betty Lou and allowed her to control her daily life, but with a great deal of latent hostility that she could not express at this point in the therapeutic process.

The Next Seven Meetings with Betty Lou

Betty Lou started off these meetings with a surface gaiety that did not successfully cover up her obvious tension. She said she was glad to be back and immediately plunged into a discussion of the problems she faced in growing up. She said she did not want to get any older because "to get older is to die." Thus she did not want to grow up. And since going to school meant growing up, she did not want to go to school. She did not want to become "big." She wanted to stay at home and be near her mother always because this meant being little, not growing older, not dying. She said, "I may be ten years old in my body, but I am still a little girl in my mind."

At the same time, Betty Lou was not happy to be little. There were times when she yearned to return to school. She told me how she watched from the window as children in her neighborhood hurried off to school. In a wistful voice, she added, "I really want to join them." I accepted these feelings without in any way attempting to alter them or influence her.

Betty Lou held tenaciously to the obsession that something terrible would happen to her mother if she went off to school. She was not ready to see this as a fear of her own separation or to see herself as a separate person in any way. It hurt too deeply to be a person. She did not deny life, but she found it extremely painful to come into it on her own. In addition, she felt that, to be a person in her own right, she must steal life from her mother. She began to reveal her own guilt over being alive. She knew her mother had had three miscarriages before she was born. As she put it one day, "Maybe I shouldn't be here. Maybe I am an accident." She suggested that perhaps she was a substitute for the unborn children of her mother.

As I have mentioned, for Betty Lou growing up really meant to die. To be brighter, keener, more aware, more in touch with life was a frightening thought for Betty Lou, frightening partly because it meant competing with her mother, surpassing her mother, being smarter, more alive than her mother. And the thought of going beyond her mother created a feeling fraught with pain and guilt. For Betty Lou, to transcend her mother was equivalent to killing her.

Thus Betty Lou was caught up in a terrible conflict with her mother, loving her and hating her, wanting her to live yet wishing she were dead. At the same time, she thought that her mother wished she had never been born. She experienced painful guilt in the thought of being an alive person.

In her contacts with me, I sharpened and clarified the split within her: the wish to be big and the wish to be little, the excitement of life and the inevitability of death, the wish to remain dependent and the desire to grow up. And in this process, in the relationship with me, I symbolized life for her. I represented a zest and vibrancy for living, a vital quality she was reaching for. Her previous psychiatrist had focused on the dying dimensions of Betty Lou, on her death wishes, on her withdrawal from life. He was technically right, but humanly and existentially wrong. He symbolized the death force, whereas I represented the life force. My conversations with her kept the focus on what she experienced in the present, from within. I reflected the side of her that wanted to live, helping her to recognize her own fear of growing up, but, at the same time, her desire to be connected with life and to emerge as a distinct and independent person. From my comments to her, Betty Lou not only became increasingly aware of the split in herself but also of her wish to become connected with life. Once she remarked, "Sometimes I have the feeling I don't want to live any more, but when I come here I know I want to live."

Betty Lou knew in advance that, at the end of these seven meetings, there would be a lengthy summer break. Toward the end, she said she wanted to keep coming. She did not want to have to stop for the summer. She said, "I am still not cured of my fears." I told her she had grown much stronger and was more ready to return to an active life. I added that her mother was growing also. She looked surprised and asked, "What was wrong with her?" I indicated that there was a lot that was wrong in their relationship to each other. Betty Lou smiled in agreement. Even so, as the last hour drew near, her anxiety increased. She minimized her progress and said that she still felt frightened when her mother was away for a long time. And, she said she did not know whether she would be ready to return to school after the summer. Several times she repeated, "Maybe I shouldn't have been born. Maybe I should have been one of the other three. There wouldn't be any problems then." At this point in our relationship, in spite of these feelings of self-doubt and inadequacy, I felt that Betty Lou was more aware of her own identity, and more alive and engaged in activity, though still experiencing guilt over being herself. She asked me, "How do people know when they are going to die?" I responded, saying, "Most people are too busy living, just as you are now, and don't have to answer such a question."

During her period of absence from school, Betty Lou was being tutored at home. One day she reported excitedly that she had passed all of her examinations and would be promoted. She enthusiastically told about the summer plans of the family: "The whole family is taking a trip together for the first time that I can remember." The change in the direction of family unity and solidarity, which began when the parents first became aware of the importance of real family life, was reflected in the plans for a joint family vacation. Each member of the family took an active part in planning the trip.

During the seven-week period of therapy with Betty Lou, her mother was becoming increasingly free to leave the home, and to do more on her own, in a natural way. While Betty Lou continued to struggle and battle with her mother when her mother wanted to go her own way, the intensity of her reaction lessened and she was becoming more able to accept separation from her mother. At the same time, her mother was finding new courage to permit Betty Lou to express fear and anger without herself becoming enmeshed in these feelings. A much more favorable climate for healthy growth had been created, so that Betty Lou could use family resources in solving the dilemma of being an individual and, at the same time, a member of her family. Both parents were finding new qualities in themselves that supported the growing up of their daughter. Therapy was providing her with a differentiating experience, where she could reveal herself as a genuine and distinct person.

The summer proved to be an enriching experience for each member of the family. The parents renewed their relationship with each other, but without the isolating and exclusive components. The family shared many activities, including a Florida vacation. In the fall, Betty Lou indicated a readiness to return to school. On the first day, she was filled with anxiety but was determined to go ahead with the plan. She said to her mother, "I'm scared to go but I'm going anyway." However, before she departed, she exacted a promise from her mother to stay near the house while she was in school. Thus, the mother was once more caught up in the old trap. But, at the same time, even while making the commitment, she became angry that she had permitted herself once again to make an unhealthy contract with her daughter. Betty Lou tried to get her mother to work out an arrangement with the school whereby she would have to attend only half-day sessions or just on her own terms, as she felt able to attend. The principal, however, refused to accept this arrangement and insisted on full-day attendance. He pointed out to Betty Lou and her mother that, if Betty Lou expected to attend school, she would have to meet the same requirements as other children, or not come at all. Through conferences with the clinic, the principal could see that the school was a battleground but not the real situation of stress. He could understand that the struggle was between two determined and anxious people, between Betty Lou and her mother, and that the issue between them had to be settled in the family. In the light of the principal's firm insistence, in contrast to Betty Lou's determination to attend school on her own terms, it was decided that Betty Lou would remain at home until she was ready to be responsible for full-day attendance. At the same time, she was told that she was expected to return to school and that it was her responsibility to do so as soon as she felt able. In consultation with the school and the family, the tutoring was discontinued because it was felt that this would heighten Betty Lou's need to return to school and keep the challenge of school constantly before her as an imperative. I did not support Betty Lou's decision to remain at home. I did not excuse her from school attendance. My attitude was not a vital issue or theme in our meetings. It was a matter that she herself had to work out. The school was a central concern in her world, but I did not get involved in the struggle as to whether or not she should return; the issue did not become a significant theme in her hours with me.

Twenty-six More Meetings with Betty Lou

My first meeting with Betty Lou in the fall came just after her confrontation with the school principal. She told me she would return to school all day if she could be assured that her mother would remain at home the entire time. I pointed out to her that her mother was no longer willing to make such an arrangement, that when she had agreed earlier she felt extremely angry; she felt trapped; she felt it was an unfair and intolerable plan. But, Betty Lou protested, "As long as I am afraid, I cannot leave my mother. I cannot go to school. Something terrible will happen to her." Eventually I broke through these fixed ideas by pointing out that she was using her own fears as a justification for controlling her mother, not because something might happen to her mother, but because once she had felt left out by her parents and now she didn't want her mother to have a life of her own. I explained that I thought she was testing her mother, that I thought she was trying to find out how far she could push her mother. I told her that, in reality, I thought she wanted her mother to show her strength, to be firm with her, to express her love by insisting that she grow up and be responsible as a ten-year-old girl. In these discussions, Betty Lou listened, accepted, and understood the underlying dynamics of her relationship with her mother. She came to understand that controlling dependence was a form of death, that life was a movement forward toward responsibility and happiness, that I would not support the regressive, backward forces in her; but that, on the contrary, I would support the vital forces of life in her, the side of her that wished to go out into the world as a distinctive person. Gradually, she came to respond to me. Increasingly, she emerged as a spontaneous individual and came to value the alive and positive dimensions of the self.

In these hours she often spoke of death, of living and dying, of birth and ageing. She was trying to solve the riddle of living. The underlying formula seemed to be, "If you remain little, if you stay dependent, if you keep unalive then life is eternal; but each time you go out into the world and live, a piece of you is dying." She asked, "Why should I go to school? Every day I would learn a little more, and grow up a little more, and die a little more." Often she said, "I wish I had never been born, like one of my sisters who died in my mummy's tummy. Then I would never have to worry." And, sometimes sadly, she would say, "If you have to die sometime, why not now and get it over with?" I spoke reassuringly to Betty Lou, "You are beginning to answer this question for yourself, not by words but in coming here. The fact that you come is a sign that you want to live. You want to do things. You want to enjoy life."

During the latter phase of our work together, I told her we had only a couple of months to work together, only a short time to help her to become a ten-year-old girl. Though, in fact, it was necessary to expand this limit to twenty-six meetings, when the time limit was first set, Betty Lou became obviously anxious, but the limit also enabled her to become more centered in the real issues and concerns, more focused in our discussions. Sometime later she remarked to me, "You know when I started to get better was when you told me we had only a couple of months for me to learn to be a ten-year-old girl. You said I had to learn to help myself. I learned when I came to see you that I would have something to do. That it was up to me to start." I responded with full acceptance and added, "Yes, and you learned to be yourself, Betty Lou, a ten-year-old girl, and not a baby nor an adult." Although my time limit was arbitrary, it proved to be a turning point in my work with Betty Lou.

Betty Lou clearly realized that she herself must participate actively in life. She must utilize her own resources in the resolution of her fears. Even so, at times, the responsibility was too much for her. She wanted to give up. She wanted to end the struggle. She began to relate her dreams. In them one idea appeared consistently: that she could eliminate all her fears through magic. Suddenly, all of her problems would vanish; suddenly, she would become a confident, free, outgoing person, mature in her behavior, successful in school, loved by her parents. She wondered too whether I did not possess magical powers by which I could cure her, by which I could bring about the desired changes in her. I made it clear that I did not have such powers but that I believed in her. I believed in her talents and capacities to make a good life for herself. I told her that in fact she herself possessed a kind of magic, that she had the capacity to choose to grow up and be a distinct and responsible person. She said I had already helped her solve some of the riddles, and, besides, she asked, "Why is it that I feel good when I come here? I am not afraid any more. But all we do is talk." I indicated that I could understand how it must seem like magic to her, but I emphasized that what made our meetings so special was that she shared with me her feelings and her ideas and that it was both the talking and the sharing that helped. I stressed that she was discovering that she was more ready to be a real person in her own right and less needing to keep her mother imprisoned. In short, our discussions revolved around Betty Lou's growth dilemma and her movement from a frightened, disabled individual into a person with interests and activities that challenged and compelled her.

At the end of the two-month time limit, Betty Lou announced that she had decided to return to school. For several weeks prior to this time, she had discussed with her parents the idea of going back to school. Throughout one hour with me, she kept repeating, with a mixture of conviction and anxiety, "I am going to school Monday." "I am going." "I am going." Obviously, she was attempting to gain more confidence to carry out her decision. She talked about possible harm that would come to her when she returned to school. I sympathized that it was a difficult decision to make, that return would be painful at first, but that I felt that she had gained in confidence and courage and that I believed she was ready to take this important step toward growing up. I also pointed out that much of the hardship and danger she envisioned was a product of her own imagination, that she was a taskmaster in creating frightening ideas and images. None of the dangers she foresaw had ever occurred but her inventing of them was a way of avoiding life, avoiding growing up, avoiding what she was ready to do and wanted to do. She asked that I repeat this idea. She said it to herself many times.

Throughout the next several meetings, Betty Lou spoke about school, describing activities and indicating a general satisfaction and enjoyment. I pointed out to her that none of the problems she had envisioned had occurred; none of the fears had arisen. She still seemed perplexed as to why she was feeling so much better. Again, she asked, "How is it you can help me if we just talk?" But this time, she did not wait for an answer. For the first time in our many months together, she began to play, to use the play materials in a spontaneous, involved, excited, and active manner, as is natural for the healthy ten-year-old child.

At the same time, along with the obvious gains, there were episodes of regression. Within Betty Lou, there was ambivalence about getting well, even a feeling of not wanting to get better, not wanting to terminate the special experience of therapy, which increasingly had come to be a vital part of her life. On occasions, she would say to me, "I'm not much better than when I first came to you, am I?" At such times, I would comment, "You really are very much better, very much happier, but it seems risky for you to say so." Betty Lou would listen but often would assert her need to continue coming until she was eighteen (she knew this to be the age limit of the clinic).

In spite of the shifting back and forth from illness to health, Betty Lou was clearly in the ending phase of therapy. Both Betty Lou and her mother, in her own therapy, were moving toward this goal. We had reached the beginning of the end of our life journey together. There were times when Betty Lou experienced considerable anxiety. Although she was feeling satisfaction in being more active, in moving ahead, in getting well, she was finding it difficult to yield to the fact that she was now being responsible for herself. She continued saying that, if she got completely well, she would become very ill again. She frequently commented that she might give up going to school. But, at the same time, I knew that school had come to have an important place in her life. I accepted her threats and suggested that whether she went to school or not was her choice but that I felt it would be a real loss to her if she stopped. Betty Lou would smile and we both knew it was part of the struggle to bring therapy to a close, part of the conflict in concluding an experience that had held such meaning in her life. Out of this process of affirming and denying her gains, we settled on a definite time for our last interview. This was also discussed with her mother, and we were in full accord. In one of our final meetings, Betty Lou described going to a class lunch. Up to this time, she had taken all of her lunches at home. On this occasion, she knew her mother would be away the entire day. Although she experienced considerable fear, she decided to attend the luncheon. It turned out to be an extremely important occasion in increasing Betty Lou's courage in being on her own. I paved the way for other school activities, such as dances and parties. She was now fully ready to leave her mother and have an independent life of her own. Once more, she referred to the time limit and the nearing of the end, "Do you remember when you said I was ready to stop and we decided on a few more times? That's when I knew I really had to get down to work and start doing what I wanted to do on my own." I agreed, saying that I too had noticed the forward spurt. In so many ways, the mastery Betty Lou had achieved was quite obvious. She was in control of the earlier fears and constraints. She had learned to live with the normal anxieties engendered by the process of becoming a differentiated individual. When we parted she said she was a little fearful about leaving, but she knew there was no backing away from her new life.

Two follow-up interviews were arranged, one a month

after ending and the other at the beginning of the new term, when she was entering junior high school. In both of these hours, she was relaxed and spoke in a natural, excited, spontaneous way about her summer experiences and her friends and activities in the new school. Clearly, the therapeutic experience was already receding in her conscious awareness, and it was becoming, as it should, an episode in her life journey toward becoming an adult.

Though I have given little detail of the mother's part in therapy, her participation, through regular interviews with a skillful social worker, gave an additional meaning to Betty Lou's hours with me. A truly differentiating quality, in Betty Lou's discovering herself as a separate but related person, and in the parents' recognition of themselves as separate, as related to each other, and as members of a family unit, gave this mother and father a livable sense of values. Both parents found that they could maintain a rich independent life alone and together, not as evasions and substitutes for their important commitment and responsibility to the family as a whole, but as expressions of interests and needs which were requirements of their own adult living. By discovering this healthy way to live individually and within the family, it became possible for Betty Lou to stop fighting for recognition and love in the home. It enabled her to become free and to use her resources and strengths in emerging as a separate and distinct person who, at the same time, could relate to her parents lovingly and with respect for their private world.

Years have gone by. Betty Lou completed a college education in her early twenties and is now happily married.

8

Initiation of an Obsessional Adolescent Boy ❦ *Eve Lewis*

ROY WAS TWELVE YEARS OLD when he first came to the Child Guidance Center. He was referred by a school medical officer, who reported that Roy was suffering from anxiety and depression which made it increasingly difficult for him to continue in school. Roy had been frequently absent in infant and junior school because of infectious diseases, heavy colds, and two hospitalizations. An attack of jaundice precipitated his present acute state of anxiety and his referral. With the onset of this illness, Roy had left school altogether.

There was no history of neurosis or psychosis in the family, but Mrs J. called herself "highly strung." She had a recurrent nightmare of being imprisoned deep underground and a tendency to claustrophobia. When Roy was an infant, our region had been subjected to many enemy air attacks. Even when bombs were falling, Mrs. J. had at times been driven to go out of the air raid shelter because she could no longer bear the enclosed and crowded space. She was an extroverted woman who mixed reasonably well in social situations. She worked part-time in a large department store.

In contrast, Mr. J. was an introvert. Although kind to his wife and children, he was somewhat detached both at home and at work. He held a superior position in a highly skilled trade. He was an isolated person in his job, having no close relationship with any of his fellow employees. Susan, nine years old, was the final member of the family. She had adjusted adequately to the requirements of life in the home and at school. She and Roy were on good terms, but by no means devoted. Her birth had not seemed to upset him in any way.

Roy was a good-looking boy, tall for his age, blue-eyed and very fair, with a sensitive guarded expression. As I came to know him in the course of our relationship, I found him to be introvertive, self-reflective, and able to think clearly within the limits of his endowment. On a first examination with Wechsler's Intelligence Scale for Children, his I.Q. was 101. On a later examination, when he was less anxious, he obtained an I.Q. of 115.

After the first test, I suggested to Roy that he and I should talk over his problems; together we would search for a way to solve them. I added that, if he wished, he could paint or draw or model as we talked.

With this as a preliminary background, our meetings in therapy got under way. We continued together through thirty-one half-hour sessions, spread over twelve months. I will present the significant episodes occurring between us. The meetings were punctuated by silences, by passing comments from Roy or myself as our experience and our relationship began to emerge and unfold. What appear to be long explanations on my part were broken by questions from Roy or by nods and grunts and other gestures to show that he understood. As we came to know each other, we began to share little jokes and to invent catch phrases for some of his difficulties.

The First Meeting: Phobias and Rituals

I began my hours with Roy by assuring him that I would not press him to return to school but, on the contrary, would respect his decision to return or not in accordance with his own readiness or wish. In my experience, removal of pressure in the place where greatest tension and disturbances are provoked ensures cooperation from the child and enables him to utilize his resources to face his problems rather than using them to battle against a therapist who attempts to force him prematurely into a situation of extreme threat and fear. Thus, I always leave the child free to make his own decision when a school phobia is a marked symptom in an emotional disturbance.

Roy received my preliminary remarks with relief. Immediately, he relaxed, settled back in his chair, looked less strained, and indicated a readiness to begin.

I told Roy that his mother had already given me a brief description of his problem in school and at home but that I preferred to hear directly from him, as I believed his own views were important and I would respect them. The adolescent appreciates a recognition of him as an individual and trusts and values the adult who genuinely listens and accepts his version of his own experience as valid. A comment like, "Yes, I know, it's simply awful, isn't it?" when spoken in an accepting human way, at once strikes the right note and registers as an agreement when a child is painfully struggling to express his secrets and his fears. And the very fact that the therapist accepts the child's statements calmly depotentializes the problem to a considerable extent.

With many hesitations and sideway glances, Roy began to

explain that his great problem was not the horror in connection with school but was a feeling of having "to do things." I encouraged him to tell me about the things he felt compelled to do. Bit by bit, his story stumbled out. He had to safeguard himself with a variety of rituals in dressing, undressing, washing, going to the lavatory, passing from one room to another or from the house onto the road. The rituals had to be carried out before he could begin to eat or to read, and in nearly every major activity of his life. He had to say his prayers again and again in a particular place and in a definite posture. I asked him if he knew why he had to perform all these rituals. He replied that he felt something awful would happen to him unless he did. I informed Roy that other boys and girls had mentioned similar rituals and fears to me and that the "something awful" for them was a fear of dying. I asked if this was so with him. Roy absolutely burst out, "Yes. It is! It is! I am often terrified of dying." The sight of an ambulance or a hearse made him feel faint. He could not bear even to hear about illness or death. Following these revealing comments, Roy picked up a pencil and began to sketch. My feeling was that he had chosen to draw at this moment not only as a way of escaping further consideration of the terror he had put into words, but also to suggest that he had blurted out the "real problem" and so had nothing further to say.

Of course, Roy's fear of death was not the basic problem. I knew for a fact that for the past three months he had been sleeping in his mother's bed, while his father, apparently uncomplainingly, had been sleeping in Roy's single room. Since I believed this to be indicative of the central problem in Roy's life, I felt it had to come out into the open. At the same time, I recognized that I might embarrass him and cause him to withdraw if my broaching of this area was not done in a gentle and sensitive way.

I spoke to him directly, but in a personal tone. "Then your fear of death explains why you are now sleeping with your mother; you feel safe when you are with her." Roy blushed scarlet and muttered, "It's only for a little time." He assured me that soon he would return to his own bed. Deliberately changing the subject, I said, "Look here, Roy! You feel compelled to do these rituals all day long, yet you know it doesn't make sense, don't you?"

Roy went on drawing for some moments without comment. Then he agreed that the rituals were senseless, but omitting them only increased his fear and pain. I told him I could understand that this could happen and that we needed together to find out how to put an end to all these senseless performances. We needed together to discover the unknown forces inside him that compelled him to "do things," terrified him with thoughts of death, and prevented him from enjoying a happy life at home and at school. I suggested that, if he could just talk freely and openly to me, that that in itself would help. I also suggested that a discussion of dreams often revealed the nature of inner experiences. His paintings too might provide us with clues to his inner life.

He was especially interested in what we could learn from paintings, so at this point I showed him a drawing done some years earlier by a nine-year-old girl. It was of a tiny figure seated at a school desk in front of a blackboard. The board was covered with a sequence of numbers adding up to an enormous sum. On the desk were a pencil, a pen, and an exercise book. All were very much larger than the figure of the child. I asked Roy if he could tell me what clue this drawing might have given me. He gazed carefully at it and then said, "It looks as if school was too much for her." I told him that he was quite right. The girl was accomplishing B. stream work, which was at the level of her potential, but she was expected by her parents and teachers to succeed at an A. stream level. The child did not understand why she felt ill every morning, why she felt unable to go to a school she hated. But she had drawn the truth for me. Perhaps he might depict his own real inner life for me through paintings and drawings. Roy was interested but doubtful. He protested that he liked school, and he strongly wished he could feel better so that he could attend again. As a matter of fact, his achievement was on a high, acceptable level.

Following a period of silence, Roy said he thought he partially understood the reason for his fear of dying. He was terrified at the possibility of fainting in school and thus of being forced back into the hospital. He could not bear the thought of being separated from his mother, of being isolated in a bed, of being prevented from occupying himself in activity. He could not bear the thought of a free, unscheduled time that would compel him to do more and more things to keep something awful from happening.

Roy's fear of isolation and hospitalization, his fear of forced removal from life, although it increased his anxiety and his need of rituals, was at the same time a healthy sign. To me it meant that Roy was seeking to remain in touch with life, that he wanted to live. Here was an inner awareness of hope and value, of direct involvement in the world, an inner awareness that his salvation lay in being able to participate in life.

Roy then turned to a different problem. He said he was becoming increasingly unhappy with the fact that now he was often losing his temper with his mother. He was unable to control himself, and he frequently worked himself into a rage against her. It left him frightened and exhausted. I said that I could understand how losing control could be a frightening experience. Sometimes "doing things" was a kind of magic against the inner feelings that might sweep one away.

This idea amused him and he smiled for the first time since we met. Sometime later, however, he told me that my explanation that his performing of rituals was a way of making magic was an important insight for him. At once, he felt that the compulsions were less mysterious and alarming.

Roy drew silently for some minutes and then related a dream he had had two nights earlier. He was in a great rage with someone; he thought it might have been his mother. He rushed out of the house, and finding his toboggan, he threw himself onto it. At once, it set off down a slope that grew steeper and steeper. He could see that the path ended in a deep pit, but he was quite powerless to stop the descent of the toboggan. He awoke in terror. To me, the dream gave further insight into his problem. The descent into the pit symbolized the urge to return to the womb of the Great Mother; his anger with his human mother arose through Roy's struggle with this image and his projection of this image onto his real mother. If this were so, in time I would have to help him to become aware of the inner situation and to see the self-creative striving implicit in his rages. As a first approach to this awareness, I said, "Anger can be good as well as bad, you know. It can be right to be angry with something that is evil, can't it?" Roy replied, "I hadn't thought of that before." Our time was up now. In leaving Roy remarked that he would continue with his drawing at our next meeting.

The Second Meeting: The Launching of the Ship

Roy began the hour in a quiet way. He completed his drawing, which was a strange, diffuse characterization of a ship. It was a crude, somewhat immature picture, with no distinction between bow and stern. The ship had three funnels and a long row of portholes. He began to paint the ship, and in the process, he completely obliterated the portholes. The middle funnel was much taller than the other two and out of it poured a cloud of dense black smoke. To me, the furious outpouring of the smoke symbolized the negative, incestuous libido. The eradication of the portholes communicated Roy's confused relatedness to outer reality. Of course, I did not interpret any of my impressions to Roy. But suddenly, as I was reflecting, Roy looked directly at me with a definitely cynical smile. I understood its meaning: he was saying, with a dare, "Now, make something out of this!" So I accepted his challenge and, pointing to the drawing, I replied, "The smoke here shows that there is energy and plenty of it. But it is terribly black. This kind of blackness often means that a person has inner thoughts and feelings that he regards as bad. Perhaps you fear your own intense feelings of anger."

Roy immediately reminded me, "You said anger could be good as well as bad." I answered, "Yes, I did. Are you trying to trip me up? Let me explain. I did not mean that anything is good or bad in itself, not even anger. It is the way in which anger is used that determines whether it is good or bad."

My comments were met with a lengthy silence but I felt that Roy was reflecting on what I had said to him. Then quite suddenly he began to speak. He began to tell me of a recent dream. In his dream, he was back in school again, extremely frightened and unhappy. As he described his dream, its meaning registered. Would I keep my promise? Would I permit him to decide when he was ready to return to school? His message communicated to me a distrustful attitude. I spoke gently and sensitively, "You aren't certain that I shall keep my word and wait until you are ready to go back to school." Roy looked me very full in the face and responded affirmatively, "People do tell lies to children. People do trick children. My mum does. She puts the clock ahead to make me go to bed early. She promises me she won't leave the house after I've gone to bed. Then she does. I come down from my room and she isn't there. She has gone out. The clock is back to the proper time."

I became poignantly aware of how we adults, driven into a corner by an importunate child, may hedge and lie as the easiest way of dealing with the problem. I could see in these moments how disturbing this could be to a child, how this could create suspicion, doubt, and distrust. So I responded, "Yes, Roy, I understand. Parents when pressed sometimes do not tell the truth. But try to see this from your mother's point of view. I am quite sure that she hates deceiving you, but you want to make a prisoner of her. She needs time alone with your father and time to visit her friends. She feels that the only way she can escape is by being sly with you. I am not saying that it is right for her to deceive you, but only trying to help you understand why she is doing it. As for myself, I can only repeat, that as far as I am concerned, when you return to school is entirely up to you. My interest is not in pushing you back into school but in helping you to overcome your fears and rituals and to win back all the energy wasted in making magic."

I then suggested that we return to a study of his painting. Pointing again to the smoke, I said that to me it represented bottled-up energy down below that was not being used to drive the ship properly. The captain was not using it to meet his needs but was putting the energy into irrelevant matters, making magic, in fact. Roy laughed at this explanation and, as our time was up, he went away, saying he was sorry for the poor man.

The Third Meeting: More Magic and More Rituals

Roy selected a large piece of clay, which he fingered and kneaded during the entire visit. He seemed especially tight inside when he began to relate what an awful day the previous Sunday had been. He was in a constant state of tension on that day; he felt compelled repeatedly to carry out rituals. He was absolutely exhausted and discouraged with the constant effort of having to do things. At last he had gone to bed, morose and weeping. Then further difficulties arose. First, he found it necessary to pray over and over again. With each prayer completed, a new element emerged which made it necessary to pray again. Then, no matter how he arranged his garments and bedclothes, he was not mentally comfortable. Over and over, he changed the arrangement. He felt he would lose his mind completely before he finally settled down and fell asleep.

For me, Roy's tension and despair grew out of the religious atmosphere of Sunday. I asked him if it was possible that what troubled him was the idea that it was God who might make something awful happen to him, some severe punishment, if he omitted any of the rituals. Roy agreed but said that he could think of nothing he had done wrong, nothing that deserved punishment. I asked if going to his mother's bed had anything to do with his fear, since there was such a tremendous amount of magic and ritual surrounding this event. The idea of magic once again amused Roy, but he was not ready to face the archetype of the angry father-god, so he quickly changed the subject.

"If I only had a dog, I could keep busy exercising it, and I wouldn't have to do all these things," he said excitedly. "But," he added, "my parents will not let me bring a dog into the house." I suggested that if he explained his reasons for wanting a dog, his parents might be willing to get him one. I spoke of the dog's naturalness and gaiety, saying that human beings also have an animal side, which is valuable just because it is natural and free. While we continued discussing ways that animals and humans are alike, Roy modeled "a man." It was a torso with a large bowed head, and it looked exactly like a fetus. I thought that perhaps this symbolized Roy's psychically unborn state or that it might stand for the beginning of a new inner life.

With the close of our meeting, Roy joined his mother. In my presence, he told her that I wanted him to have a dog. Since I felt that this was an issue between them, an issue for which Roy must remain responsible, I pointed out to him that he must discuss this with his mother, that it was a matter to be settled between them.

The Next Three Meetings: Roy's Animal Nature

These hours with Roy revolved around Rex, the year-old terrier which Mrs. J. had purchased immediately following my last session with Roy. I remarked that there were now two kings in his home, Roy and Rex. But we soon found that Rex was kingly only in the way in which very young infants exercise dominion. We decided that if Rex represented Roy's animal side, this must be very young indeed. He himself recognized that in some ways he was very much dependent on his mother. I said, "Yes, indeed, you still feel that you have to sleep with her." He took this well and without embarrassment. He mentioned how Rex liked to lie in a truck while Roy pushed him about "like a baby in a pram." In other ways, he recognized his own immaturity. Bearing in mind that I must ultimately help Roy to see why and how he was failing to live his life in accordance with his talents and endowments, I emphasized that growing up was not an easy task. In simple terms, I told him about psychological types and of the fact that some people are born with the ability to come out into the world without fear, while others, like himself, would by nature find facing outer reality, at times, extremely difficult. It was this attitude of reservation and fear that made it seem safer to hide behind one's mother or some other grown-up. I explained to Roy that, given such a nature, one was not automatically doomed to be burdened or destoyed by it, but, on the contrary, one could live creatively by accepting and honoring it. The innate attitude is natural and valuable if it is not carried to extremes.

Roy mentioned an incident with his mother when he became extremely angry with her. While he was reading a book, he wanted her to turn the pages for him. She refused, and he responded with rage that reached such a pitch that he lost control. I told him I thought this was another example of his immaturity, that he was like a young infant crying with rage because his bottle was not ready, and that, although this represented a problem, it was not the end of the world. If he could recognize it as such and attempt to come to grips with it in its real form, perhaps this would be a first step in growing up.

Seventh Meeting: The Constructive Use of Anger

Roy began this meeting by making with clay a model of a boxer, which he painted. The model was remarkably spirited and lifelike. He commented that it looked just like a gorilla and waited for my reaction. For me, the model was an externalization of Roy's own shadow side. It represented the image of the 100 per cent brutal male, from whom women instinctively shrink. It was difficult to reconcile the image of the model with the quiet, anxious, handsome boy who sat beside me. Of one thing I was certain, I could not baldly say, "This gorilla-boxer is really what you are rejecting in yourself; it is what you are always trying to magic away." I approached this dimension of Roy by referring to his relatedness with his dog, "In your creation of a gorillalike boxer, you show me that the animal side of you is coming on. The babyish Rex has turned into a very unbabyish gorilla." Roy looked alert as I spoke. He listened attentively as I continued. I pointed out the ways in which animals and human beings were alike, how they shared similar emotions and behaved in similar ways. I pointed out that as human beings grew up from infancy to adulthood, the primitive impulses had to be modified and expressed in more acceptable ways. The problem was that often, through the process of growing up and becoming socialized, children began to think of their animal nature as bad, as evil, and they sometimes tried to eliminate it altogether. I told Roy that I thought this was a mistake. I told him that, to remain whole as human beings, it was important to retain our animal natures and use these natural energies in creative and constructive ways.

Roy said that he could understand just what I meant. Then he grinned broadly and said, "But I still do not see how getting angry can ever be a good thing." To this, I explained, "You're interested in boxing. You know that, when a boxer hits his opponent in anger and gives him a foul blow, the boxer is disqualified. But when he puts his aggressiveness into a constructive determination to win, he uses his anger in a socially acceptable way." Roy nodded affirmatively. As he was leaving, he handed me his model of the boxer and asked me to take good care of it.

Eighth Meeting: A Touch of Therapeutic Significance

Roy began the hour by telling me that during the week he had discovered how to be a good boxer, how to put his anger into constructive actions. In moments of rage, he had chopped up wood for the fireplace; he had kicked his football about; he had shadowboxed. In the process, he came to realize that he had forgotten about his rituals. At such times, he no longer had to make magic. He had more time for his own important interests. I took this opportunity to show him another consequence of his compulsive behavior. I explained to him, "How right you are, Roy! Making magic is horribly time-wasting. It fills one's life with meaningless actions and is used to avoid anything important. You can dodge all responsibility with the excuse that you have to 'do things' from morning until night." Putting aside further discussion on this need to magic away his fears, I then asked Roy what he really wanted to do.

He answered my question saying that he would like to take up scouting again. As he talked, he modeled a scout camp. He was certainly not ready to return to school yet, but he could revisit the scout hut. I felt so encouraged by this hopeful sign of active return to life that I spontaneously, warmly, put my hand on his shoulder and told him that I wished him luck in this venture. Usually, I am careful not to touch adolescents at all, and I immediately wondered whether I had not made a mistake. I was, therefore, quite relieved and joyful when Roy did not shrink away from me; indeed he leaned toward me and, for the first time, genuinely smiled. *I realized that, in this spontaneous moment of touching him, I had accepted the shadow in Roy which I had previously rejected and found unpleasing.* As he left, I said jokingly, "Be sure to take the gorilla-boxer to the scout hut with you. He could become a very energetic and valuable member of the troop." Roy was delighted with the idea and with the moment we shared. He went away making unrestrained sparring movements.

Tenth Meeting: A Test of Freedom and Courage

In this meeting, Roy recounted his experiences in the scout hut. The scouts had been studying tracking and Indian life. Roy told of a dream in which his home was attacked by "red Indians." But, in the dream, although he was frightened, he did not go to pieces. He held together. He talked about the Indian way of life and said that he admired the freedom and courage of the Indian. Then, with a provocative smile, he said, "And the children don't have to go to school." This gave me an opening to discuss with him the matter of being ready to suffer in order to mature. I reminded him that Indian boys had to pass some very stiff tests, had to leave blood behind, so to speak, in growing up. Then they were ready to enter the world of adults and warriors. Roy listened attentively and caught the meaning in my message. He was busily engaged in modeling a pipe of peace. I remarked that, sometimes, when you have a battle with someone, it can be settled amicably. Perhaps he wanted to smoke the pipe of peace with his enemies. Perhaps the gorilla-boxer was turning into the free, courageous red Indian, and now he was coming to terms with it. Was he accepting his forward-striving animal nature instead of having to magic it away all the time? Roy understood my thought and stated that he was not able to give up any of the rituals as yet, but they were receding in importance. He now had to repeat each ritual only once or twice, rather than over and over again.

With the completion of this meeting, the Easter holiday began. I suggested to Roy that, when we met again in three weeks, we could look more deeply into the magic and the rituals and see what still had to be controlled by them.

Eleventh Meeting: The Crocodile and the Return to School

Roy was particularly quiet and uneasy in the first minutes of our meeting, after a three-week interval. He reported that he had not returned to school for the beginning of the new term nor had he been able to sleep apart from his mother. After telling me this, he began modeling a crocodile, making it with a wide-open mouth. He then told me he felt increasingly anxious and worried. At first, he had liked coming to see me because he felt safe in my room. But now he was experiencing a sense of panic and physical illness. It began just before his vacation and had at this moment reached a peak. He couldn't breathe in my room. He felt shut in. He experienced a feeling of gloom, darkness, stuffiness. After a prolonged silence, I suggested that he speak freely, whatever thoughts came into his mind. He told me he had seen a crocodile at a local zoo during the holiday. To him it was a horrible creature lying quietly, completely still, creating a deceptive loglike appearance, waiting for a victim whom it would swallow alive.

I told Roy that I thought this was an especially important incident and I would like to attempt to explain its meaning. Part of him wanted to grow up, return to school, and live a normal active life with all of its discomforts and joys. But part of him wished to remain a baby, enclosed in a warm, motherly atmosphere. This was the struggle going on within him now, the struggle between the darkness and the light. This was what it was like to be swallowed whole by a crocodile, darkness and comfort, but at the same time stuffiness and a wish to emerge into life. This was the situation he was experiencing in my room, at this very moment, a feeling of darkness; yet, in actuality, the room was flooded with sunshine which beckoned him. A look of amazed understanding and acceptance spread across Roy's face. Immediately, he stood up to go, with an expression of determination and decision. Our time was not up, but Roy was definitely bringing the meeting to a close. I told him that I would pass his house in a few days and would bring his model to him. Roy said airily, with the door half open, that he would be glad to have the crocodile, but that he might not be home when I called. *The next morning he returned to school.*

Though Roy had taken an important step toward self-recovery, I still felt that I had to help him face the archetype of the Great Mother. But, for the moment, I was satisfied to have used the model and his feeling about my room to symbolize the unconscious into which the backward-drawing infant was pulling him. Roy could face the conflict between the forces of immaturity and regression and the forward-striving sources within himself. But he still had to come to grips with the Great Mother which was behind his inability to get out of his real mother's bed.

Twelfth Meeting: The Angry God

Roy was proud that he had returned to school and was able to remain there in spite of the increased discomfort and anxiety. His rituals returned in full force, though not with the same degree of frequency. The fear stayed with him that, if he omitted even one ritual, he was faced with disaster and death. Why should this fear, this ominous danger persist?

I reminded Roy of our conclusion that he thought God was angry with him and that he was afraid God would make bad things happen to him as a punishment. He commented, "Yes, I used to think that. It's funny, I *know* now that it isn't true, but I still *feel* that it is."

I suggested that we consider when God was angry in the Old Testament. I explained as simply as I could that the Israelites had been chosen by God to live a certain way of life and to serve Him alone, to hold no other gods before Him. God became angry with the Israelites when they fell away from this commandment, when they broke the pattern and searched back after other gods. But when we really examine the Old Testament, we see that the anger is always followed by forgiveness, not punishment and retribution. The person must recognize his backsliding and be sorry for it. He must atone for it. Then I exclaimed, "Isn't it ridiculous to think that such a God would punish a boy unless he always put on his left shoe before his right or unless he pointed his pen at a particular knob on a cupboard before putting it down? Isn't it ridiculous to think that you need to make magic against God?"

These explanations seemed to hit home with Roy. At this moment he sneezed, and spontaneously I said, "Bless you!" Then I added, "There! Now I am making magic. We all do it at times." Roy laughed out loud and left the meeting chuckling. My involuntary piece of superstition had made the whole question of magic a little comic and thus less alarming. At all events, he resolved to end the rituals, and though he experienced considerable anxiety at first, he continued living with the feeling, facing the issue, and taking responsibility himself for his actions. Following this meeting Roy performed no more rituals, though he was, at times, aware of the impulse to do so.

Thirteenth Meeting: The Image of Mother and Father

In the meetings with Roy, I had looked for an opportunity to constellate the image of the good father. At the same time, I recognized that, in approaching this theme, instead I might activate the image of the angry, exacting father.

By this time I had a clear picture of Mr. J., not only from Mrs. J.'s interviews with the psychiatric social worker but also from Roy's spontaneous remarks. At times, he had complained about his father's insistence on tidiness, extreme politeness, and perfect table manners. I understood from our reports that Mr. J. was not neurotic although he was overparticular, fastidious, and, at times, too demanding. Certainly these attitudes did not constructively aid Roy in dealing with his compulsions. At times, Roy spoke rather wistfully of his many friends who went fishing with their fathers or who were taken by them to football and cricket matches. He said that his father never cared about any of these activities. He cared only about reading and gardening, neither of which he shared with Roy. Mrs. J. communicated that her husband did not think that the raising of children was his responsibility. He felt that his task was to provide materially for them but that the nurture, training, recreation, and *schooling* of the children were tasks for mothers and teachers. In his own way, he was fond of the children but rather remote and undemonstrative. Finally, and perhaps most significant, Mr. J. was entirely content to go on sleeping alone in Roy's room. Neither he nor his wife saw anything odd or questionable in a boy of twelve sharing his mother's bed. Consequently, I finally concluded that there was little in the home to constellate the image of the father who is proud of his children, able to enter into their world, and concerned with their progress toward maturity.

Yet in spite of the apparently impoverished father image in the home, Roy's activities in therapy were highly reassuring. His interests again and again pointed to a masculine identification. In this meeting he had turned from modeling to paint a most phallic-looking space ship, a greatly inflated masculine symbol, prepared to attack the heavens. In referring to the space ship, I said, "So Dan Dare is off again!" Roy seemed surprised that I knew this popular figure from a boys' weekly magazine. He remarked that his father thought comics were rubbish. I explained that sometimes men outgrew comics, but that most women admired adventurous men, even in comics. At this point, I had in mind Jung's description of the mother of the hero, in which he states:

Man leaves the mother, the source of libido, and is driven by the eternal thirst to find her again, and to drink renewal from her; thus he completes his cycle, and returns into the mother's womb. Every obstacle which obstructs his life's path, and threatens his ascent, wears the shadowy features of the "terrible mother," who paralyses his energy with the consuming poison of the stealthy, retrospective longing. In each conquest he wins again the smiling love and life-giving mother.[1]

It must, I thought, be my function to constellate this image in Roy's mind. But I soon realized that I must create and clarify the image of the good father who helps his son discover the life-giving mother by progressively drawing him into the world of men. This became primarily a matter of accepting, valuing, and sharing Roy's own self-chosen activities as he created and painted spaceships, bombers, battleships, cricket and football matches, and racing cars. We often talked about airmen, sailors, and sportsmen.

During these weeks Roy's compulsions finally disappeared. His fear of dying no longer held such power over

---

[1] Carl Jung, *Psychology of the Unconscious* (London: Kegan Paul, 1933), pp. 235–236.

him. He attended school regularly and enjoyed the many scout adventures, including a ten-day camp expedition. The one problem that still persisted was Roy's continued dependence on his mother and his retreat into his mother's bed. This was an attachment which his mother, in her own way, was encouraging. As Roy evolved more and more healthy patterns of relating and living, his mother began to manifest unconscious disapproval and resistance. She came late for her own appointments and was obviously responsible for Roy's constant tardiness. My colleagues and I felt that this was not so much due to her fear of losing Roy as that Roy and I were very close to understanding a crucial problem which was also her own. She knew we were working on his infantile mother fixation, which was precisely the net in which she was caught up with her own mother. It was this situation, their mutual inability to separate from the Great Mother, that was holding Roy back from a full restoration of his talents and powers.

Twenty-Third Meeting: Facing the Problem of the Great Mother

Although we skirted the issue of the Great Mother many times before this meeting, it was an area in which I had to tread warily. But, in this meeting, we came to grips with the problem openly and directly. At an opportune moment, I asked Roy why he continued to sleep with his mother. He said that his mother was lonesome because she missed her mother and, therefore, she needed him. But, as for himself, he could return to his own room anytime he wished. When we explored this further, he admitted that he too abhorred the thought of having to be quite alone at night. I knew that he was struggling to move forward in all areas. I pointed out to him that being alone at times was inevitable, that it was a requirement of living. I explained that growing up was always a struggle and that to be a man he would have to leave the security of a protected childhood behind. I added that both his parents wanted this for him. They looked forward to the time when he would leave the dependent, childish path and become a real companion to them. Roy was interested in this idea, that emancipation from his mother could result in a mature friendship. I stressed the fact that a new kind of relationship with his mother could be rich and rewarding, not only for him but for his mother as well. Roy listened and seemed to be reflecting upon my statements.

At the end of this meeting, Roy told me he had been given four demerits for "horse-playing with other boys." My comment slipped out, "Good for you. I bet they are the first you've ever been given." He answered, "Yes. But I'm sure they won't be the last."

Twenty-Fifth Meeting: The Fear Is the Wish Inside-Out

Roy was now coming to see me only once every three weeks. Just before this meeting, he had fallen off his bicycle, cut his face badly, and dislocated an elbow. In spite of this frightening accident, Roy's fear of dying did not return nor did the rituals. But a new and distressing problem emerged: Roy was now afraid that his mother might be killed in an accident. He became extremely anxious whenever she was out of the house for any length of time. I decided the time had come to discuss this fixation with him. I reminded him of our talk about his crocodile model and how my room had seemed dark and stuffy to him. We had understood from this theme that the growing resources in himself were in conflict with inner pressures and pulls to remain a baby. He wanted to be mothered, and at the same time he blamed his mother for keeping him a baby, for imprisoning him in the dark, and for being the key by which he could escape fear and return to light. The image of an imprisoning mother became fixed in his mind. It became painted over to cover Mrs. J., even though she did not wish to keep Roy dependent on her, did not want him to remain a baby.

I wanted Roy to understand that the growing aspects of himself came to hate the picture of the possessive mother, and that the feeling, at times, was very intense. So the fear that his mother might be killed was actually a wish that she would die, a wish to escape once and forever the imprisoning mother. I re-emphasized that anger could have positive implications, but that his anger was directed toward an imagined possessiveness, a fantasied mother, that he was attacking a pictured mother concocted out of fear and desperation. Roy responded immediately to my explanation, saying that he understood what I meant.

Twenty-Eighth Meeting: The Initiation

Though much change had occurred in Roy's school and personal life, he had still not given up sleeping with his mother. I realized that, *though his parents were passively willing for him to mature, there was not sufficient strength of determination and conviction in either of them, actively to initiate him.* Mrs. J., though making progress in therapy, was still caught in her own fixation; Mr. J. was, as ever, remote, absorbed in his own world. I, then and there, in this meeting, suddenly, spontaneously, acting under the strongest sense of need, took it upon myself to initiate Roy in his growth toward independence and maturity.

I asked Roy to consider once again his red Indian dream. I reminded him that Indian youths had to undergo severe tests before they were accepted as warriors by the men of the tribe. I detailed to him some of the ordeals that the Navaho Indian had to meet and master. I explained that all primitive peoples introduced their youths into maturity by setting arduous, painful tasks which had to be struggled with, endured, and eventually conquered. The whole purpose of these ordeals was to help young people to realize that they could not remain infants but that fulfillment of initiation rites in the achievement of manhood required effort and exertion. Young people learned these lessons for themselves. They accepted their terror and suffering and *they did not run away or hide.* They stayed with the tasks, endured the ordeals, met the requirements of life to growing maturity. They accepted everything because it proved to themselves and to the community that they were worthy to be called men and women. I said to Roy, affirmatively, and with conviction, "I am absolutely certain that the time is coming, and coming soon, when you will go back to your own room, not because you are no longer afraid, but even though you are still very frightened indeed, you will take this step as a requirement of growing up, of becoming a man."

Roy did not speak a single word. Although our time was not over, he jumped up, clattered down the stairs, climbed on his bicycle, and hurriedly rode away.

I was not at all sure of the meaning of this outburst. And, in the next twenty-four hours, I spent much time reflecting and wondering and worrying whether I had not been precipitous, whether my initiation was more in the nature of a psychic death rather than a new birth. But, the next day, the merit of my spontaneous action was confirmed. *Mrs. J. telephoned to say that Roy was back in his own room.*

Now all of Roy's original problems had been resolved. He did not again return to his mother's bed. The separation was, at first, quite painful, but he had stuck it out and was glad to be on his own. Roy and I met a few more times and then agreed that he would come and see me once each term just to report on major events in his life. He came two more times and then decided to terminate our meetings altogether. He felt he could manage his life on his own.

Nine years have passed since Roy attended the clinic, but I have up-to-date news of him. There has been no return of the neurosis, except for a slight tendency to compulsions on the eve of important examinations. He is nearing the end of his apprenticeship in a highly skilled trade, having passed his examinations with an average mark of 80 per cent. He rides freely about on a motor bicycle and has spent some holidays in Europe with friends. He is particularly fond of a special young lady whom he hopes to marry when fully qualified in his occupation.

9

Individual Psychotherapy as an Obstacle to Growth ❧ *Clark Moustakas*

IN EXPERIENCES WITH CHILDREN, the element of surprise is always present. Call it an unpredictable mood, a sudden, capricious impulse to change, an ability to choose a new direction in a moment of decision, a deliberate effort toward a new life, or the sudden spontaneous awakening of a mysterious substance or dimension of the self. I am pointing to an event in which a child unexpectedly and suddenly transforms himself from a passive, frightened, undirected, defeated individual to a person in control of his life, with a sense of purpose and direction, with a new sense of determination and freedom to be.

The kind of change I am describing occurred in Tom, a nine-year-old boy, who was referred for therapy by his elementary school principal because of poor grades, social ineptitude, withdrawal patterns, and general immaturity. Tom was placed in group therapy because he seemed first and foremost to need to establish affirmative contacts and friendships with other boys. Initially, he provided a benevolent, imaginative leadership, not only suggesting activities, but assigning duties and roles. These activities were generally war games that started in a rather mild and somewhat peaceful way, but soon became intense and vehement. As the attacks became more violent, Tom tried to reprimand and control the others. He would preach and moralize. But, once the other boys were aroused in battle, they ignored him and carried on intense campaigns against each other. When the wars stopped being peaceful, when they became wild and destructive, Tom stopped being a leader and temporarily withdrew to a corner of the room out of the range of "fire." However, he would usually recover before the hour ended, and, through a forceful flow of ideas, he would influence the action of the group in a more tranquil direction.

Throughout the year, Tom continued to be the leader in the group, but he was able to direct the others only as long as their aggressions remained within proper bounds. On one occasion, Tom suggested that they destroy all the books in the playroom (two boys in addition to Tom were failing in school). Once this activity got under way, however, and the boys proceeded to scribble in the books and cut pages in them, Tom felt ashamed and withdrew. When the intensity of emotions reached an explosive peak, when the group became really destructive, even if he had initiated the sequence of activity, Tom would withdraw to an isolated place in the playroom.

When I attempted to interpret to Tom this pattern of manipulation and withdrawal, he would become visibly agitated, run around the room, start a raucous conversation with another boy, or initiate a noisy game. It soon became clear to me that he was afraid to face himself, afraid to recognize his own feelings of hostility, afraid to be responsible for his influence and his actions. Occasionally he would begin to express his real feelings, but if I encouraged him in this, or attempted to clarify his feelings, he quickly changed the subject. When it seemed that I was on the verge of breaking through the tight pattern of our relationship, one of the boys would always interrupt us, and the moment was lost. With one frustration after another, with one failure after another, unable to meet Tom on a meaningful and genuine basis, I decided to see him alone, in individual therapy.

Just before his summer vacation, an urgent call came from Tom's home. His parents were deeply upset that his teacher had decided to fail Tom. They were opposed to the idea that he must repeat the grade. Accordingly, a conference was scheduled with the principal of Tom's school and the parents. At this meeting, it was decided that Tom would be probationally promoted in the light of his superior intellectual capacity, his strong opposition to being failed, and his own resolution to study in earnest during the summer. The school crisis was a real shock to Tom, and he was manifestly disturbed by it.

One other decision was made in the conference. Tom was to be promoted to a teacher in the fourth grade who was a relaxed, sensitive person, who regarded children as individuals, and who respected their interests and unique differences.

With this background of tension and drama, Tom departed from group therapy and plunged into his summer program of study, tutoring, and camp.

I was completely unprepared for the change in Tom the following October when he walked into the playroom for his first interview. He came into the room with a distinctly different sense of confidence and spoke to me in a clear, direct, and articulate way. Immediately, he began to tell me of the tremendous strides he had made over the summer and during the first six weeks of school. The following is a verbatim account of our first talk.

(*Holding a stack of books.*) I want to show you what I'm doing in school. (*One by one Tom discusses each of his classes, explaining his assignments in detail and commenting on his progress. He illustrates the progress by working out problems from each of his textbooks.*)

Life in school is certainly different from last year.

My work has been coming along real, real well. I've been getting lots of A's in arithmetic, spelling, and in all my other subjects.

You seem to be excited about what you are learning this year.

I have a real nice teacher. (*Pause.*)

Did the tutoring help?

I think it really helped.

And are you continuing?

Yeah. Every Monday night Mr. Barrett comes. It helps a lot. (*For the next ten minutes Tom explained concepts and aids he had learned from his tutor. He illustrated a number of arithmetic methods on the blackboard. Then he continued with other matters.*)

My spelling is coming along too, also my social studies and my language.

No problems at all in school this year.

No trouble at all. Our teacher makes work enjoyable.

After reaching a real low point last year, you're beginning to soar now.

I enjoy reading too.

Remember the day you heaped all the books in a pile and said you'd like to burn them?

Not any more. I like books. I've also learned to use the dictionary, and let me tell you that book comes in real handy. (*Pause.*) When we have quizzes, I score points for our row now.

You save the day instead of making blunders.

(*Emphatically.*) Uh-huh. (*Tom then talked about his camp ex-*

periences, his pleasant association with other children, and his close relationship with his cabin counselor.)

Now I've told you about my summer. It was fun. It was just perfect. (*Long pause.*) I heard some real good jokes at camp. Would you like me to tell you? (*Tom relates jokes during the next fifteen minutes. Then he discusses two exciting boat trips he took with his father.*)

It's time for us to stop now.

My gosh, is it? I've talked the whole hour.

In our second talk, Tom continued to speak about his school experiences with the same heightened enthusiasm. The last half of the hour, we threw darts together. He was not particularly concerned about winning or losing. Up to this time, he had assiduously avoided any game which involved competitive behavior. Yet he was now throwing darts without being concerned over his own self-adequacy, without concern with success or failure, but thoroughly enjoying the game.

It was evident during these first talks that Tom's involvement and commitment were with school and not in his contacts with me. His underlying resentment in being forced to come for therapy flared out openly midway in our third session. Since this half-hour represents the substance of the existential encounter between us, I have quoted extensively from the verbatim transcript. I initiated the conversation.

School is enjoyable when you are successful in your work.

It's fun. Especially, if you have a real nice teacher.

A lot depends on the teacher.

Yeah. A good teacher can make learning interesting and fun.

But, Mrs. Stewart (*speaks the name contemptuously*) last year! Boy! That was awful!

You didn't like her, and she didn't like you.

She didn't like me at all!

Is that why you destroyed your arithmetic book?

I scribbled in it and ripped pages out of it. I *hated* arithmetic. BR-R-R-R-R!

You hated it so much you wanted to destroy it and forget about your bad experience.

I felt like burning it but then I decided to mark it up. (*Long pause.*)

Now you don't feel like destroying your arithmetic book or any of your books.

Books are helpful now. They come in handy when you have a nice teacher. . . . I'm having *so* much fun in arithmetic. (*Long pause.*) I still think it's a waste of time. (*Pause.*) A *big waste* of time.

You mean coming here?

Yes. I'd rather be in school.

Do you really resent coming here?

That's about it. (*As Tom talks he is kicking against a wood cabinet, banging with the back of his heels. As his voice rises in anger, the banging becomes louder.*)

You'd like to stop coming here.

The sooner the better . . . coming here IS JUST A WASTE OF MY TIME!

Then why do you come, Tom?

Because you guys said so.

Who said so?

You, my mother, my dad. (*Pause. Disgustedly.*) Oh, I don't know who.

Do you know why your parents decided, together with me, that you needed to come here this year?

(*Tom is really exasperated now. He screams in anger.*) Why? I don't know why. It's just a waste of my time!

And you think your parents want to waste your time?

NO! NO! But I don't learn anything here, and I can be learning in school.

Yes, I understand that you would rather . . .

(*Interrupting.*) C-o-r-RECT!

But why do your parents bring you here?

(*Tom bangs with considerable vehemence.*) Why! I can't see any reason at all for having to come here. Look what I'm doing—sitting and banging and rocking.

Maybe the banging is helping you express your anger.

(*Shouting.*) I *admit* it! *I am* angry. I don't want to come here any more. (*Tom gestures in desperation.*) Boy! Last year, it was different. I hated school last year. I wanted to come here all the time. But this year, I like school. I hate coming here. I hate this place. Honestly (*with tears in his eyes*), I really could be in school right now. I could be learning. I could be with my friends.

Instead of wasting your time here.

YES!

What is it you really want, Tom?

To learn, to be like the other kids, to study with them. I'm not putting on an act. I really mean what I'm saying.

I know you do, Tom.

Coming here is a waste of time. I have important things to do in school. In other words, I want to stop coming here completely. (*Pause.*)

Well, Tom, I think we can arrange that.

Like when?

After I talk with your parents.

Okay. But not in six months.

No. Not in six months. Very soon. (*Long pause.*) You say your parents have not told you why you're coming here. Would you like to know?

Yes, I would.

You remember last year, you were failing in school. The picture was pretty grim for you. Your teacher had decided not to pass you. You were upset. We decided it might help you to talk things over with someone. You had gotten behind in school. You yourself wanted tutoring.

She never helped me. I *hated* her. She made fun of me.

I know that's how you feel, Tom, but from her point of view, she tried. She felt that she tried to help you but that you rejected her help.

She didn't try. She never cared about me. I found out: *Stay out of her way.* And I did.

So you felt that she was completely at fault.

No, not completely. But she made it worse. Gol, everything I did was wrong. She made me feel I didn't know how to do anything.

I understand that, Tom. But you wanted to know why your parents bring you here. And one of the main reasons is that you were unhappy in school and failing.

Yeah. That was last year but not any more. (*Long pause.*) You will talk with them?

Yes. I will. Just remember you've thought this all out and know what you want to do. They may need a little time.

I couldn't get it into their heads.

Have you tried? Have you discussed this with them?

Not exactly.

Then how do you know they wouldn't listen? How do you know they would be against your decision not to come any more?

Because they think this is a big pleasure.

But you haven't even talked with them.

They'd try to brainwash me.

Tom, you feel too strongly about not coming here; I don't think anyone could brainwash you. But remember their problem was this: *How could a boy with your ability be failing in school?* They knew it was partly that your teacher didn't or couldn't give you what you needed but they also believed that something was wrong inside you, that you didn't believe in yourself, that you had the feeling that you didn't measure up to other kids.

I don't feel that way any more.

No, you don't. You have changed. You're sailing ahead now. I think your parents will listen to you.

I don't want anyone putting the brakes on me.

No. And your parents don't and I don't (*Pause.*) want that either.

I really miss school. I bet the kids are having a blast. Everything is fun this year.

I'm sorry, Tom. I don't like depriving you of all that joy. I'm sure your parents and I will work it out. In the meantime, I plan to visit your teacher. Perhaps you could talk with your parents before we meet again.

Okay. I'll try.

In this dramatic hour, Tom revealed his growing openness and directness. He faced up to the issues involved, conveying his real feelings, and standing his ground with courage and forcefulness, in his confrontation with me. At the same time, he is able to recognize that he was partly responsible for the problems that occurred in his relationship with his previous teacher. Tom himself explained the change in his attitude and behavior in terms of self-determination, self-exertion, and a positive relationship with his present teacher. Obviously school has a new meaning; it has become an exciting place for the first time in his life. In short, for Tom therapy has become an obstacle in this new life, and he is frustrated and resentful about being forced to continue.

The next time Tom and I met, we continued in a similar way. First, I told him that his teacher had reported marked improvement in his school achievement. Then we discussed my conversation with his parents.

Now I want to tell you about my talk with your parents. They were in full agreement with your decision to discontinue your meetings with me. We thought you might come one more time after today and then stop altogether. Is that all right?

Yes. I talked with them too. This time they listened and didn't try to change my mind.

You see, Tom. Your teacher listened, your parents listened, and I have listened to you too. We all want to do what is right for you, what you really want for yourself.

Yeah. I couldn't believe it.

That's understandable after what you've been through. Of course, you know I'm not just saying good-bye once and for all. I hope you will come and visit me from time to time. (*Long pause.*) Tom, I would like to share something with you that has been on my mind for some time. I tried to talk with you about this last year. There were many times when you started to talk about your family or about your teacher or about yourself, but, when I encouraged you to express your feelings, you got upset. You changed the subject. You used the other boys to escape facing me. I felt you were afraid to look into your problems.

Uh-huh.

In short, I felt you were running away from yourself. You weren't being honest with yourself or with others.

I told you I couldn't talk to my parents. They didn't listen. They always wanted to change my mind. And my teacher made me feel I . . . (*Pause.*)

Was no good.

Yeah.

But, Tom, I didn't feel that way. I really wanted to listen to you, to know you. You were unhappy, and I was concerned about you.

But I didn't trust you. I couldn't talk with you then. I felt I had to do it myself and not lean on anybody.

I see.

All the teachers I had until this year made me feel I was stupid or something. They weren't interested in me. (*Pause.*) I couldn't talk to you. Not then.

I know that, Tom, and that's what impresses me now. You talk to me so freely. You have opened up with your feelings. I don't think you're running away from yourself any more.

Uh-huh.

I think you're able to face up to your problems. There may be times when you will want to talk with your teacher if you run into difficulty in school or with your parents when there are problems at home, but I don't think you'll get into the kind of jam you were in last year. (*Pause.*)

Yeah. She's interested in my ideas. But I couldn't talk with Mrs. Stewart.

I understand how you felt with her, Tom. But can you in any way realize how she must have felt when you, a person with abilities, were not learning, when she was not getting results with you.

It was a miserable mess.

Yes, for both of you.

Uh-huh.

Mrs. Stewart must have felt as much a failure with herself as she did with you.

Uh-huh. (*Long pause.*) I don't know what else to say.

Perhaps it has all been said, Tom. (*Pause.*) We have about seventeen minutes. Would you like to play a game?

Okay. Let's throw some darts. (*This activity continues to the end of the hour. Tom is relaxed and thoroughly enjoys the game.*)

We met one more time during this sequence of interviews. In the final session, Tom initiated a series of games that we played with much delight.

At the request of his principal, I made a follow-up visit to Tom's school at the end of the semester. He had continued in the same direction, strengthening his achievement background and his relations with other children. In the next two years, Tom called me four times for appointments. In every respect, he had continued to grow as a real self. He spoke with enjoyment of his experiences in school, his friends in the neighborhood, and his interests in science, shipbuilding, and the Civil War. His mother called me from time to time and spoke with great pride and enthusiasm over the wonderful life Tom was creating for himself, in school and at home. As Tom was completing the sixth grade, his principal called to say that he had achieved a place of real leadership in his class; his principal described him as "a boy fired-up with ideas and filled with imaginative projects." He was exerting himself toward his goals and achieving at a high level. Obviously, Tom had found himself and was proceeding in a consistent way toward increasing self-realization.

Who can say what brought about the transformation in Tom. His family and school did not simply fashion and mold him toward a new destiny. Certainly, the individual therapy did not bring about the sudden, dramatic change. Perhaps there is no full answer or explanation. Perhaps what happened to Tom is outside the realm of theory and therapeutic process. Somehow, he stopped letting life control him, and he began to shape and determine his life, to meet it on his own terms. He realized that his life need not be formed by pressures and threats of defeat and failure, but rather that it could emerge and be determined by his own sense of value and interest and positive commitment. Tom took hold of himself. He began connecting with life and its requirements. He began making decisions for himself and seeing them through. Tom knew what he wanted from life, and he proceeded to actualize his wishes and interests in his own way. As he once remarked to me, "I felt I had to do it myself and not lean on anybody." Well, Tom did it himself and he was unwilling to let anyone get in his way. He was unwilling to let either therapy or his parents impede his growth.

While Tom was living in the present and seeing achievement and success in the horizons of the near future, his therapist and his parents were living in the past, seeing the isolated, thwarted child, afraid to express himself and feeling somewhat less than others; they were seeing the Tom who was a failure in school and who, having reached a point of total futility, began to deface and destroy his books. They were worried, and the therapy provided a security and safeguard for them. But not for Tom; he proved in his own way that for him therapy was an obstacle to growth—a waste of time, a big waste of time. Perhaps, at best, it initiated a process of self-discovery, but Tom had to continue the process on his own.

My delay in seeing Tom as a new person was fostered by the commitment I had made to therapy. I was waiting for Tom, waiting for the therapeutic process to unfold, to take its course and bring about a spontaneity and an integration that would enable Tom to live in accordance with his real self. I looked for a unique process with Tom as I do with every child, but it simply did not happen. There was no therapeutic process, unique or otherwise, which could account for the changes in his social and personal behavior.

Sometime between the day Tom left me at the beginning of the summer and our first meeting in the fall, he became a self-emerging, autonomous individual, who was meeting the requirements of life in his family and in his school through self-exertion and self-involvement. Somehow, Tom made a commitment to himself to meet life directly and openly and to master the problems of living without outside intervention or help. Possibly the group therapy enabled him to make this commitment. Certainly, the shock of school failure and the realization that he was floundering precipitated his decision to take hold of himself and meet his responsibilities to home and school. Undoubtedly, his tutor and his teacher made available resources by which he could learn and grow in situations that had suddenly become meaningful to him. The rest is all Tom's story, a story connected to his own self, the work of a core of inner resources, aptitudes, and potentialities meeting the challenges of life and achieving harmony in the world, making academic gains in knowledge and skill, growing new feelings of self-confidence, and developing a sense of direction and purpose. Once this happened, Tom was soaring and, as he put it, he did not want anyone putting the brakes on him. He could speak openly and listen carefully, but he stood by his own wishes and decisions, his own perceptions and ways of viewing life. At the same time, he recognized the part he played in contributing to the self-defeating experiences of the past. For him, the nadir was reached at the end of three years of constant frustration and failure in school. There was only one way to go, and that was forward. Once he made the decision to straighten himself out, to do what was right and necessary for himself, once he realized what kind of restrictive and damaging world he was creating, he simply decided to call halt. He brought his resources to bear in conquering his fears and self-doubts. In brief, he became a different Tom with a strength of determination that would not be denied. Thus, reluctant as I am to admit that the therapy was not the primary ingredient in bringing about the personal and social changes in Tom, reluctant as I am to say that a therapeutic process did not actually facilitate his self-growth, this seems to be the only valid conclusion. Tom grew himself, and he was his own catalyst in that growth. He simply stopped being determined by life, by the pressures and threats of his school and his home. He began to determine his own being in the world and to shape this being in accordance with his own beliefs and wishes and convictions.

> The data included in this study, taken from transcriptions of tape-recorded interviews and stenographic notes, were made possible by a grant from the Social Research Foundation. I wish to thank S.R.F. and Dr. Irving Sigel for making this resource available.

10
The Child Meets the World
Antonia Wenkart

THE QUESTION "What is man?" has gained new urgency and momentum. Out of the multitudinous aspects of human life, certain essential features have been singled out to represent human existence. Definitions of man in terms of the instincts, will, and rationality no longer satisfy the quest of man for a comprehensive grasp of his essential nature and the meaning of his existence.

We now know that we can understand man as an integrated being only through knowledge which comes from a study of man in his world. We can appreciate man as an individual only by recognizing that man is and has his being in relation to the world.

The newborn infant enters the world as a particular and unique individual. The predisposing conditions for growing as an individual and for relating are both present from the very beginning, sometimes running parallel, sometimes fusing with each other. From the start, the infant is drawn toward making connections in the world, toward making contact with people, places, and things. He uses his body and all his senses to meet the world. He uses his voice and gestures to make his wants known. He contributes to life not only by bringing satisfaction and delight to those who hold and nourish him, but also by bringing a unique and distinctive being into the world, a being that never before existed.

Outside his domain, the world is a vast and chaotic space. It is purely external territory to him. Yet it *is* the *Mitwelt*, the world we all share, and the desire quickens in him to take his place in the communal domain and be a part of this world. His first grasp of objects in the world diminishes the vastness of space for him. Although the infant cannot distinguish the form from the movement of objects, this very fusion helps to bring order to the chaos. As he actively participates in this *Mitwelt*, he transforms the space into a socialized universe where he can breathe and expand beyond the confines of his physiological smallness. Subjective participation in the world at once establishes a structure and a center of his existence as a self and at the same time contributes to a growing sense of relatedness.

People and objects serve as a means of orientation in the world, enabling a young child to place himself, to find his own position, and begin to establish a distinctive identity. In this effort, there is both relating and separating, reaching out and returning.

The child's vehicles for expanding into the world, besides his senses, are his voice, his thoughts, his feelings, and his fantasies. From the other direction, the sociocultural order exerts a drawing-out power, inviting the child to come join in the living that surrounds him. Even as the world with its people and objects and conditions wields great influence upon the child, he makes his own impact on the world as a new and vital force. Thus the child assumes his place in the world and becomes part of the world. It is a two-way process, a two-way experience whereby the young child begins to bring order and unity and wholeness into what is initially a diffuse, chaotic universe. He begins to put down roots, to create a home for himself. While he is developing a unique self-hood within the reality of the world, the young child is sustained by a mediating, subjective reality. The mediation is based on sensory perception and maintained by intelligence and memory. These dimensions of the self, combined with imagination, are integrated into experience and contribute to the child's sense of substance and consistency.

The child experiences himself as the center of his own world. He harbors feelings of sureness, presence, and being, which are sometimes mistaken by adults for egocentricity and omnipotence. The focus of the growing child, however, is centeredness and connectedness—not selfishness and manipulation. Aside from extremely disturbed states, the self of the young child is never so completely isolated or removed that it is cut off from the bloodstream flowing to and from the self toward others. Subjectively, the child does not represent himself as disconnected from others. Individual and social, inner and outer, subject and object, world and child —all merge into one unified integrated being.

Growing into the societal world calls for the acceptance of all the social institutions and organizations that lay down the laws of conduct by which we all are bound. The world of institutions differs, however, from the historical-cultural world, where traditional goals and values prevail. They have an order of their own and are independent of the agents that have established and transmitted them. Hence as the child grows older, he faces not only the requirement that he make good in this *Mitwelt*, but also the problem of defining for himself what is good.

At this time, the child often does not value anything for itself but only for its effect on others. He finds that both the definition and evaluation of himself depend on the company he keeps. The world is a communal domain of self and others in which the child tries to be what he ought to be, as "ought" and "should" are defined for him by his parents and the other significant adults in the world.

Self-hood, however, is never totally taken up with the roles assigned by society. The child establishes and maintains his own identity, makes his own impact on his immediate world, and at the same time he accepts certain functions and roles. He learns to appreciate the rights of others. He respects others, but he does not abandon his own position.

To distinguish "Being" from the specific individual being, we must perform a dialectic division, thereby achieving a fictitious cleavage between the self and the world. As he grows in self-hood and identity, the young child perceives, explores, and tests objects. He gauges the distance from himself to objects and people. He grasps them through his intellect as well as his sense of space and then incorporates them into his body of experience; he engages in transition and moves to new levels of Being. Such newly entered territories are full of tentativeness, ambivalence, and vacillation.

The child, being himself, is continually enhanced by becoming himself. This entails transforming passive and formless perceptions into active and expressive ones. The child is not merely a coordinator of sensations, as an electronic computer is a coordinator of impulses. Perceiving with his senses, he moves into space with them. He experiences reality in a new way, expanding into space and making the world his scene of action. He moves, stands, crawls, and walks. Each of these events carries him into a larger space and puts him into contact with new aspects of the world. By standing, by rising to the peculiarly human posture, as Straus says,[1] the child opposes the force of gravity. He comes face to face with others. He stands before and he

---

[1] Erwin Straus, "The Upright Posture," in *Phenomenological Psychology* (New York: Basic Books, 1966).

stands against—thus distinguishing himself from all others.

Even before he can walk, the young child finds and feels himself as a body in space. He thrusts himself into the world with his senses—exploring, scouting, holding, seeking, and finding ways to make reality his own. As he expands into space, moving into it and taking it in with his senses, experiencing again and again, he gains an appreciation of both his separateness and his relatedness. Gradually, he learns that the world is a true dwelling place, a space in which he can live comfortably. He is a born explorer, growing in a continuum of experience. His first voyage of discovery is his own body. Through a process of testing and savoring, he gains a sense of connectedness with his body. "This little piggy went to market," is the familiar refrain of a game in which the child's fingers and toes are affectionately touched and designated one by one, giving the child not only a sense of connectedness with his body, but also of relatedness with the person who is playing with him.

Soon the child gains a sense of body image consisting of an outline in space and the full occupation of this space. The sense of having a body and being a body develops not only through physical exploration, through grasping and touching, but also through mental vision and gazing upon one's own body. Merleau-Ponty[2] says that vision is a vital experience in this development:

> Vision is an act of two facets. To look at an object is to inhabit it, and from this habitation to grasp all things in terms of the aspect which they present to it. . . . But insofar as I see those things, too, they remain abodes open to my gaze, and, being potentially lodged in them, I already perceive from various angles the central object of my present vision.

Body image is a composite of an individual's corporeal existence and the expression of his right to take his place in

---

[2] M. Merleau-Ponty, *Phenomenology of Perception*, translated by Colin Smith (London: Routledge & Kegan, 1962).

the world. It is molded by his own views and attitudes and related to his prevailing preferences. Mental and muscular activities pursued with speed or sluggishness are decisive. Success or failure in establishing a social position finds its counterpart in the shape and volume of the individual's body image.

Goldstein[3] stresses the relation of a person's movement to his background. He says that for the normal person movement has a background. Every movement with its background has moments of a unique totality. The body and its shadow belong together, as the hand of a sundial belongs to the sun, as a touch belongs to the skin. Tactile and visual experiences are integrated in such a way that it is impossible to gauge the contribution of each sense. In the infant and young child, there is a simultaneous fusion of several processes—motor, sensory, and cognitive. Separation and integration go hand in hand, alternate, or occur simultaneously.

The physical and conceptual vicissitudes of the child's experience of his body are spiced by all the physical pleasures and aches that remain his exclusively and are not transferrable. Impressions that are not incorporated into a body of experience and knowledge are out of the frame of the world shared with others. These impressions are uncommunicable, inexplicable, and beyond comprehension—autistic.

The young child relates to the world by his senses. In his own mind, while he copies the gestures of a sensible object, he imagines and creates something that is still the object of his sense, but no longer outside. The object comes to him, but its image becomes him. "All impression," says Proust [4]

---

[3] Kurt Goldstein, *The Organism* (New York: American Book Co., 1939).

[4] M. Proust, *Remembrance of Things Past* (New York: Random House, 1927); quoted by Georges Poulet, *Studies in Human Time* (Baltimore: Johns Hopkins Press, 1956).

"is double—half developed in the object and half produced in ourselves." There is no transition between the instant in which the child sees an object and that in which he grasps its details, yet there is a moment of sensation and a moment of imagination. In every instant of time, each perception is related to the previous ones, each sound related to the result—leading to a total discovery. Sensory perception lays the foundation for meaningful experience. Touch and taste coincide in such a way that the subjective and objective aspects of an object mingle. The inherent quality of a percept and the child's curious investigation merge into a single experience.

A child can become what he envisions himself to be. Image helps to transform desire into reality. Although desire can change objects and influence the turn of events away from their natural sequence and consequence, in the growing child there is a balance between normative, adaptive tendencies that aim at sustaining life and creative acts that promote life. To see, to hear, to see clearly, to hear distinctly, to savor what one is seeing or hearing moment by moment —such concrete motifs dominate the relation with the environment. Through repetition, continuity, and concentration, a demarcation is made of one object from another, of one person from another in geometric and lived-in space. The identity of the I, the individual person, also grows out of this demarcation. The time element involved is the "Now" of the present, the outstanding definiteness out of all infinity. The overwhelming multitude of possibilities and diversities tears at the focus of the child. But he must choose. Being as experience has no limits, only points of contact. For the sense of totality, unity, and completion, the child himself has to set the limits.

Gradually, the child learns to distinguish among phenomena, between the animate and the inanimate, between animals and people, and between persons. The stuffed dog does not jump away when the little child shouts at it, but the live puppy may. When the child calls to his mother, her voice responds in a way that resembles his own calling to her more than the puppy's bark does. Papa sounds different from mama; sister and brother make still other kinds of sound. The child discovers not only the particular presence of others but also the differences between them and the possibility of relating himself to all of them, however different they may be.

The child also develops a sense of the continued existence of persons and objects even when they are out of his sight. Nearly everyone has played peek-a-boo with a child at one time or another. There is a significance in this activity beyond the fun of the game. By moving so as to shut out experience and admit it again, the child gains a new sense of stability and movement. He acquires a sense of himself as separate from the world and an awareness of what is not before him at the moment. He distinguishes what is in view from what is recalled. The child remembers the person or object, and their reappearance validates his memory, giving him a concrete experience of continuity. Thus the child discovers that he can move out into time as well as space.

The infant and the very young child perceive only present time. To them Now is always. From this comes the child's experience of bliss. It is a unique feeling of wonder and delight. The child can know bliss, can have entire and untroubled pleasure in being Now—the moment which is complete and without limit. Unaware of past time or time to come, unrestricted by the one and not made anxious by the threat or promise of the other, the child is afloat, borne along on the ocean of time present. The experience of existence in a state where time is unlimited is of such a quality that the adult maintains his nostalgia for it all his life.

The time continuum, extending into space, is a promising source of endless possibilities. The child's first ventures into this continuum are indelibly fixed upon him, either with the enchantment of a marvelous discovery or the foreboding of a dangerous encounter. For each event, there is a different time sense. The inner structure of time is subject to many changes, but the one feature of order and continuity prevails. Days filled with active experience, with no waste, quicken the tempo and rhythm of life. Fully experienced time rolls along steadily.

The young child often has an insatiable desire to prolong experience, to prolong time, to continue what he is doing at the moment no matter how urgent the adult calls or his own bodily needs. He is so totally involved in his present world that he cannot bear to break off making mud pies or arranging a doll's carriage or shouting and racing up and down as he plays at being an airplane pilot.

Experienced time has been contrasted with measured objectified time in that it is subjectively unique and varied in its tempo and rhythm. Temporality suffers a decisive change in the solipsistic world of a sick child. Time does not flow but is impaled on the past and becomes inextricable. It has a special hold on the frightened child. He tries desperately to get acquainted with his time in order to be able to discard past events. Only then does he feel he can dare to move on to new experience.

The child adds a third dimension to his time through role playing. He begins to grasp the future, to experience not merely what is absent but what is yet to come. He puts himself in touch with some of the possibilities for his own growth: he transcends the present and envisions the future. The child is able to leave off the socially assigned role of girl or boy for a moment and play a chosen adult role, thus bringing the future into the total present of childhood.

By pretending to live in that future, each child develops a concept of time to come, of growth out of the constriction of his current experience. Each child begins and pursues the creating of his own time.

Through role playing the child enlarges his experience. Roles are often played unwittingly. Some roles are *assigned* by society, such as the role of boy or of pupil. Others are *assumed* in playfulness and out of determination. Children play school for the sake of facilitating coexistence, to manifest concerted efforts. But they also take on roles in order to grow in their uniqueness, to grow up to the call of duty, to show that they can be responsible.

In Rainer Maria Rilke's *Stories of God*,[5] one tale tells how the thimble came to be God. Deciding that anything could be God, the children chose a shiny thimble which each child in turn was to carry for one day a week. On the whole, the arrangement worked out quite well. Everyone could see at once who had God, for that particular child walked about more stiffly and solemnly and wore a Sunday face. And though the thimble had not changed a whit, under the influence of its great dignity, the very thimbleness of it seemed a modest cloak hiding its real form.

Of all the vehicles for participation in the world, sound may be the most important to the child. The infant is born with a cry. The sound of his voice fills the room. Out of a soundless envelopment, he emerges into the world of animation. Out of silence, he will travel through sound to sign to symbol.

Sounds from the outside hit a special selective sensitivity in the child's auditory perceptions. Babies wake with a start in response to sudden noise. The uniformity of quie-

---

[5] Rainer Maria Rilke, *Stories of God,* translated by Nora Purtscher-Wydenbruck and M. D. Herter Norton (London: Sidgwick & Jackson, 1932).

tude is first disturbed by noises. In time, the quiet empty space of the outside world is populated and animated by a diversity of sounds and voices. The emptiness has changed into a fullness of the rhythmic ripples of friendly voices, an overall rustle in the distance sprinkled with accents of shrillness here and there.

Into the time and space expanse, the infant enters the world with his first cry. Later, with his cooing, he starts to use his voice as an instrument. The immensity of distance diminishes as the child develops his voice and receives the expressions of others.

Sounds and echoes stimulate response. Sounds as they approach the child are vibrant reminders of ongoing activities. They fill distant places and bring them closer. They animate empty space. They modulate the airways in a full-range orchestration. It is not surprising that the child chimes in—first trying to reproduce sounds, then producing and creating sounds that delight him because he is able to participate and contribute to the liveliness of the world. Above all is the wonder that he experiences as he gets in touch with others and elicits their responses.

The general background of sounds and voices and the immediate environment of a friendly address help to establish intersubjective communication. Repetition of sounds and later of words prolongs the time of the young child's expressiveness. Dialogues with himself establish his own identity and differentiate the roles he plays. Through language, the child grows in self-hood and in relatedness. With his language, he formulates his being in the world.

Language is the exquisite mediator between feeling and thought, thought and action, initiative and determination. It gives form to the desire to contact others; it gives shape to sentiment; it carries the meaning of one's intent; it is a source of happiness and accomplishment when one succeeds in expressing appropriately and exactly what one intends to express. Ontologically, it is the structure for facilitating the grasp of evanescent thoughts. Impressions that might otherwise be transitory are registered and stabilized in language.

The young child learns to speak first by imitating sounds. Then the meaning changes the sounds into signs and symbols. Symbols have a life of their own. They are fraught with meaning. They have content. They extend in time. They are born in the world of relationships and are uniquely human. The child learns by means of language to formulate his own thoughts. He learns to use common denominators in order to be understood. He experiences his own lived time and operates with past memories and future anticipations, couched in language.

The essence of languages lies not only in its function of a vector in the transition from percept to concept or from soliloquy to dialogue, but also in the fact that language is itself experience, for speaker as well as listener. Language is the ever-present potential of fulfillment, or, as Boss[6] puts it, "human *language* in its deepest meaning has to be regarded as a primordial *existentialium* of human *Dasein*."

Children's private language and secrets are used to engage in a playful testing of reality. Experimentations as to what may be shared and what has to be reserved for one's own consumption increase self-confidence in one's own exclusive possessions. Language used as steppingstones from the child's enclosed confinement does not always develop in an uninterrupted way. Children babble to hear their own voices, to practice the sequence of thought, and for the sheer joy of making sounds. The young child often

---

[6] Medard Boss, *Psychoanalysis and Daseinsanalysis* (New York: Basic Books, 1963).

uses words effectively, if not conventionally. One four-year-old, describing his day at kindergarten, confided, "Now I have two friends and three unfriends."

The language of the child who is alienated and fragmented fails to establish links and bridges from one experience to another, within himself and within the world. Natural phenomena frighten these children. They reveal a lack of familiarity with experienced space and a disturbance in present time. They find themselves in a strange island of isolation where no communication prevails.

There is a resemblance between the adult failure to grasp reality and establish relatedness with it and the autistic child's failure to make himself at home in his living space. In our day, the failure of integration can be seen all through our culture. The characteristic fragmentation of modern experience is vividly presented by the artist who has cast aside traditional modes of presenting experience. Like the child who may still be striving to grasp his world wholly, to develop all the dimensions of the space and time of his existence and to integrate that experience until he is one with it, so the modern artist, a man among men, shows how experience has been split asunder and men have not been able to develop a continuing relatedness, a genuine connection with their existence. The artist presents us with a world of truncated objects. These parts may be placed into interesting arrangements, but they cannot portray and render his world as a whole because modern man does not fully occupy his living space, nor is he fully connected to the flow of time around him.

Nevertheless, this is not the way life begins. For the infant, there is no fragmentation, no alienation, no separateness. His world has no real divisions. The infant is all he is and he is all. He exists in an eternal present. He moves into the world very soon, with his body, his voice, and his senses.

The world becomes his dwelling place, unless he feels rejected and cut off from the world. He brings order into the world. He reaches out—touching, grasping, making connections with life. By being lovingly responded to, by being nourished and valued, he develops responsiveness in kind. He builds bridges to objects and to people.

By distinguishing between what is under his skin and what is outside, he develops a sense of self and a sense of others. He learns to separate himself from objects and people, but he also learns to stay whole, to remain connected, to stay related—as long as he is cherished and valued for himself.

The child growing in a healthy way expands into and grasps the world and time. He develops an increasing capacity to convey and receive from experience. He comes to expect response from the people around him and in turn responds to them. A two-way movement grows between the child and the space he occupies. Even as he separates himself from that to which he responds, he remains related at the same time. In the very act of becoming aware of his individuality, the capacity for relatedness develops. Isolation and alienation are terrifying experiences; in relatedness there is peace.

In *The Little Prince*,[7] Saint-Exupéry tells of the lamplighter whose job it is to provide daylight and dark for all the small planets. They revolve so rapidly that the lamplighter is kept busy continually darting about, turning on the stars and putting them out again. To the young child, adults must often resemble the harassed lamplighter who does nothing but hurry himself and push others into meaningless hurrying along with him. In reality, as in fiction and

---

[7] Antoine de Saint-Exupéry, *The Little Prince*. Translated by Katherine Woods (New York: Harcourt, Brace & World, Inc., 1943).

especially from the child's point of view, the demand for haste and the call to duty leave no room for joy. Such demands are perplexing to the young child. For he quite literally "has all the time in the world."

11

Existentialism and Experiential Psychotherapy ❃ *Eugene T. Gendlin*

THE ARTICLES IN THIS BOOK have a humanity and a gentleness. In these newer therapies, people are perceived as human beings and not as containers of machinery. One can bear the thought of sending a child to a therapist who speaks and feels as these do.

In this chapter, I want to introduce the new formulations of existential and experiential theory. I shall try to state what existentialism has contributed to psychotherapy and to outline and illustrate experiential therapy. I will use the chapters in the present volume as examples of the "existential" approach.

Experiential Theory

In the new thinking, human experiencing is approached directly rather than studied after it has been translated into theoretical machinery. Therefore, theory for the new therapies is different in kind. It not only involves different concepts but a new way of using concepts. Both concepts and experiences enter into this theory in a very special kind of interplay.

The existential approaches use concepts as "pointers" that refer directly[1] to felt experience. That sounds very modest, and it is. Yet, the use of concepts as pointers to felt experience is the steppingstone to a new theoretical outlook.

For example, the articles in this book share a common outlook. Yet, they employ a huge range of different theoretical concepts. The authors themselves come from radically diverse theoretical orientations. A few phrases from the articles illustrate this diversity: "existential moment," "pattern of neurotic interaction," "acceptance," "alienation," "explore analytically," "separation anxiety," "the Great Mother." Clearly, what these authors have in common is not their theoretical vocabulary!

If you take any of these phrases as well-defined concepts (and each is a well-defined concept in the context of its proper theory), then, of course, they are highly inconsistent with each other. The implications which follow by theoretical logic from one of these concepts are very different from those which follow from another. Since these authors share a common approach to psychotherapy, they are not using their concepts in accordance with original definitions. This divergence accounts for the impression that existentialism in psychotherapy is no more than a protest movement against theory and that it combines under its aegis a diversity of views united only by the refusal to think clearly—thinking clearly (logically, theoretically, that is) would reveal definite inconsistencies.

This confusing picture is altered when we see that these

---

[1] Eugene T. Gendlin, *Experiencing and the Creation of Meaning* (New York: The Free Press of Glencoe, 1962); Eugene T. Gendlin, "A Theory of Personality Change," in Worchel and Byrne, eds., *Personality Change* (New York: John Wiley, 1964).

therapists employ concepts, not chiefly via their logical-theoretical implications, but in a different way. I can illustrate this new way by means of the gentle example of the articles in this book.

These authors do not reason from concept to concept through logical chains. Their reasoning is not based on theoretical concepts as such. Rather, they use concepts to point to and differentiate directly felt experiencing. This new use of concepts turns theoretical orientations into mere vocabularies. A few decades ago, these concepts were not "vocabulary," but fundamental forces, entities, or constituents of personality. Each theory viewed the nature of man differently, with different practical applications. Yet, today, something is the same in all these different theoretical writings. Something transcends the differing vocabularies (indeed, makes them merely "vocabularies"). It is the direct reference by each concept to specific differentiations of felt experiencing.

Let me say more exactly what I mean: One of the authors in this book, Allen, tells of a little girl who did not want to go to school or even separate from her mother because she feared that great harm would come to her mother. In one of the interviews, the child told Allen that her mother was really her twin. Allen writes: "The feeling of separation aroused a feeling of being nobody, at best a twin, but with no adequate confidence of being a unique and distinct person." Here is an "interpretation" via the theory of separation anxiety and birth trauma. It seems to be a totally different interpretation than that of another author in this book.

Discussing a little boy's insistence on sleeping in his mother's bed, this therapist, Lewis, interprets the behavior as a difficulty in "facing the problem of the Great Mother." We recognize the Jungian interpretation. Yet, throughout these experiences, we know what both therapists are talking about; it is the same thing! We are unconcerned about their theoretical differences. We do not relate separation anxiety to birth trauma, as the theory would. We do not ask: Is it really birth trauma or is it an archetype? Notice, as I now cite two more statements from these same therapists, that it is difficult to know which expression is Jungian and which is Rankian. "I pointed out . . . that being alone is sometimes inevitable, that it was a requirement of living . . . the fear that mother might be killed was actually . . . a wish to escape once and forever the imprisoning mother." "To be brighter, keener, more aware, more in touch with life was a frightening thought . . . to transcend mother was equivalent to killing her."

Our direct words about experiencing, our direct differentiations of experiencing, do not depend upon conceptual definitions. As we differentiate experiencing directly, and, rather finely, we may occasionally use theoretical terms, newly invented words and old words that have differentiating power when referring to feelings.

The articles in this book use case reports and are naturally full of descriptive detail. But descriptive detail is really meant, and the concepts have meaning only in terms of descriptive life. The meaning of the concepts is precisely what they point to; it is not based on theoretical definitions. Existential thinking does not move from concept to concept through logical implications. Rather, it moves through experiential detail, through differentiations that make experiential sense and that enable further experience. In existential child therapy, the steps of discussion are steps of experiencing, not steps of conceptual derivation. The experiences are not defined by the concepts, but, on the contrary, the concepts are defined by the steps of experiencing.

The descriptive detail is not merely an "application" or

"manifestation" of conceptually defined entities. At one time, the detailed texture of experience was considered "epiphenomena," manifestations of conceptually defined forces, entities, psychologic factors. In the newer use, you might say the concepts are the "epiphenomena," pointers whose sole meaning consists of the experiential texture at which they point, and which help us to differentiate so that we may directly feel and know the experiential steps in therapy as the therapist discusses them.

This method, of course, requires concepts. It is a use of concepts, but a different use than the chain which moves: concept—implication—concept—implication—concept. It is a chain which moves: experiential step—concept —experiential step—concept.

These steps of experiencing (of differentiating and moving from feeling to feeling) must make direct experiential sense to us. They are always much more specific than any theoretical concept. Therefore, we could not possibly gain the sense of these steps by means of a theoretical concept. On the contrary, the theoretical concept, as used, gets its meaning from the detailed steps we must first directly feel.

Current developments in psychotherapy have obscured the lines between different orientations. For example, contrast psychoanalysis and client-centered therapy. What a sharp difference that once seemed to be! Today, looking back, we see the similarity: Both were highly formal denials of a real relationship. One role-played a relationship of transference; the other role-played a perfectly neutral acceptance. We see two of a kind—artificial, formalistic avoidances of genuine interaction between two people. The patient's real feelings were considered invalid (transference). The analyst's feelings were also considered invalid (counter-transference). Similarly, in client-centered therapy, it was a mistake for the therapist to interject his own feelings into the therapeutic situation. Today, client-centered therapists make "genuineness" the first condition[2] for therapy and therapist-expressivity[3] and spontaneity[4] main therapeutic factors. Psychoanalysts are also moving toward real involvement and commitment as persons, with less reliance on technique.

A second main trend that cuts across orientations is emphasis on directly felt experience instead of insistence on certain special contents. For example, in classical analysis all difficulties had to lead back to Oedipal sexual conflicts. Few analysts today would construe psychotherapy so narrowly. The other orientations also place less emphasis on contents once held as necessary for successful therapy. Concepts, such as self-perception, power drive, separation anxiety, archetype, sexual conflict, and interpersonal reactions no longer fix the direction and movement of therapy. Today, there are many different "orientations," but they do not differ along really essential lines. What appeared to be major differences in the essential personality determinants now seem more differences in vocabulary. Today, whatever the theory, the directly felt process in the patient is basic. The patient can oblige his therapist and express his felt experiences in any one of the content languages.

The present explorations in psychotherapy reflect a pe-

---

[2] Carl R. Rogers, *On Becoming a Person* (Boston: Houghton Mifflin, 1951).

[3] Eugene T. Gendlin, "Subverbal Communication and Therapist Expressivity Trends in Client-Centered Therapy with Schizophrenics," *Journal of Existential Psychiatry*, IV (1963), No. 14; Eugene T. Gendlin, "Schizophrenia, Problems and Methods of Psychotherapy," *Review of Existential Psychology and Psychiatry*, IV (1964), No. 2.

[4] J. M. Butler, "Client-Centered Counseling and Psychotherapy," in D. Brower and L. E. Abt, eds., *Progress in Clinical Psychology* (New York: Grune & Stratton, 1958), Vol. III. *Changing Conceptions in Psychotherapy*.

riod of transition. The new essential dimensions, shared very broadly by some therapists in all orientations, are *the relationship process between two humans and the therapeutic feeling process*. Both of these dimensions are experiential in character. For this reason, I am calling the new therapy "experiential therapy." In every orientation, today, we find discussion for and against the new emphasis, in contrast to the technique forms on which we once concentrated so heavily.

I have already mentioned how the chapters of this book illustrate the direct experiential way of talking about and proceeding in therapy. Let me now discuss how these chapters emphasize the experiential relationship and the individual's feeling process. These chapters point at the concrete living personal relationship, something that is much more than two people and their individual patterns, more than what each thinks of the other or how each sees the other, more than units of meaning communicated from one to the other. Martin Buber as quoted in "The Existential Moment" says of the therapist that "if he has really gathered the child into his life then that subterranean dialogic . . . is established and endures." This is no mere professional relationship to a patient; it is a life relationship of two humans. They both live really there, in the "reality *between* them." And this reality is a "subterranean" connection and interaction. It isn't merely something perceived and communicated, or specific reactions of one to the other. It involves one's whole ongoing aliveness. Poetic language —but we have no well-established technical terms for it. We all know, for example, the concrete sense of being looked at by another human being, when someone looks *at* us. That is not what he really thinks or what we wish he would think, or how we wish he had seen us. It isn't this or that perception he may be getting. It is the live, direct sense of existing in the "reality between" ourselves and him, of being seen by him, and of meeting him in his seeing.

I believe that successful psychotherapy of any type has always centrally involved this concrete type of encounter. Yet, there has also been a great deal of artificiality, of therapists limiting their involvement as persons (as if it were an error betraying the therapist's weaknesses, needs, or softness), much painfully distant dealing with patients as though with forceps. Therapists have often felt they had to sit behind screens of various kinds—fully seeing the patient, but themselves neither visible nor visibly involved in an encounter.

But the fully real relationship involves the therapist's own person and hence his weaknesses and fears. Therefore, case reports of such relationships are quite personal. And so, these chapters each are quite personal. They include, as Dorothy Baruch says, ". . . the things I've wanted to put into other books, but which were. . . . Not to be spoken of," for example, the children's "crazy sounding but poignant longings" and "the fear of our own feelings." Both therapist and child, in these chapters, are fully rounded and fully human persons. Only recently have case reports reflected this kind of human encounter. After all, one use of the word "clinical" and "case" is as a cliché for impersonal oblivion of humanness. No one likes to be treated "as a case" or to be looked at "clinically"—as if we all knew that, when the therapist looks at us "clinically," he is in some way violating our person! There is no longer such inhuman formalism here: a theme running through content and manner of these papers is the directly felt encounter and the concrete way in which it involves the therapist as a person.

But why call it "subterranean"? Only because it involves our total, live, ongoing being rather than this or that message or analytic tool? More than that: because this concrete encounter easily and constantly transcends words. For example, what a shock to find, after many pages in one of these chapters, that the little boy *for the first time* speaks to the therapist! And all that went on with both of them, as described over these many pages, none of it involved the child's speaking? You look back over the pages and, yes, it could be, you see it was . . . silent. In a similar way, Moustakas' experience with Jimmy: "[he] saw the bottles of blood, his body tightened visibly throughout, and a dark look of violent dread crossed his face . . . a foreboding expression . . ." and "I remained with Jimmy. . . ." "As far as it is humanly possible . . . I was there. . . ."

"The physician tried to convince him that the needle would hurt him only a little. . . . He screamed repeatedly. . . ." "During this time, I held his hand. . . . I did not talk about the realities involved." So much action, without words, all of it direct living connections, specific, eventful, concrete.

Or, there is Alexander's Jerry, a supposedly retarded boy who "struggled through almost the entire . . . Wechsler-Bellevue with little or no response. Everything I said, everything I showed him, seemed beyond his comprehension. . . ." "Yet, I could not stop." (And Alexander did not stop, but went on to the Block Design test, trying on and on.) "But this time there was a difference; he was able to copy the third demonstration. Then . . . he was able to complete the next five designs. . . . Jerry appeared to be a different boy. He seemed to relax."

What is happening here? A relationship: a concrete interaction, a different boy. What is being said—how was it achieved? What technique was used? What of the facts shown in the Wechsler-Bellevue? What kind of facts are such facts, and what kind of facts are "he was able to copy the third demonstration" and "the next five designs . . ."? What is a person? What kind of facts? And, again, what different thing is a person-in-relationship, and what kind of facts are these different ones that grow out of a relationship?

In these relationships the individual is already, in these moments, ongoingly, a different person differently involved and differently alive than he was as a lone set of facts.

The chapters in this book describe many other ways of portraying this same theme. Here is one author's clear tracing of how the individual is what he is in interaction, and how he changes in the moments in which the interaction is concretely different. Colm describes the older brother Bobby and the little Gavin:

> And I saw Gavin slowly, slowly moving his foot closer against the big, complicated building that Bobby had just erected for an army barracks. Bang! It collapsed by "accident." Bobby instantly became the monster and threw a stone. Gavin cried out *desperately* and ran to me for protection.

If the therapist is temporarily drawn into the child's pattern of provoking unreal acceptance, pity, or protection, he must catch this in himself, and make it a useful experience for the child, and for himself.

> I said, "Oh shucks. . . . Poor little Gavin (*pause*) or (*pause*) really like superman? . . . could wreck even big Bobby's building *and* could make Mom come and scold Bobby and comfort *him*." . . . An embarrassed . . . smile came from Gavin. At this point, I gave him a short hug—not before, when he had tried to force me into protecting him.

Sometimes, in these chapters, therapists know and describe moments when it is clear and self-explanatory by just what steps the relationship changes the individual. At other times therapists equally well know these moments and describe them in finely caught detail, yet only the child's unfolding is visible—the why is mysterious. The *general* explanation is the same: it isn't that the interaction affects the individual and then makes him different. In the very ongoing of that interaction, he is already different.

The therapists sometimes know and can say just what kind of change they bring, in what way they make the interaction (and the changed person in that interaction) into something more positive, more alive, more free and lifeworthy. At other times such "making positive" is not specific nor known to the therapist. It happens nevertheless. It is a function of the nature of two people connected, open, honest, and struggling. To be helpless, hopeless, isolated, unloved, lost in weirdness—we call these things negative; but no "value judgment" is required of the therapist in order to alter these negatives in the patient. The very nature of finding oneself concretely seen, felt, connected, and one's every feeling and motion responded to constitutes finding oneself no longer helpless, hopeless, no longer isolated, unloved, lost in weirdness. The concrete mode of living is already different. The words with which to perceive and say what has changed, these can come later. For example, in his chapter, Allen writes: "I reflected the side of her that wanted to live, helping her to recognize her own fear of growing up, but, at the same time, her desire to be connected with life and to emerge as a distinct and independent person. . . . Once she remarked, . . . when I come here I know I want to live."

That is what a relationship does! Always the *positive* being of the person is concretely extended and made real. But this is no "value choice" of accentuating the positive. It does not mean at all that one welcomes positive feelings and plays down negative ones. In the case above, it was just as important to respond to "her own fear of growing up." The making real of the person's positive being lies in the concrete relating, in the response and welcome to every shade of feeling, in the kind of ongoing person-process made by such responding. Precisely "the side of her that wants to live" is made real and alive as *she* is responded to in whatever she may be up against. A responded-to person is already a more positively alive one, than the dulled, life-blocked, hardly ongoing, lone facts of the person were.

Similarly, Lewis tries to help the boy ". . . see the self-creative strivings implicit in his rages." She remarks, "Anger can be good as well as bad, you know. It can be right to be angry with something that is evil, can't it?" Or, note her positive view of the boy's refusal to go to school for fear of fainting and having to return to the hospital. "He could not bear the thought . . . of being isolated in a bed. . . ." (The boy slept only with his mother in her bed.) The therapist calls it "Roy's fear of isolation, . . . his fear of forced removal from life. . . ." Does this therapist see only the silver lining? Is she unaware of the pathological and negative character of all this? Hardly. She calls it "his infantile mother fixation," but she sees it as "holding Roy back from a full restoration of his talents and powers." Consider the phrase "holding Roy back." It is a phrase describing something negative, and yet it surges with the positive, which is to be released, allowed, made real, made ongoing.

These concrete existential encounters make the positive ongoingly real, and it hardly matters whether a therapist's design is quite conscious and clear, or whether he has no design at all—except precisely to relate responsively and connectedly. That subterraneously includes all possible positive designs. For example: ". . . I responded to him in ways which told him that a strong adult who knew the realities of life was his honest ally . . ." (Kogl); or "I give myself to you without fear of losing myself" (Baruch); or "The therapist never loses touch with himself as a person . . . (and brings) to the child the full resources of a real self . . ." (Moustakas). The experiential relationship, the existential encounter, then, is fully and mutually personal and not just professional; it is much more than verbal, it is a concrete interplay and connectedness; and in the very ongoing of this kind of interaction the individual is already different and more fully and positively alive.

These themes run through every chapter of this book. And, literally as a corollary of concrete relating, another pervasive theme concerns the experiencing process in the individual. The concrete relationship involves humans as experiencing and feeling persons. And so, the individual is ongoing as a new and different process of experiencing, of feeling. Not this or that content, but the type of process determines illness or health.

The very contents of an individual are different depending upon what kind of feeling process he is—and the relationship determines that. Baruch, in her chapter, speaks of children's "preposterous giant imaginings." "A child must pathetically hide inside him the monstrous things." Yet, these are normal! Baruch pleads with us as parents and therapists to give "attention, more hearing, more understanding that goes forth in quiet peace to meet our children's feelings." In this way, she tells us, "the normal problems of childhood remain normal." These "monsters" of childhood, as such, don't create trouble. Rather, it is the way in which the child is responded to, and allowed to exist as an ongoing being—that determines sickness or health.

Similarly, Colm's Bobby and his "monster" dreams. As the little Gavin goads him, "Bobby instantly became the monster. . . ." And, when Bobby experiences himself in a different interaction, no longer as unwanted and goaded, "the monster dreams disappeared."

These concrete relationships change the individual just because an individual isn't these or those facts inside, but always an ongoing feeling process in interaction. The monsters aren't "psychotic contents." They are as human as having your block building kicked over by your sneaky little brother who competes for your mother's love. They are the consequence of being isolated and unresponded to as children. They "disappear" in a relationship as a distinct person emerges. Or, as Wenkart states, in her chapter, "By being responded to lovingly, by being nourished and valued he [the child] develops responsiveness in kind; he builds bridges to objects and to people."

What is the individual? Not these or those factual contents but the felt, ongoing process. Moustakas describes it in "The Existential Moment" as "an entirely unique and particular substance which is his own . . . an essence which can be recognized and called forth in the encounter." The encounter calls it forth, it brings it about that "the person feels his feelings . . . ," is more fully alive as his own unique substance, and is just thereby and just in that way changed from how he was before!

Insight plays a great role in this feeling process which transcends content. But, in these chapters, it is not an insight brought up dead, like a long-drowned fact from the bottom of the unconscious sea. As Allen puts it, "the child's inner life is revealed in such a way that the child participates directly and actively in the resolution of his own conflicts and problems." Throughout these chapters, recognition, "helping him to see . . . ," this is insight that stems from the concretely felt flow of ongoing inner life. The payoff and truth directly bring an immediately experienced release, a more fully being alive, concretely. This is insight which emerges out of felt experiencing and leads right into a movement of that experiencing.

The Theoretical Questions

How, now, shall we formulate these themes more exactly? There is great promise but also danger in the new experiential psychotherapy. The promise is for genuine therapy and a genuinely human science of man. The danger is a therapy without theoretical perspectives and trainable principles. Existential psychotherapy can look like a mere rejection of theory and precise thought. No such rejection is implied here—only that the main concerns and the very method of thought are still in the process of being formulated, and they are different from older theories.

Having pointed to some of the main themes as exemplified in these chapters, let us formulate these more exactly. We must develop a theory of experiential process and experiential steps. Experiential process plays a central role in at least three related respects: in the function of experiential steps, in the interpersonal relationship, and in the individual during psychotherapy.

The individual during psychotherapy could not change in personality if he did not engage in directly felt experiential steps. If we think of his experiential steps as merely an experiential version of conceptual steps, then we cannot explain how he changes. Suppose he and we describe accurately how it is with him now, the what and why of his painful, self-defeating patterns, the factors which have made it so and keep it so. Suppose he remains only within what logically follows, what is logically consistent with this way of being. He would never change. To remain consistent with —that means precisely not to change. Any account of how someone changes and resolves difficulties must involve a process that moves beyond what can follow consistently from how the individual is.

For this reason, the older theories failed to define the change process in the individual. Freudian theory, for example, calls the change process "working through," an admittedly chaotic, little-understood struggle in which the individual "somehow" overcomes what the theoretical diagnosis represented. The theoretical diagnosis explains why and how the individual came to be and had to remain as he is. If the experiential process of the individual did not move through steps other than those which could be deduced from the diagnosis, the diagnosis would continue to fit him. He would not have changed. The experiential steps cannot possibly be only concrete versions of consistent conceptual steps. Thus, our theory must not portray experiential steps and resolution as if they were logical steps. Patients and therapists employ not only concepts, but also experiential steps. We do not want merely to "intellectualize" or "rationalize"—neither *in*, nor *about* psychotherapy.

I call this reliance on experiential as well as conceptual steps the "experiential use" of concepts. In "experiential use," concepts, words, or other symbols have a vital function, but a different one than that of leading directly (by logical implication) to other words or concepts. Steps of experiential differentiation intervene between one concept or set of words and the next. Rather than leading by implication directly to other words or concepts, there is first a directly experienced effect. Something directly felt is newly noticeable. That newly noticeable experiencing then leads to further concepts. The new conceptualization "makes sense"; it follows understandably *from* the preceding concepts, yet one could not have gotten to it by any conceptual implications *of* the preceding step.

One can, and often does, move directly from concept to

concept by conceptual implication. But therapeutic change and resolution occur because of those times when one moves via intervening experiential steps.

An experiential use of concepts still requires that concepts retain their logical precision and meaning—for that is what has the power to refer to experiencing. It is an error to drop logic, language, definition, and logical precision. That leads to arbitrary emotionalism, not to experiential steps. It is true that there is here a difficult philosophic problem,[5] just how to know what aspects of a conceptual construct one employs to refer to experiencing, as against those aspects one ignores for the moment, as being experientially irrelevant. To so use concepts systematically involves a systematic method. For the moment I want only to point out that a glorification of "ambiguity" and "inexpressibility" is not in order. Concepts and intellectual differentiations play a vital role both in psychotherapy and in civilized man generally. We cannot differentiate experiencing and move along experiential steps unless we are willing to grant concepts even more precise and specific power than when we use them abstractly. For example, recall how often in psychotherapy the client struggles for the exactly right way of stating something he feels. Many statements may be rejected as "not quite it," even though conceptually they seem to be the same as what he finally asserts is "exactly it." That exactly right statement has a powerful experiential effect. The person may visibly relax, exhale deeply, and feel released and deeply relieved, often despite the fact that the statement asserts something awful. The "felt rightness" (as we usually call it) of such a statement is obviously not at all arbitrary. Not any and all concepts or words will do. Only just exactly these words have this effect

---

[5] Eugene T. Gendlin, *Experiencing and the Creation of Meaning* (New York: The Free Press of Glencoe, 1962).

of experiential movement. We experience this effect as "the words are exactly right; they feel true"; just this is a deeply felt experiential movement and change. A few minutes or days later, it thereby becomes possible to conceptualize quite a different experiential step. That new conceptualization may well now contradict the one that felt so true, and just because of the change made by this "feeling true." Thus the process of felt experiential steps is involved not only in our own experiential use of concepts, but also in the client's change process in therapy.

This process of felt steps helps to explain the value of the personal relationship in psychotherapy.

Again, the old method of conceptual machinery fell short. Just as the change process within the individual is a mystery if only constructs and their implications are considered, so also, without the experiential process, it is a mystery how the interpersonal relationship creates its powerful change-effects.

Freud explained how the patient repeats his self-defeating patterns (the "transference"), but he did not explain why the patient ever ceases this repetition, how he ever becomes different, how the transference is "handled" or "overcome." More basically, it was said that the presence of the therapist in a close transference relationship "changes the libidinal cathexes" or "alters the dynamic balance." Today, with our new experiential way of using concepts, we need not object to these terms. The personal relationship indeed changes the "dynamic balance," we may agree. We say "of course it does." We aren't even thinking of "dynamic balance" as the theoretical construct it is, with all its conceptual implications of bound forces and hydraulic economic complexes. We are not using the definition of "dynamic balance" when we easily assent that, indeed, a personal relationship of a certain sort can alter the dynamic balance. We can let this phrase stand as a pointer to what we feel directly: the way in which one's whole manner of being alive feels and is different, depending upon toward whom and with whom we live, feel, and express.

In the words of Allen, in his chapter in this book (Allen who has done so much during the last thirty years to bring us just this insight): "Therapy exists to the extent that it is a meaningful and unique life experience." The therapeutic change, resolution, working through, overcoming of repetitive and limiting patterns, occurs not from more exact revelation of how the patient is and came to be as he is, not from more and more fully showing him that he must be as he is, and must react as he does. It comes from making this now ongoing relationship into a new and different concrete life experience for him, a kind of experiencing he could not be, and was not, until now. Thus, the effects of a personal relationship must be understood as the new and different experiential process that a genuine relationship makes possible.

Existentialism

Previous theories looked upon the interpersonal relationship second; they considered the individual first. The individual was explained (his behavior, personality, feelings, and so forth). Then, when two individuals met, they "communicated," or "interacted." Such interaction was explained in terms of basically individual entities. Behavior was explained out of individual motives, drives, patterns, or tendencies. Outside "stimuli" set off patterns or forces in the individual, and these determined his behavior. The individual was regarded as a self-contained box, and his internal machinery determined his feelings and acts. Existentialism overthrows these kinds of perceptions and interpretations.

Being in the world and being with others is the first consideration of existentialism; the individual as a separate entity is explainable only in the second place. In America, Sullivan[6] effected a similar theoretical revolution, although in different terms and not quite as thoroughly.

For existentialism there is no "subject' within, separate from the "objects" outside. Our language and habits of thought have been guided so long by British Empiricism that even existentialists sometimes fall back into just those modes of thought which existentialism most opposes. For Husserl, and phenomenology since then, the basic term is "intentionality." This word means that experience as we have it is always about something, toward something, in reaction to something, of something, with something, never *just* an entity inside our heads or bodies. Phenomenology rejects the theory that we see "percepts," that we think "images" and "sensory traces" or "nervous stimulations." Husserl, in examining directly-given experience, found that he just never saw a percept. No one has ever seen a percept. We always see a tree or a person or a room. We always see something outside us (even dream images are like that), never a percept in our heads. We always feel angry at what someone did because of what happened to us and what we must now do. We never feel anger as just something subjective, an entity within, unrelated to the world we live in. What we actually experience eliminates the old barrier between the objective (geometrically conceived atoms and physical forces outside) and the subjective (entities or forces inside). Husserl found that the whole human world was really implicit in our experience and that the supposed entities within were mere theoretical constructs.

The individual's gut-felt experience (for example, "I am all tense and tied-up") is no mere internal entity (like a

---

[6] Harry Stack Sullivan, *The Interpersonal Theory of Psychiatry* (New York: Norton, 1953).

swallowed rock) but implicitly contains a whole texture of concerns about situations, reactions to others, perceptions of things and people. The following speech illustrates the many situational conditions and perceptions implicit in what may seem to be purely internal entities, being tense or afraid or ashamed:

Oh, I'm so tense because I know I am going to have to talk about X and I don't want to because of what you'll think of me . . . and what I'll think of myself, I guess I am ashamed, really, because I did this awful thing, but really that isn't the main of it, it's that I had to do it not out of meanness but because I was afraid to stand up to him because I'd have to fight and so it was really out of fear I got pushed into it, and having to admit that is worse than just what I did, and I was afraid to admit that. Boy, *was* I tense.

In the old theory, we talked as though "affects" (internal entities) were "attached" to situational stimuli. The formula we used is "I am tense because of X" and the "because" bridged the artificial gap between the subjective and the objective. But, this "attached affect" hides the real way it is. Notice, in the few lines above, first tension was "attached," then "fear," then "shame." These different emotional colorings did indeed come and go, but the individual was really explicating one felt chain of experience. As he told why he felt tense, he no longer felt tense, but instead, ashamed. Nor was he merely "tense" as an entity within. He was tense at the prospect of having to discuss something with someone. He did not merely have shame as an entity within. He was ashamed at being pushed into certain things through fear. His "fear" was not an entity within but a being afraid of having to fight.

It is an essential character of felt experience, that it is internally differentiable,[7] that it may, after moments, turn into

---

[7] Gendlin, "Experiencing: A Variable in the Process of Therapeutic Change," *loc. cit.*

a long chain of complex situational and interpersonal aspects. Experience is not something "within," but something interactive, implicitly containing many aspects of the situations one lives in.

Existentialism defines human beings as being "in the world." It defines subjective or individual experience not as something within, but as "in the world." It defines the individual human as a being here (Dasein). This means he is concretely sentient. Existence is always yours, mine, his. It is the concrete ongoing living we feel and are. It implicitly contains how we are alive and geared into our situations.

Other persons are perhaps the most important aspect of the world and the situations we live in. Human beings are always a "being-with." [8] (Loneliness is no exception; in fact we can feel lonely only because being-with is an essential aspect of human beings.)

Being-with and being-in (situations, the world) are not mere "traits" of humans. They are what it is to be human, they are human "being." Much as Sullivan had altered theory from individualized entities to "dynamisms" (ongoing exchanges between people), so also existentialism portrays human nature as first and essentially an ongoing living in and with. What we feel and do stems not from inner self-contained machinery, but rather from what is felt toward and done toward people and things, to bring about situations, to alter them, to realize possibilities we foresee and avoid possibilities we fear. If you take away from human beings this aspect of a "projected" world (of fearing, caring, worrying, planning, arranging, being glad at, or avoiding), nothing is left, since all feeling, thought, and behavior is being in the world. The past is nothing but a texture of feelings and behaviors that were once fears, cares, concerns, and al-

---

[8] A. Burton, "Beyond the Transference," *Psychotherapy: Theory, Research, and Practice,* 1 (1964), No. 2; M. Heidegger, *Being and Time* (New York: Harper & Row, 1962).

terations of situations, avoidances and acceptances of conditions we lived in. True, all that is over and settled, and we can recall it as though it were fact, but it is still this peculiar type of being which, unlike a thing on the table, is never just what it is but always something else, something worried about or desired or cared for or done because of.

One false version of existentialism makes it into the subjectivism that existentialism opposes. Another false version makes it into an emphasis on the present, as though there were a present that did not consist of creating and being concerned about a future. Indeed, existentialism holds that the past does not make us what we are, but this is because the kind of "are" applicable to human beings is fundamentally the way we are in the world, always a possible way of being about to act or be affected. Human beings "are" never just here, in the room, but they "are" writing a paper about—— because—— and for——; they are getting something in order to do something with, waiting for someone, or avoiding someone, or resting from, or being lonely for. Of course, humans have their factual aspect (facticity). A human in a room is just here and cannot, without transportation, suddenly be in England. As a factual "thing" he can be shot, hit, or transported. But as a human kind of being, he is thinking about, feeling affected by, angry at, glad in, lonely for, close to, concerned about, and happy with.

It is therefore not the case that I know only myself (as an entity within) and can know you only via my analogous inner entities. Rather, there is no entity-self within but only the ongoing self in the world. I know directly how you affect me because the kind of being I am is a being affected in the world, a being-in and a being-with. I know myself secondarily from out of relationships, from out of my ongoing being-in and being-with.

When you communicate to me, existentialism implies, you

do not rearrange some old entities within me; you affect me in ways in which I have never been alive before. What you stir in me are not entities that sit waiting in me like marbles or rocks or pictures or pathways. I do not first have a given machinery-like nature and am then affected by what happens. I am always, only, a being affected by what happens. It is not the case that you act, and then I perceive your act, and then I react to your act out of my own constitution. Rather, as soon as you act, I am already this being affected by you. There is much to be said about how individuals have differing perceptions and reactions, how they remain within certain limitations and repetitious structures, how they avoid aspects of their human ongoing—indeed Heidegger makes such avoidance the most common mode of being human—but just as loneliness is possible only for a "being-with" type of being, so also avoidance and inauthenticity are possible only for a being-in type of being.

Individuals are not boxes full of entities into which a therapist tries to put new entities (information, example, insight, values). We have no way to get such entities into somebody. Personality change is just this shift of a person from being unable to learn, to take in, or to perceive accurately to being able to do so. Hence, even if information, example, insight, and values are "communicated" from therapist to patient, the question of change is: What happens in psychotherapy so that the patient "becomes aware," "learns," "accepts," "takes in" from his living what, at first, he was unable to be aware of, or learn; what happens to alter his self-defeating patterns?

If the essential nature of human beings is conceived of as a being-with and a being-in, then it is most easily explainable that people change when their surroundings change, that people are different when they are with someone different. If there is a puzzle, it is how we avoid being alive in new ways, how we repeat patterns that are not a being affected by the situation or person, here, now. (For this reason existentialists discuss at such length the avoidant "bad faith" or "inauthentic" modes of being.)

This is not to say that there is no separate, individual, self-based personality, but only that personality is not a thing. We have our separate being as selves—but only as we carry it forward by our actions, thoughts, gestures, and moves (all of them *at, in,* or *toward* situations). When we think or say what we feel or are, we do not "dig up" contents of self that were lying down under there but, rather, we have this ongoing being this or being that only as we complete it in action, in process, in symbolizing, in feeling. To the extent we are able to so carry forward our own process, to that extent we are separate and independent selves. Conversely, in those respects in which another person carries our experiencing forward in ways we alone cannot, in those regards we are not separate persons.

But, we cannot conclude from this that an optimal person would be able to carry his own experiencing forward in *every* respect in which it *could* be carried forward with others in a relationship! Every new individual who relates with me may carry my experiencing forward in ways that then seem terribly valuable and essential to what I (then) feelingly am. There is no set, limited, exhaustive list of what I am or could be in all respects! Again, humans are not set things! They have no exhaustive table of contents. But, an optimal person does carry forward his own experiencing (responds to himself with action and thought) sufficiently to constitute a broad ongoing process of experiencing, even when alone in his room, or for years in a lonely forest.

The view of human beings as entities or containers of entities comes from physics, from Galilean science, from the absurd (but highly fruitful) assumption that nothing is real except mathematically behaving masses and energies. But should we really accept as basic the type of construct that inherently assumes that people are not part of reality? Aren't we once and for all here, and part of reality? For some sciences it may be fruitful to assume that humans do not exist, but that is not a fruitful assumption for a science of man. Yet it is the assumption implied in a type of construct still often employed in studying human behavior.

Philosophy often sounds very arid and abstract because it is a discipline of discussing *types* of constructs. No one asserts that people do not exist. But many will persist in a type of construct that fits physical reality only if the humans who live in it, and study it, are first abstracted away. Existentialism poses the possibility of types of construct based on human modes of being, rather than on subsistence apart from human living.

Thus humans should not be conceived as containers with thinglike entities within (like a box full of individualized forces, energies, contents, experiences, drives or motives, wishes or needs, archetypes or repetition compulsions, instincts or nerve patterns, anxiety bonds or repressions, power drives or conflict equilibria, laws of thought or firing synapses, representations, images, percepts, or sensory traces). This is not to say that one or another of these construct systems might not generate fruitful hypotheses or lead to behavior predictions. But a more fruitful science of man must adopt more human-fitting types of constructs than that of the thing in the container.

Existentialist philosophers are giving us alternative types of constructs. Sartre,[9] for example, states that "thirst" is not a thing inside. It is my "drinking from a glass" which "haunts" how I am now (it isn't actual, yet it isn't unreal

---

[9] J. P. Sartre, *Being and Nothingness* (New York: Philosophical Library, 1956).

either) . . . a possibility that I *feel* and call thirst. Another example: "A belief" is not an entity, a content. It is just as much the "believing," an ongoing process. The process can never be separated off, so that entity-like contents exist as such. The process always "surpasses" whatever seem to be the entities, the beliefs, the emotions, the thoughts. Contents are "made to be" by the process and sustained by it.

We "interrogate" ourselves inwardly to discover what we feel, wish, are. This "self" we interrogate is not an "inhabitant" inside. In one respect it is "present" (our directly-felt bodily concreteness), in another respect it is "absent." (We must ask ourselves, dig, project questions "down there.") Sartre calls it the "absent-present," deliberately portraying it as one process, rather than as two separately existing things (like the Freudian down under, and the Freudian ego). There are no contents or "laws of consciousness" (there is only consciousness of laws and contents). The process as concretely ongoing is always more basic. The type of construct that fits such phenomena always needs hyphens in English, because it combines what had previously been split into two thinglike entities, and because it presents this combination, not as a tying together of two things, but as an ongoing process.

When we conceptualize or express how we are, what we feel, what our feelings imply, we are not digging up things which were down under there in just the same shapes as they now have, when we express them. Rather, to "dig up," to "express," these are ongoing life processes. They make meaning, rather than simply finding meaning already there. This may be expressed by the hyphenated pair "facticity-surpassing." There is always a given situation I factually find myself in, but to think, feel, interpret, react, explicate, perceive it, there is a process that alters what the situation is for me. Situations do not exist apart from me. A situation is not purely physical attributes, but human relational factors, what I can and cannot do, need, expect, achieve, use, avoid, and so forth. All the "attributes" of the facts as "situation" are in terms of someone's living, doing, using, and avoiding, altering, or failing to alter. But this means that there are not already given finished facts in us, or around us. Rather, to say how I feel is a living process that "surpasses" what was given when I began to talk. And, to tell you how I feel is, of course, a different being-in-the-world, than to say it to myself or some other person.

Existentialism is phenomenological; that means it aims to explicate directly what we concretely are, live and experience. Often, very abstruse constructs are coined, and these make existentialism seem like any other abstract conceptual-assumption system. Existentialists struggle to emphasize that they do not impose or assume their schemes to be in experience as such. Everything we say, both in theory and in personal self-expression, is a "lifting out," a "making be" of order, meaning, pattern, and situation, a "surpassing" in the very process of concrete living and doing, speaking, and thinking.

Thus they use words like "preontological" (that is to say, before ontology or philosophy is formulated), "prereflective" (before one reflects upon it and fashions a content that is reflected on), "preobjective" (before given objects are precisioned out, fashioned as objects) to convey the concrete flow of sentient living. All philosophic assertions are an explicating, a precisioning, "based on" the concrete on-going living and feeling process.

Yet, this seemingly complicated way of describing concrete experience can be misleading. Many readers of existentialism do not realize the simple, obvious, concrete reference to their own "gut sentience," which these technical phrases attempt. Then it seems that existentialism is simply vague, "ambiguous," and one is invited to glorify the ephemeral as something described only by negative phrases (like God's negative attributes): It cannot be reduced to analysis; it cannot be reduced to words; it cannot be presented as lawful; it cannot be predicted; it is ever new, unique, unexpected, irreducible and hence incapable of being thought about clearly. This is an error. What is intended is the directly experienced, felt sentience which you are all the time, and out of which you live and look through your eyes. Nothing is more ordinary and known to you than your concrete sentient "being here"—in its "preontological," "predefined" concreteness. Only from out of it do you genuinely express yourself or genuinely make the specific contents and patterns, emotions and chains of explication, experiential steps and reactions that you find as you explicate phenomenologically (and these are always about the world, others, situations, what you want, fear, might do, hoped to avoid, and are affected by). Thus the crux of existentialism is this formula that humans exist without defined essence. Humans have as their being just their existence (ancient philosophic words for that alive felt sentience you are).

The crux of existentialism, however, is not merely to assert that concretely felt experiencing is basic, but to put all concepts and thoughts into direct interplay with it. Phenomenological assertions are "based on" direct concrete existent living. What does "based on" mean? What is this peculiar interplay of the patient's living-and-formulating that we call genuine psychotherapy? How is it different from the mere mongering of verbalizations or concepts that we call intellectualizing? The difference lies in a peculiar relationship between directly felt sentience and words or concepts.

"Being-in-the-world" is *concrete*. It isn't something general; it is always your existence, or mine, or his. "It is my 'here,'" says Heidegger. He explains: it isn't this or that mood, but the very possibility of mood or quality of feeling. Feelings are our ways of being affected in the world, more exactly, the very possibility of being affected. What we are is feeling—an "openness to being affected" (Heidegger). Similarly, Sartre points out that our feelings are "possibilities," possible actions in the world. We interrogate what seems like ourself, down under there (the "absent-present"), but these possibilities are really the stuff of the body. We *feel* our possibilities before we shape them and verbalize them.

Experiential Psychotherapy

In the last section I presented what the philosophy called existentialism contributes to psychotherapy. But, it is also true that psychotherapy contributes greatly to existential philosophy. Felt concreteness is difficult to describe philosophically, whereas in therapy we are continually working with it and familiar with it. The work of Jung, Rank, Allen, Rogers, and others (coming directly from psychotherapy) joins with the philosophical existential trend. Both streams are going to make up a new philosophy and psychotherapy.

In psychotherapy, the concretely felt is so familiar that we define therapy as just this. We call it "rationalizing" or "intellectualizing" or "externalizing" (not therapy) if an individual talks and explains without the direct participation of his ongoing experiencing. We call it genuine therapy only when he freshly phrases his ongoing feelings, or otherwise symbolizes them, reacts to us from out of them, and lets his feeling process evolve and move in relation to us. As practicing therapists, we do not merely intellectualize, and we wish our clients to do more than that. Why, then, as theorists, should we remain on a merely intellectualized plane? Existentialism succeeds if we equate "existence" with "experiencing." For the client, the ongoing sentience is the basis of what he says and does in therapy, and it is what we try to respond to interactively, it is what we try to maximize, to free, to permit its fuller ongoing.[10]

Those who work with children (and with adult schizophrenics too) have always emphasized the experiential, and have always looked at words, gestures, play activity, and all symbolic activity generally as growing out of concretely ongoing sentient experiencing. It is not what is said or what is painted that does the effective changing of the personality, but rather it is the living experiential process of so speaking to someone and of so painting.

When an individual expresses accurately for the first time how he is, just then and precisely in so doing he is no longer that way. The accuracy which he feels so deeply—the physically sensed release of the words which feel exactly right—this very feeling is the feeling of change, or resolution, of experiencing moving a step forward.

From this carried-forward experiencing, from this new step, everything now looks somewhat different. Solutions may not be in sight. What was said earlier (perhaps with deep-felt rightness) may now be false or irrelevant. The whole scene may have changed. The issues and questions may be different, they may be worse than one had thought, yet it always feels good and enlivening to have the experiential process carried forward.

To say how it is does not simply represent, but it creates, it moves, it carries forward; it is a process of living.

No wonder, then, that a similar process is possible with nonverbal symbolizations. Therapists of children have always been ahead of others (for example, Allen or Rogers) in pointing out that psychotherapy is an experiential process.

---

[10] Gendlin, "A Theory of Personality Change," *loc. cit.*

Not only can playthings and dramatized situations symbolize experiencing and carry it forward; the other person's responses, too, can be considered as symbolizing and carrying forward the patient's experiencing. We are using the word "symbolizing" here in an odd but true way. Symbolize here does not mean represent in symbols. Symbolize means for external events (words, acts, others) to so fit the individual's implicit preconceptual feelings that the process is carried forward.[11]

I prefer to call this view of psychotherapy "experiential," since the "concrete existence" existentialists speak of is really experiencing.

I have described three closely related contributions of existentialism to the current developments of psychotherapy: (1) the relational being-in-the-world and being-with character of human beings as the primary type of construct with which to study human behavior; (2) the concrete sentient life process of an individual as not reducible to entities, pictures, contents (supposedly within), but rather as a feeling process; (3) a mode of thinking in which concepts and words are "based on" felt experiencing directly, precisioned or lifted out, creatively fashioned, not merely represented conceptually, but directly felt as a result of being thought about and differentiated in this way.

To discuss these three points I have already had to add a good deal of more therapeutically-oriented experiential theory. Let me make my own further steps clearer by discussing them separately:

As I mentioned earlier, in the United States existentialism came late upon the therapeutic scene. The contributions of Otto Rank, J. Taft, Frederick Allen, George H. Mead, Harry Stack Sullivan, Frieda Fromm-Reichmann, Carl G. Jung,

---

[11] Gendlin, *Experiencing and the Creation of Meaning, loc. cit.;* Gendlin, "A Theory of Personality Change," *loc. cit.*

Carl A. Whitaker, John Warkentin and Thomas P. Malone (they first coined the term "experiential psychotherapy"), Paul Federn, Abraham H. Maslow, Carl R. Rogers, and many others had already created a major movement in the experiential direction.

I will quote now from just a few sources to illustrate earlier trends toward what we have been discussing. First, Jung:

> According to this definition, the self . . . transcends the powers of imagination to form a clear picture of what we are as a self. . . . Thus we can, for example, see ourselves as a *persona* without too much difficulty . . . [but] the self remains a superordinate quantity. [The self is] . . . an actual, living something, poised between [conscious and unconscious]. . . . I have used the word "sensing" in order to indicate the apperceptive character of the relation between ego and self.[12]

Thus Jung points both to the concretely sentient, felt nature of experiencing and to its noncontent character, the way contents (ego, persona) are only aspects of the concretely "sensed" process. Similarly, Rank says:

> As long as one makes the feeling experience as such, in which the whole individuality is revealed, the sole object of the explanation and understanding, one finds one's self on sure ground, and also, in my opinion, insures the only therapeutic value, that is, to allow the patient to understand himself in an immediate experience which, as I strive for it in the therapeutic process, permits living and understanding to become one.[13]

Only in recent years are these views really understood by most therapists. To cite one of those who moved developments in this direction, Rogers wrote:

---

[12] Carl G. Jung, *Two Essays on Analytical Psychology* (New York: Meridian, 1956).

[13] Rank, *loc. cit.*

As the individual perceives and accepts . . . more of his organismic experiences, he finds that he is replacing his present value *system* . . . with a continuing organismic valuing *process* . . . (the individual) examines . . . in terms of a more basic criterion—namely, his own sensory and visceral experiences.[14]

Rogers developed a method of responding to "feeling" (this word is not yet in the index of the 1951 edition, however). The "reflection of attitudes" he discusses soon became known informally as "reflection of feeling." In client-centered parlance a "feeling" was always something like "You resent her criticism" (p. 28), something which the client *feels* viscerally as he speaks, but which he probably does not know conceptually, or say. Client-centered therapy is a method of doing regularly and systematically at every step what Rank described in more general terms in the sentence above. It depends upon the therapist using all his words to phrase and point at the client's ongoing, not fully formulated experiencing, something directly felt, yet upon explication always about living in situations, reacting to, feeling about, worrying over, fear of, and so forth.

Even when the therapist is not at all clear about just what the client directly senses and feels (and when the client is not at all clear about it), both persons can point their words at it. It is concretely felt. Both people's attention and symbolizing "carries forward" this experiencing process, as I formulate it today.[15]

Words, acts, other people's reactions . . . all "carry forward" the experiencing process, and that is what man is: a sentient, interactive organism. Like the oxygen and food we take in, like the CO_2 and feces we give off, the life process is inherently an interaction. Even the animal's physical

---

[14] Rogers, *loc. cit.*
[15] Gendlin, *Experiencing and the Creation of Meaning, loc. cit.;* Gendlin, "A Theory of Personality Change," *loc. cit.*

structure dies and disintegrates when it ceases to inhale and exhale, to push against the ground and bury feces in it, to ingest food and circulate blood whose very internal content consists of external oxygen and food particles. The sentience of this live body is its complex ongoing (not "in" the environment like a thing lying in a container, but "as" ongoing process, much like the water is not "in" the river, but is the river). Our experiences are not "in" us. We are our felt experiencing. Whatever we bodily feel is already highly organized. To put words or points or action to it "carries it forward" further, "surpasses it," so that words do not render it, but are "based on" it, in relation to it, explicative of it, in a direct interplay with it.

Not all words and responses have this effect of "carrying forward." Only very few do; everything else affects us, to be sure, but not in a way of making the ongoing experiencing move forward more fully and broadly. When that happens, there is a release and relief, a powerful bodily felt effect which convinces us of the accuracy of what was said, or the rightness of what was done, even just as we change by this very movement, being carried forward.

One example, among many in this book, of "just the right words" comes from the dialogue between Philip and Dr. Buhler. Philip has been describing the various ways in which his parents try to force him into a dependency relationship and try to make him feel guilty. Struggling to achieve a sense of clarification, he expresses this attitude: "I guess it comes back to the fact that I don't trust my parents." Dr. Buhler enables Philip to reach the next step in awareness, responding: "They have made you feel that strings are attached." Philip adds: "That's putting it well. . . ."

That the words or symbols "fit" or "feel right" means that what is said or symbolized or done was already *implicit* in experiencing earlier. But "implicit" does not mean "in the same form as explicit, only hidden." Rather, it means not yet formed, not yet ongoing fully, and therefore amenable to many different ways of being formed (though these many ways are still few, compared to all the possible words, deeds, and responses which do not fit, and would leave the aspect implicit and unlived).

When even one experiential step occurs (when some words, gestures, symbols, responses, actions, or events have carried experiencing forward in some respect), then there is a felt change, a shift. One feels at least a slight release, a "give" in the felt referent, and thereafter new aspects arise and can be referred to. True explanations which do not carry experiencing forward are worthless when compared to one even slight *referent movement,* that felt sense of "give" in what we feel, after which arise new facets and changed aspects of our feelings and situation.

A feelingly accurate statement or symbol (even if it makes little conceptual sense, or seems awfully obvious, like "I don't know what to do, that's what I feel now") can have this effect of referent movement. As a result of referent movement, there is *content mutation,* that characteristic way in which the contents shift in the therapeutic process. Often, even one slight, felt referent movement takes the process in a totally unpredicted direction, all the parameters of the discussion change, the decision at which the client seemed about to arrive is now irrelevant or different, the whole scene changes.

Experiencing never consists of sheer emotions (the affect-tonality reified into a thing): joy, fear, anger, etc. Rather, *experiencing is always internally differentiable and explicable.*

We should not confuse intensity of emotion with experiencing. Anxiety can double one up, shame or guilt can make one weird and intensely pained. Schizophrenics whose self-processes have largely stopped feel intense and weird discomforts. Primitively structured sounds and pictures occur. In dreams (where interactive experiencing is also curtailed by sleep) the same sort of static imagery occurs. Whenever the process of felt ongoing living-in-the-world is narrowed and inhibited (sleep, hypnosis, poisons of all sorts, stimulus deprivation, isolation), these peculiar phenomena occur: instead of functioning as the apperceptive sensing of ongoing living, the shape of feeling and sensing becomes weird and frightening, psychotic and primitive, the body's own life process without full interaction in the human world.

When the apperceptive flow of differentiable felt experience is narrowed, then words and events are not interpreted by an ongoing feeling process. Reactions and interpretations are no longer modifications of this felt sentience, as we are accustomed to have it. Rather, it is all dark and dank, swampy and silent, stuck and dully painful. Passively, with only little ongoing sentient flow, an individual still watches the rampant specters. But these are weird childlike imagery. Such imagery is very, very much akin to the small child's imagery when he is left alone at night for a long time. His interactive process ceases, his capacity to respond to himself in human in-the-world ways is not great enough to carry his own experiencing forward and, instead, very psychoticlike imagery appears. Respond to the person (or the "psychotic contents") in an adult way but similarly to the way you would respond to a weirdly frightened child, and an ongoing human process will replace the psychotic material. That "material" is not "contents" in him, but a manner, a mode, that mode in which there is too little ongoing *inter*action-with.

For the same reason we should not turn away from someone who is "latently psychotic" because we fear (as the contents-in-people theory implies) that the psychosis will "erupt." Psychosis is not an entity in people that erupts.

Whether psychosis occurs or not depends on whether one helps or fails to help carry experiencing forward.

The fear of incipient psychotic material arose because so many therapists employed methods in which psychological entities were "dug up" and symbolized without response to the individual, his feeling process, his personal relating to the therapist. Many patients did become psychotic as a result of *such* therapy. They felt their effort to relate warded off and defeated, their ongoing experiencing further deadened inside themselves.

We should never avoid what an individual *implicitly* feels because we fear he cannot take it. He is already taking it! The question is: "Will you enable him to live it with you or only alone (two entirely different sorts of experiential processes)?" But, this principle applies only if we respond personally, if we refer concretely to exactly what the individual feels and if we go with him the steps in which—with our help—he explicates it.

But we must make responses not only to what he seems to say and do, but also the sort of responses which first make personality, the picking up of a child, the touching gently on the shoulder, the expression of some of our feelings to him, the spontaneity of having another person be with one. Therapy too often consists only of clarifying conceptually the admittedly inadequate and undeveloped machinery he has. In contrast, to respond to what another feels carries experiencing forward because experiencing (feeling) *is* an interactive ongoing-in and with.

Similarly, at times we express our own feelings toward him (the content seems different—it seems to be about us), and the carrying forward effect occurs. Expressing our feelings does not just tell about entities in us. Rather, expressing our feelings toward him is an interactive process and constitutes what occurs in him as much as in us.

Therapist expressivity and carrying forward concerns *the*

individual's ongoing process. It is a carrying forward and reconstituting of his life process that cannot be done without a genuine other person genuinely responding with the whole gamut of his feelings to the patient's whole gamut of feelings. We know best with children that this is a personality development process. With children we do not expect everything to be "in there" already. However, such a relationship requires that the therapist's feelings be expressed as clearly his own, and the child's as clearly the child's own. To protect another's freedom we do not need to paralyze ourselves. That would give him only a useless emptiness instead of a full relationship in which he is free. We need to express our feeling reactions and then still let him be free— by virtue of the fact that these reactions are our own. They don't preempt *his*. We point again and again at his, ask about them, make room for them, refer to them—even at a time when, perhaps, he remains totally silent and neither expresses anything of his own feeling life, nor has it at all clearly.

Today, the main parameters of therapy are the experiential process in the patient, and our carrying it forward directly by living as people toward him. In ourselves as therapists (out loud, when possible) we must do with our own ongoing experiencing what we try to help the client do with his: we must differentiate it, we must explicate it. We must not just blurt out: "You bore me," or "Why do you never say anything important?" Instead, we must ourselves carry forward our own experiencing for a few moments in a chain of content mutation and explication. For example, "I am bored. . . . This isn't helping him. . . . I wish I could help. . . . I'd like to hear something more personal. . . . I really would welcome him. . . . I have more welcome on my hands for him than he lets me use . . . but I don't want to push away what he does express. . . ." The resulting therapist expression now will make a personal interaction, even if the client says nothing in return. The therapist will say something like: "You know, I've been thinking the last few minutes, I wish I'd hear more from you, more of how you really feel inside. I know you might not want to say, but whenever you can or want, I would like it." Or, to the silent, unwilling schizophrenic: "I don't know how you felt when the aids pushed you in here so roughly, but I felt bad about it. I hate seeing you pushed and shoved." Or, "I know *I* am going to feel a lot better when you're out of the hospital and we can meet in town, but I guess it's no simple thing to you. You haven't said how *you* feel about it." Or, "Gee, am I glad to see that they gave you back your shoes. How I have hated seeing you in those rags they had you wear instead. Are you glad too?"

If there is one rule which encompasses the many we are still formulating, it may be: Let us conceive of the individual as not fully formed sentient experiencing, and pay attention to it, respond to it, refer to it, and make room for it, even when silent and without shape. Then let us respond from our own persons in whatever way is immediate and plainly real for us, but quickly again make room for attention to the newly moving experiencing in him which we thereby create. For no one can predict what will come next and can be referred to next by him, in this newly ongoing further process.

How radical this sounds for adult therapy, how obvious it sounds for therapy with children! It is what each illustration in this volume exemplifies. Those who work with children know instinctively to respond to children with a real self, know to pick them up rather than only talk at them; know to make positive what seems negative (we hug the child that cries and pounds at us with fists). We respond to experiencing if the child lacks the words; we respond to fashion positive interaction rather than only explaining what is lacking.

In summary: Therapy must be "experiential," experiencing is always internally differentiable (never just this or that set of contents, always a moving directly felt process). Change comes through directly felt experiential steps. Interpersonal relationships carry the experiencing process forward, if the therapist expresses his own actual reactions (as clearly his own) and at the same time gives room, attention, and reference to the client's felt reactions as the client's own. Our words (in theory and practice) must refer to this felt, as yet not carried forward sentience of experiencing. Words, in practice, and in theoretical statements must refer to what we directly feel. We can call that "experiential theory" and "experiential psychotherapy."

❦ References

1. Burton, A. "Beyond the Transference." *Psychotherapy, Theory, Research and Practice*, Vol. 1, No. 2, 1964.
2. Butler, J.M. "Client-Centered Counseling and Psychotherapy." In D. Brower and L.E. Abt (Eds.), *Progress in Clinical Psychology*, Vol. III. *Changing Conceptions in Psychotherapy*. New York, Grune & Stratton, 1958.
3. Gendlin, E.T. *Experiencing and the Creation of Meaning*, New York, Free Press of Glencoe, 1962.
4. Gendlin, E.T. "A Theory of Personality Change." Chapter in *Personality Change*, Worchel and Byrne (Eds.), Wiley, New York, 1964.
5. Gendlin, E.T. "Experiencing: A Variable in the Process of Therapeutic Change." *American Journal of Psychotherapy*, Vol. XV, No. 2, 1961.
6. Gendlin, E.T. "Subverbal Communication and Therapist Expressivity Trends in Client-Centered Therapy with Schizophrenics." *Journal of Existential Psychiatry*, Vol. IV, No. 14, 1963.
7. Gendlin, E.T. "Schizophrenia: Problems and Methods of Psychotherapy." *Review of Existential Psychology and Psychiatry*, Vol. IV, No. 2, 1964.
8. Gendlin, E.T. "Values and the Process of Experiencing." In *The Goals of Psychotherapy*, A. Mahrer (Ed.) In Press.
9. Heidegger, M. *Being and Time*, Harper & Row, New York, 1962.
10. Jung, C.G. *Two Essays on Analytical Psychology*, Meridian, New York, 1956.
11. Rank, O. *Will Therapy*, Knopf, New York, 1950.
12. Rogers, C.R. *Client-Centered Therapy*, Houghton Mifflin, Boston, 1951.
13. Rogers, C.R. *On Becoming a Person*, Houghton Mifflin, Boston, 1961.
14. Sartre, J.P. *Being and Nothingness*, Philosophical Library, New York, 1956.
15. Sullivan, H.S. *The Interpersonal Theory of Psychiatry*, Norton, New York, 1953.

Index

Abt, L. E., 211 n.
adolescent, 45–47
adolescent boy, obsessional, 152–176
adopted child, background of, 78–79; rejection of, 95
adult, lying by, 160; as quasi-family member, 47
adult–adolescent relationship, 46–47
affect-tonality, 241
ageing, fear of, 146
aggression, 21–23, 122, 126, 129
aggressive play, 125
Alexander, Eugene D., 119–133, 214
Allen, Frederick, 134–151, 208, 216, 219, 224, 235–237
all-or-nothing attitude, 134–135
Ammon, Jean, 52, 68, 70
"angel" role, 86–87
anger, 21–25, 32; constructive use of, 163, 174, 217; subjective, 225
animal nature, in obsessive adolescent, 162–163

anxiety, 32, 41, 136–137, 152, 241
apperceptive flow, 242
authority, dislike for, 114
automobile, owning and driving of, 115
awareness, existential, 1–2

background, of adopted child, 78–79; movement and, 196
Baer, Melvyn, viii
Baruch, Dorothy W., 30–44, 213, 218
becoming, in child, 193–194; failure and, 122
bed-wetting, 35
"being-in," 227–229
being-in-the-world, 224–225, 227–228, 274–275
being-with, 227–229
belief, existential, 232
Bernstein, Harvey, 63
Betty Lou, existential therapy with, 134–151
bliss, experience of, 198
Block design test, 120, 214

blood cancer, 10
blood transfusion, fear of, 11–12
Bloomberg, Claire, 101
Bobby, existential therapy with, 79–101, 215, 218
body image, 195–196
books, "burning" of, 178–180
Boss, Medard, 202
boxing, interest in, 164–165
brain damage, 57, 66
Brower, D., 211 n.
Buber, Martin, 3, 212
Buhler, Charlotte, 102–118, 240
Burton, A., 227 n.
Butler, J. M., 211 n.

Campbell, Nadine, 60, 70
car, owning and driving of, 115
"carrying forward," 240, 243–244
Cavanaugh, Bob, 67, 71
centeredness, 193
change, capricious, 177–180, 187–188, 215–216; versus consistency, 220–221; therapeutic, 224; as "working through," 221
child, background of, 78–79; body awareness in, 195; focus of, 193; ignorance of adult about, 31; language in, 202–203; meeting with world, 191–205; role playing in, 199–200; sensory perception in, 196–197; sound and, 200; timidity of, 33; value system of, 110–111
Children's Center, Napa State Hospital, California, 46–77
child–therapist relationship, commitment in, 29; in existential moment, 2–3; hostility in, 20–21; sharing in, 6
classroom, growth in, 130; *see also* school
claustrophobia, 152
client-centered therapy, 210, 239

Colm, Hanna, 78–101, 215, 218
commitment, of child, 18; to honesty, 110; of therapist, 4, 20
competitive behavior, 181
concepts, experiential use of, 222
confrontation, in experiential therapy, 5
connectedness, 193
constructs, philosophical, 231–232
content mutation, 241
counter-transference, 210
crocodile, symbol of, 167–168, 173
"cut-off" feeling, 97, 106

Dasein, 202, 227
death, discussion of, 89; experience of, 26; fear of, 146, 155, 157, 171–172
death wish, 141–142
delinquent behavior, 46–47
depression, 152
desire, reality and, 197
despair, cut-off feeling and, 97, 106
destructiveness, 21–23
dishonesty, 109
drawing, expression in, 128, 155–160
dream, of deep pit, 158; of empty house, 98; magic powers in, 147; of "monster," 83–85, 218–219; of red Indians, 166–167, 174–175; static imagery in, 242
"dressing-up," 34–35
dying, *see* death
dying self, in living self, 9–29
dynamic balance, 223

Elgin, Joan, 69
Ellicott, Roseanne, viii
emotionalism, 222
empty house, dream of, 98
encounter, existential, 218

epiphenomena, 210
existence, experiencing as, 235–236
existential crisis, father–son relationship and, 108–110; therapy in, 102–118
existential dilemma, 25
existential encounter, 218
existentialism, 224–235; and experiential psychotherapy, 206–246; phenomenological, 233; versus subjectivism, 228
existential limitation, 78
existential moment, 1–7, 219
existential therapy, with Betty Lou, 134–151; with Bobby, 79–101; with Gavin, 79–101, 215; with Ron Jennings, 48–77; with Jerry, 119–133; with Jimmy, 9–29; with Philip, 102–118; with Roy, 152–176; with Timmy, 34–44; with Tom, 177–190
experience, differentiable, 241–242; in existentialist theory, 227; feeling as, 243–246; "gut-felt," 225–226
experiential process, theory of, 220–224
experiential psychology, 206–246

failure, value and, 122
family, absence of unity in, 135; adoptive, 79, 100–101; emotional crisis in, 103–104; versus individual, 144; puritanical, 80; rejection by, 135–136; unethical practices in, 109; ward as, 47–48
father, grief of, 13; temper outbursts of, 104; *see also* parents
father–daughter relationship, 136
father image, 170–172
father–son relationship, 75, 83–84, 170–172; existential crisis in, 108–118

fear, experienced, 5, 41, 226; of feelings, 33, 213; as "wish inside-out," 173–174
Federn, Paul, 238
feeling, existential, 235; experiencing as, 225–226, 243–246; pure, 2
feeling process, therapeutic, 212
feelings, fear of, 33, 213
felt experience, 225–227
"felt rightness," 222
finger painting, 37–38
"foolish" feeling, 106
Fromm-Reichmann, Frieda, 237
frustration, fear of, 79
fulfillment, potential of, 202

Gavin, existential therapy with, 79–101, 215
Gendlin, Eugene, viii, 206–246
gentleness, emphasis on, 206
God, concept of, 200; punishment from, 161–162, 168–169
Goldstein, Kurt, 196
Great Mother, "problem" of, 168, 173, 207–208
group psychotherapy, 49
growth, versus individual psychotherapy, 177–190
guilt feelings, 99, 118, 161

Heidegger, Martin, 227 n., 229, 234–235
home, as garden, 45
homosexuality, fear of, 35
honesty, commitment to, 110, 113
hospitalization, fear of, 157
hostility 21, 118, 122–123; of adolescent, 45–46; in child–therapist relationship, 4
human beings, as "being-with," 227; as "containers," 230–231
human life, features of, 191–192

Husserl, E., 225
hypnosis, 17

I, identity of, 197
ignorance, adult's, 31
independence, value attached to, 115–117
individual, versus family, 144; meaning of, 219
intentionality, 225
interaction, concept of, 224
interpersonal relationships, 224
insight, 5, 16, 219
I.Q., 120, 153
I–thou relationship, vii

Jennings, Ron, existential therapy with, 48–77
Jerry, existential therapy with, 119–133, 214
Jimmy, existential therapy with, 9–29, 214
Jung, Carl G., 171 n., 208–209, 235, 238
juvenile delinquent, 46–48

Knapp, Pauline, viii
Kogl, Richard C., 45–77, 218

language, experience through, 201–202
leukemia, 10
Lewis, Eve, 152–176, 208, 217
life–death dilemma, 25
limitations, acceptance of, 78; struggle against, 79
Little Prince, The (Saint-Exupéry), 204
living, creative, 99; limitations of, 78
love, 31–32; search for, 78–101; in teenager, 116
lying, 110–111, 160

magic and magical powers, 147, 160–162, 169
man, world and, 191
Maslow, Abraham H., 238
masturbation, 31, 35
maturity, process of, 173–175
Mead, George H., 237
mental retardation, 120
Merleau-Ponty, M., 195 n.
Merrill-Palmer Institute, The, viii
Mitwelt, 192–193
"monster" role, 83–85, 218
mother, aggression toward, 125–129; attack on, 103–104, 129; fears for safety of, 137–138, 141, 145–146; "perfect," 80; separation anxiety about, 208, 211; sharing bed with, 170, 208–209; symbolic killing of, 209; transcending of, 209; *see also* parents
mother–child relationship, 80, 103–104, 129
mother–daughter relationship, 136
mother image, 170–172
mother–son relationship, 170–172
Moustakas, Clark, 1–7, 9–27, 177–190, 214, 218–219
movement, background and, 196
mutuality, 3

Napa State Hospital, California, 46
negativism, 68
newborn infant, as individual, 191–192
nightmares, 83
Norton, M. D. Herter, 200 n.
Now, awareness of, 198

obsessional behavior, in adolescent, 152–176
O'Connor, Mike, 56–57
Oedipal conflict, 211

Old Testament, God of, 169
omnipotence feeling, 101
outpatient therapy, 67

parents, anxieties of, 30–31, 80–82, 136; loss of confidence in, 112; lying by, 160; therapist's conference with, 139–140; *see also* father; mother
patience, 20
patient–therapist relationship, existential, 212–214, 242–246; *see also* child–therapist relationship
peer group, adolescent and, 47
penis, exhibition of, 38–39; holding of, 93; size of, 93–94
perception, abstract, 120
"perfect" mother, 80
person-in-relationship, 215
phenomenology, 225, 233
Philip, existential therapy with, 102–118, 240
phobias, obsessional behavior and, 152–176
play therapy, 9, 14–18, 81–82
"poor me" attitude, 92
positive, "accentuating" of, 216
Poulet, George, 196 n.
prayer, 161
problems, running from, 175, 186
problem-solving, 124–125
Proust, Marcel, 196
psychoanalysis, 210
psychological tests, 120–121
psychosis, "eruption" of, 242–243
psychotherapy, in existential crisis, 102–118; experiential, 206–246; individual, 177–190; as living experience, 134–151; orientations in, 211–212
Psychotherapy with Children (Moustakas), 15
punishment, guilt and, 161

Purtscher-Wydenbruck, Nora, 200 n.

rage, 21–23
Rank, Otto, 209, 235, 237–238
rationalizing, 235
reality, desire and, 197; and existential moment, 212; subterranean, 212–214
referent movement, 241
rejection, by family, 135–136; by father, 83–84; fear of, 79
retarded child, 120
Richards, Tom, 66
ridicule, fear of, 30
Rilke, Rainer Maria, 200
ritual, obsessive, 155, 158, 161–162
Rogers, Carl R., 211 n., 235–239
role playing, 199–200
rootless feeling, 97
Roy, existential therapy with, 152–176, 217
running away, 175, 186

Saint-Exupéry, Antoine de, 204
Santa Claus, "dishonesty" about, 105, 110
Sartre, Jean-Paul, 231, 235
schizophrenia, 241–242, 245
school, failing in, 184, 189; fear of, 135–136, 148, 208; leadership in, 187; teacher and, 131–132, 181–182
self, dying and living, 9–29; existential, 232; internal warfare in, 16
self-confidence, 126, 189
self-consistency, 18
self-denial, 80
self-determination, 185
self-disclosure, 2
self-healing, 14
selfhood, vii, 4, 7, 193–194

self-mutilation, 68–70
self-punishment, 99
sensory perception, 197
separation anxiety, 208, 211
sexual conflict, 211
sexual intercourse, model of, 95–96
sharing, in child–therapist relationship, 6
Siegel, Irving, 190
silent dialogue, world of, 119–133
sister, aggression toward, 129
Smith, Ronald Gregor, 3 n.
social institutions, acceptance of, 193
Social Research Foundation, 190
sociocultural order, 192
sound, 200–201
stealing, 110–111
stepfather, 75
stimuli, behavior and, 224
Stories of God (Rilke), 200
Straus, Erwin, 194 n.
stuttering, 102
subjectivism, 228
subterranean reality, 212–214
suicide, 50, 53, 68
Sullivan, Harry Stack, 225, 227, 237
superego, 123
superman role, 88, 94
surprise, element of, 177
symbols and symbolizing, 202, 237

Taft, J., 237
teacher, relationships with, 131–132, 181–182
teenager, love experience in, 116; world of, 45–46; *see also* adolescent
temper tantrums, 93
tension, fear and, 226

therapeutic experience, assessment of, 131
therapeutic feeling process, 212
therapist, adolescent and, 47; commitment of, 4, 20; existential moment and, 3
therapist–patient relationship, 212–214, 242–246; *see also* child–therapist relationship
therapy, client-centered, 210, 239; as living experience, 5, 134–151, 224
Thomas, Keith, 56, 61
tics, 34–35
time, experienced, 198–199
Timmy, existential therapy with, 34–44
Tom, existential therapy with, 177–190
totalist attitude, 134–135
tranquilizers, 69
transference, 210, 223
traumatic experience, neurosis and, 103–104
truth, shock of, 30
twin fantasy, 138

value choice, 216
value judgment, 216
value system, 111, 117

Warkenten, John, 238
Wechsler-Bellevue Scales, 120, 214
Wechsler International Scale, 153
Wenkart, Antonia, viii, 191–205, 219
Whitaker, Carl A., 238
Woods, Katherine, 204 n.
"working through" concept, 221
world, as jungle, 45; meeting with, 191–205; of teenager, 45–46
World War II, 103